The Wisdom of Words

The Wisdom of Words

Language, Theology,
and Literature in the
New England Renaissance

Philip F. Gura

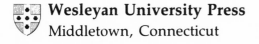 **Wesleyan University Press**
Middletown, Connecticut

Parts of chapter 1 appeared in "The Transcendentalists and Language: The Unitarian Exegetical Background," in Joel Myerson, ed., *Studies in the American Renaissance, 1979,* and Twayne Publishers has kindly permitted the use of that material. Parts of chapter 4 originally appeared in the *New England Quarterly* ("Henry Thoreau and the Wisdom of Words," March 1979), and the author gratefully acknowledges permission to incorporate those sections into his text.

Library of Congress Cataloging in Publication Data

Gura, Philip F.   1950–
   The wisdom of words.

   Bibliography: p.
   Includes index.
      1.   American prose literature—19th century—
History and criticism.   2.   Religion and languages—
History.   3.   Symbolism in literature.   4.   Theology—
19th century.   5.   New England—Intellectual life.
I.   Title.
PS368.G87   810'.9'15   80-25041
ISBN 0-8195-6120-7

Distributed by Harper & Row, Publishers

Manufactured in the United States of America
First Printing, 1981
Wesleyan Paperback, 1985

For my parents,
Oswald E. and Stephanie Gura

Contents

Acknowledgments

Tracing one's intellectual lineage always is humbling, especially if the preparation for one's efforts has taken over a decade. I would like to believe this volume began in Holyoke Center 952 at Harvard University when Richard I. Rabinowitz urged me to major in American history and literature rather than in French. In the course of my interview he discovered that I knew of Thoreau (even had read in his journals!), and Richard was convinced that I should study in the same program in which he then was tutoring. I succumbed and the next summer followed him further, sixty miles west, to Old Sturbridge Village, where he soon would become director of museum education. Many special hours of my life were spent immersed in early American folkways at that museum, and this study owes much to the kinds of knowledge to which he there introduced me.

Three of my teachers provided a focus for my intellectual development. Among many other things, Alan Heimert taught me how to read theological language. Joel Porte introduced me to the study of American romanticism and nurtured my interest in the philosophy of language among transcendentalists. By generous and unfaltering example Daniel Aaron displayed the commitment necessary to become a serious student of American civilization.

Howard M. Munford, as chairman of the Department of American Literature at Middlebury College, believed enough in a young graduate student to hire me and so first allowed my ideas and enthusiasm to be tested in the class-

Acknowledgments

room. To him and his gracious wife, Marion (the only woman I have met who bears comparison to Sarah Pierrepont Edwards), I also owe an introduction to John Conron, whose intellectual toughness has taught me to roll with the academic punches. The Reverend Arnold McKinney, formerly associate dean of students at Middlebury, provided sympathy and understanding displayed countless times at *Fire and Ice* and *The Alibi*.

Hans Aarsleff, Sacvan Bercovitch, and Lawrence Buell kindly read and commented on this manuscript, and many of its thorny passages have been clarified by their particular kinds of wisdom. Over the years Richard Morey and Donald F. Eaton have encouraged my scholarship immeasurably, taking time from their busy lives to humor my peculiar interests and presumptuous demands. Carolyn Dameron has had the patience and good nature to bear with me through this book's various revisions, and her typing and editorial skills have saved me countless hours. My wife, Leslie, has seen me go to the study too many times but always believes something will result from all those hours.

The Council on Research and Creative Work at the University of Colorado generously supported this work by granting me a research fellowship in the summer of 1978.

Philip F. Gura
Boulder, Colorado, 1980

Among persons of more conceit than intelligence, it is not uncommon to hear the study of language represented as being, under almost any form, a dull and frivolous pursuit. It may be so to those whose attention is confined to arbitrary rules, founded on the mere forms of words; but when we consider the faculty of speech as the distinguishing gift of the Creator to our race: as interwoven with all the wants, enjoyments and improvements of man: as the index to the progress of society from barbarism to refinement . . . what benighted man, rejecting the bounty of his Maker, shall come forward and say that the study of language is dull, or low, or unprofitable?

William S. Cardell, *Essay on Language,
as Connected with the Faculties of the Mind,
and as Applied to Things in Nature and Art* (1825)

Introduction

In his *Journal* Henry Thoreau once reminded himself that there were "a great many words" that were "spurious and artificial" and could be used only in a "bad" sense because they signified concepts no longer "fair and substantial." He remarked that men who used words like "church" and "judiciary" no longer stood "on solid ground" because such terms were not "genuine and indigenous" and had no recognizable roots in human nature. At the beginning of this study of language and symbol during the American Renaissance and, in particular, of how these concepts evolved in new directions because of the intellectual context in which they were embedded, it is wise to consider how language and symbol themselves might now qualify as the kinds of terms Thoreau berated as made primarily by "scholars" for their own private use. Because these words have become so hackneyed (so much so that one wing of academia is intent on defining an entirely new vocabulary for examining works of literature and other cultural "artifacts"), for a literary critic to attempt to show how these concepts were understood by writers as varied as Emerson, Thoreau, Hawthorne, and Melville might be, in Thoreau's inimitable phrase, as vain as "towing a sinking ship with a canoe."[1]

Adopting another cardinal trait of cranky Henry Thoreau—he was as stubborn in his convictions as he was honest in assessing his contemporaries' shortcomings—I intend, however, to resurrect the topics of language and symbol; for, though they remain at the heart of the literary and philosophical achievement of the American romantics, *why* they

became overriding concerns still is inadequately understood. Scholars of American romanticism have underesti-
mated how the writings of our classic American authors, in
both form and content, reflect the same intellectual transformation (albeit with some American twists) that the critic
M. H. Abrams has documented for English romanticism in
such works as *Natural Supernaturalism: Tradition and Revolution in Romantic Literature*. To study early nineteenth-century
attitudes toward the meaning and function of language, and
how they related to other parts of the "New Philosophy" of
the English and Continental romantics, makes one realize
how much, in Abrams's words, "the characteristic concepts
and patterns of Romantic philosophy and literature are a
displaced and reconstituted theology, or else a secularized
form of devotional experience."[2] This is not to suggest that
I am merely rehearsing the arguments for the moral and religious bias of writers like Emerson or Melville. Rather, by
studying their attitudes toward language (particularly religious vocabulary), I want to show how our writers addressed
the question of the ambiguity inherent in the gesture of
human speech and so began to move in their writings, as
well as in their philosophy, toward a concept of symbolic
discourse.

The study that comes closest to suggesting the issues I
intend to raise is Charles Feidelson's *Symbolism and American
Literature*, a path-breaking volume that, though it emerged
from the claustrophobic years of the New Criticism, makes
readers aware of the importance of the intellectual context
in which the American symbolist tradition originated.[3] More
importantly, Feidelson stresses how Emerson and his contemporaries grappled in secular terms with many of the same
theological questions addressed by their Puritan forebears,
particularly with the typological or "symbolical" use of the
world's manifold objects. For all the brilliance of his sections
on Emerson and his contemporary, the Reverend Horace
Bushnell, however, Feidelson does not go far enough in ex-
plaining *why*, at that particular time, the topic of language
was debated with such intellectual ferocity. The profound
interest in what words could mean and in how they could
be used with a new force to create, if you will, a "secular

[4]

scripture" forms the rootstock of the later flowering of New England.

During the period under consideration, for example, the study of language (especially of its origins) was a vital topic with humanistic implications increasingly difficult for our generation to comprehend. When the study of language is mentioned, students whose sole exposure to its modern theory consists of a hazy incantation of "psycholinguistics" or "transformational grammar" find it difficult to conceive how in the nineteenth century the study of language mattered in any practical way or how the budding science of philology had repercussions in such disparate areas as education, theology, and art. Hans Aarsleff, whose *Study of Language in England, 1780–1860* serves as a useful reference point for parts of this book, touches the heart of the matter when he explains that language study, even when called philology, was not merely "a matter of knowing the forms, syntax, phonology, historical relationships, and other aspects of particular languages." The questions involved were of larger significance. "What, for instance, was the origin of thought? Did the mind have a material basis? Did mankind have a single origin? Was the first language given by revelation or had man invented it in the process of time?"[4] If we can understand why the men involved in investigations of language and its symbolic potential considered their work an attempt to answer such questions, their dedication to what in retrospect seems like inane or, at best, antiquarian wordplay comes into meaningful focus. Moreover, when we consider how our modern notion of the heuristic value of symbolism can be traced to a concern with the possibility of an intrinsic ambiguity to *all* speech, the philosophical debates over language between 1800 and 1860 become even more significant.

The study of language in early nineteenth-century America, then, must be viewed as an inextricable part of the cultural matrix from which our classic American writers emerged. Because it was not the hobby of marginal figures but rather an occupation for such important artists as Emerson and Thoreau, it offers the student of intellectual history an opportunity to trace the manner in which these American thinkers refashioned contemporary ideas into innovative and fruitful forms. That most of the premises on which they based their reasoning were false is not at issue; as Aarsleff wisely cautions in the introduction to his work, any comprehension of how nineteenth-century theories of language and symbol bore fruit must be preceded by our "gaining the proper depth of historical perspective" without reference to or misguidance by "the later accumulation of scholarly opinion and assignment of influences."[5] No matter how little truth the various theories contained—as we shall see, some were quite farfetched—the results of adhering to one belief or other about the origin and function of language were central to the creativity of some of our most important literary figures.

This study establishes the cultural context from which discussions of language and symbol originated among certain American romantics. We often have been reminded that many of the main figures in the American Renaissance were involved in religious and philosophical controversy—even if on a private level, as in the case of Hawthorne's psychological struggle with the ghosts of his Puritan ancestors or of Thoreau's skeptical stance toward his Christian neighbors. What has not been shown is how the terms of theological debate, particularly with regard to the accuracy and implication of scriptural revelation, when coupled with the influence of Continental romanticism, were transformed into premises with deep reverberations in epistemology, theology, education, and literary form. What began innocently enough as attempts to discredit the varied interpretations of biblical language that had contributed to the rise of denominationalism ended by clearing the way for a fully developed symbolist theory of language and literature.

In making this claim I am not suggesting that the American romantics' interest in language—which, after all, must be a concern of philosophy and religion in any age—derived solely from the contemporary debates described in my first two chapters. I do not deny that the basic philosophy held by many American romantics, one grounded firmly in Neoplatonic suppositions, was the strongest influence toward the adoption of a symbolic mode in their literature.[6] But be-

[6]

cause many of the figures I will be discussing—particularly Emerson, Thoreau, and Bushnell—were at some point in their lives engaged in soul-searching dialogue as much with the various Christian sects flourishing in the nineteenth century as with the tenets of English and Continental romanticism, I contend that the denominational struggles of this period contributed to an environment in which one's whole manner of expressing "truth" had to be renovated, even if one were not affiliated strongly with any particular religious group.

Hawthorne and Melville themselves never were concerned with specific philosophies of language, a topic that held unending fascination for people like Thoreau. But they, too, were heirs to an age characterized by an increasing skepticism regarding man's ability to decipher, let alone justify, the ways of God to men. Given the developments in biblical criticism on the Continent, as well as the increasingly acrimonious bickering among Protestant sects in the years prior to 1850, it became more and more apparent (especially in New England's intellectual centers) that the truths of the Christian religion were to be understood not literally but symbolically. To hold that scriptural language and the wisdom it represented had one ascertainable meaning was a position maintained by intelligent men only with great difficulty, for the Bible had come to be seen as the written result of poetic or ecstatic inspiration that did not unerringly follow the rules of human logic or experience.

Such a situation left profoundly religious men like Hawthorne and Melville unable to investigate theological problems through the sentimental or moralistic modes they might have used twenty-five years earlier. The world they inhabited, with all its confusion over the "right" meaning of religious language and dogma, could no longer be embraced through the stock formulas of Catharine Maria Sedgwick or William Cullen Bryant.[7] The American romantics needed a prose style commensurate to the complexity of the 1850s, and the pathway to such a style was marked by men who had come to see that truth was to be described only as a shimmering, ever-shifting premise, never to be held firmly

[7]

in hand. For the most part, these harbingers of the symbolic mode were theologians or philosophers whose interests were far removed from the realm of imaginative literature.

In saying this I do not intend so much to assign direct influence as to suggest how an initial controversy over the most seriously considered language, that of divine inspiration, led to the gradual adoption of new modes of thought and perception that better served to explain the moral complexity of nineteenth-century America. In 1800, for example, it would have been blasphemous for any Trinitarian to assert that a triune God was not so much a real as a symbolic concept; but, from 1849 on, Horace Bushnell made precisely such assertions from his Congregational pulpit in Hartford, and by the 1860s they became the foundation for the new liberal movement in Protestant theology.[8] The imaginative distance between these ideas of an essentially "poetic" theology and the philosophical romances of Hawthorne and Melville, in which the elusive and ever-ambiguous nature of transcendent experience was to be suggested through new literary devices, is not as great as one might assume.

The story I wish to tell, then, has many strands. It originates in the ecclesiastical history of the early years of the nineteenth century, especially in the rivalry between Trinitarian and Unitarian Congregationalists. The first participants were primarily ministers, men who ranged from poorly educated preachers who spent hours in their mill-village parsonages puzzling over the meaning of such words as *Gehenna* to the intellectual giants of nineteenth-century scriptural studies, men like Andrews Norton of Cambridge and Moses Stuart of Andover who ordered their lives around settling permanently the controversies over doctrines like the Trinity. Their disputations, often carried on for months in the pages of such periodicals as the *Christian Examiner*, were the starting point for an innovative reexamination of the meaning and function of language. These debates culminated in the formulations of ministers like Bushnell, who in 1849 published his "Preliminary Dissertation on the Nature of Language as Related to Thought and Spirit" as a preface to *God in Christ*, his radical reinterpretation of the Trinity based on a belief in the symbolic nature of religious dogma.

[8]

Introduction

Even prior to Bushnell's formulations, another group of men were conducting their own reexaminations of language. Like him, these thinkers—among them James Marsh, Sampson Reed, and the young Emerson—had been influenced by Continental romanticism as well as by the new scriptural studies; because of their Neoplatonic vision of the world, they were prepared to view language in ways different from their Unitarian brethren. Under their attack the psychological temple constructed so patiently by John Locke (and defended so tenaciously by his followers in the Scottish Common Sense school) ominously began to teeter. Swedenborgian mystics and transcendental idealists claimed that innate correspondences existed between the worlds of matter and spirit; if this were so, who was to say whether or not the roots of all languages, supposedly based in sensory experience, might not originate in the intuitive experience available to all men? And might not this argue for a kind of universal language, the sounds of which too many men had forgotten how to hear?

By the late 1830s the first evidence of such philological concepts became noticeable in realms other than speculative philosophy. Schoolchildren in Boston, for example (and even the formidable Horace Mann, commissioner of education in Massachusetts), were being encouraged to attend to the philological speculations of educational innovators whose ideas were spread by Bronson Alcott and Elizabeth Peabody, members of the transcendentalist circle. Seeking the most valid way to nurture the spiritual capacities of children, these pedagogic prophets settled upon the theories of such philologists as Charles Kraitsir, a Hungarian immigrant whose lectures on language were drawing crowds in Boston. His contention that all languages could be traced back to a few root utterances suggested to some of his followers that all mankind may, indeed, have had a common origin in divinity and that the seemingly fragmented nineteenth century had more unity to it than many had come to suppose.[9] Some educators thought that, if children were inculcated with concepts such as his, people might return to the days before Babel and so inaugurate a verbal millennium in which all would speak the same Christian language in tongues of fire.

Besides appearing in such areas as theology and education, the new speculations on language and symbol became visible in the imaginative literature of the day, a development discernible in the essays of Emerson, whose career epitomizes the transferral of a concern with religious language to the realm of literature. Moreover, we see an even more obvious adoption of wide reading in philology to the purpose of art in Emerson's friend Henry Thoreau. His propensity toward verbal wit and wisdom became so complex that entire passages in *Walden* (1854) depend on an understanding of contemporary philology. Working with Kraitsir's theories, and linking them to an idea of a language of nature, Thoreau invested his literary style with a figurative power rarely equaled among his contemporaries.

Two writers whose works do measure favorably against his, Hawthorne and Melville, also were influenced by transformations in the perception of religious language and symbol. Such connections as the critic can detect among Thoreau, Hawthorne, and Melville are best discovered in the sections of *Walden* that display an intricate and sophisticated use of philological speculation: It is not that large a leap from the railroad cut passage in the "Spring" chapter of *Walden* to the "Doubloon" chapter of *Moby Dick* and the various scaffold scenes of *The Scarlet Letter.* All these passages are marked by the intrusion into the work of a metaphoric consciousness that regards the world as raw material for suggesting what Hawthorne termed "the deepest truths of the human heart," truths that hitherto could be discussed with the cut-and-dried logic of religious argument but that now came under the province of a method of allusion that could be termed symbolic. If the way in which an individual saw the world was determined not by some absolute standard of truth but rather by one's temperament (what Emerson called "the colors of the spirit"), there was slight possibility of men's agreement on topics as profound as the nature of God. For a whale to be both divine and evil at the same time bespeaks a conceptual leap unimagined fifty years before *Moby Dick.*

Melville's great novel may seem far distant from a discourse on the doctrine of the Trinity, but they both are products of an age characterized by an increasing inability to accept what one might term "static" descriptions of religious

Introduction

(or, for that matter, psychological) truth. The symbolic masterpieces of American literature that emerged in the 1850s were as much products of an environment that saw the adoption of highly poetic rendering of theology as of an increasingly complex technology, the development of a new natural science, or the reorderings of American society along class lines. In this sense, to claim that *The Scarlet Letter* or *Moby Dick* was the result of a "breakdown of Calvinism" is correct, but what has gone unnoticed is how that breakdown was as much linguistic as conceptual.

This introduction, then, indicates only the outer parimeters of a study of a highly complex cultural development; specifically, how the study of language created a climate in which the possibility of symbolic discourse was entertained and ambiguity was regarded as a viable mode for discerning truth. The ideas of philosophers and philologists that were not particularly germane to this development are not discussed in any detail; this is not a study of the history of the philosophy of language in America. Nor is the study of language in the post–Civil War period, when philology became a more sophisticated science, a concern, for this book describes a specific intellectual milieu and not the relationships, if any, among modern theorists and their precursors. The integrity of my study resides in its adherence to the interests and judgments of the period under consideration. It is testament to the originality and imagination of the figures here considered that they offer, even within their historical limits, theories and projections that continue to excite our verbal and philosophic imagination.

Words are only human instruments for the expression of human ideas; and it is impossible that they should express anything else. The meaning of words is that idea or aggregate of ideas which men have associated with certain sounds or letters. They have no other meaning than that which is given them by men; and their meaning must always be such as the human understanding is capable of conceiving.

Andrews Norton, *A Statement of Reasons for Not Believing the Doctrines of Trinitarians* (1819)

Chapter One

The Word of God, within Reason
Unitarian Scriptural Exegesis

When in 1839 the American lexicographer Noah Webster delivered an address to the members of the New York Lyceum, he stood before them as the acknowledged dean of American language study. The publication of his first important work, *A Grammatical Institute of the English Language* (1783), had come but a few years after his graduation from Yale; by 1806 he had issued *A Compendious Dictionary of the English Language*, a volume he later still regarded as a preliminary study. The year 1828 had seen his monumental *American Dictionary of the English Language*, a tome that assured his ascendency as an American Dr. Johnson whose pronouncements on language always would fall upon open ears.[1]

Observations on Language, and on the Errors of the Class-books, his address to the Lyceum, is most interesting because of his emphasis on the peculiarly religious nature of his life-long interest in words. In eloquent phrases he explained how he had always "attempted to correct the obvious inaccuracies of language," not just to make the English tongue more civil but, more importantly, to aid the cause of the Christian religion, because "the sacred scriptures, containing all the true knowledge of the Supreme Being . . . ought to be explained in plain, intelligible language." His long attempt to codify the American dialect was only what he believed it was "the duty of Christians to countenance," for his work allowed people to learn as much as possible of the Supreme Being and his demands through the proper understanding of his revelations to men.[2] Literacy, Webster thought, was mean-

ingless if not employed in the general calling of compre-
hending the Bible.

What seems extraordinary about this disclosure is that
a man who was such a popular (and financial) success should
have avowed so religious a motive. But Webster was artic-
ulating what for many had become a familiar concern. "The
evils proceeding from the improper use of words," he declared, are much greater "than men generally suppose."
"They may not affect the common intercourse of society
. . . but it is believed that a misapplication of terms, or the
use of indefinite terms, sometimes leads to serious mistakes,
both in religion and government."[3] This note of seriousness
stemmed from Webster's fervent belief that the "popular
errors" that originated from misunderstandings over words
were "among the most efficient causes of our political dis-
orders." More telling was his subsequent comparison to support that proposition: He noted that "a like evil" had long
existed in contemporary theology, a fact "which no person
seems to call into question."[4]

His auditors knew precisely what he meant when he
alluded to the theological infighting of the day. Since the
early part of the nineteenth century the proliferation of Protestant denominations had created an environment of intense
competition for Christian souls, with appeals made to the
new nation's citizens through various interpretations of
scriptural doctrine.[5] The problem of such schisms, of course,
was not novel; even in America, to say nothing of Europe,
questions of doctrinal purity had caused long and bitter disputes, for example, the case of Anne Hutchinson in the
Massachusetts Bay Colony in the 1630s or the vicious bifur-
cation caused by the Great Awakening in the 1740s. But the
early years of the nineteenth century became a special case,
primarily because of the way America's unique political system treated ecclesiastical matters.

The concept of religious voluntarism, developed as a
corollary to the United States Constitution, contributed to
an environment in which competing denominations had to
prove their validity and usefulness if they were to survive
in the rough-and-tumble religious politics of the day.[6]
Looked at another way, this ideal of religious voluntarism

[16]

resulted in a sense of moral confusion as Americans of all classes had to decide to which group to bring their allegiance. People had to justify, for example, why they were Baptists rather than Universalists, or followed Presbyterian church structure rather than Congregational. The answers to such questions, hitherto easily procured when one religious group was "established" in each colony or region, were now sought assiduously in Scripture. The word of God provided the Law. All that was needed were biblical scholars who could definitively render the ancient languages into the vernacular, a project underway with varying degrees of emphasis at least since the days of Luther.

But it was precisely here that further problems arose. In response to the increased need for a reliable understanding of scriptural language, there developed new schools of textual criticism, established on the Continent by such biblical scholars as Johann G. Herder and J. G. Eichhorn, which suggested that the Bible was as much figurative poetry as objective truth and so was to be read not just with blind faith but with historical and philological imagination.[7] If the Bible were not the absolute word of God but the word of God brought to men and imperfectly or metaphorically translated by them, where did that leave people who sought in Scripture an undeviating standard of truth?

The confusion into which Christianity was thrown by suggestions that the Bible was to be treated like any other literary text was not easily dispelled. What form was baptism to take? Would there be everlasting punishment for all sinners, or universal salvation? How great a degree of freewill did man possess? Ministers of various denominations burned their lamps low to try to find answers, but controversies continued unabated, fueled by the new wave of proselytization that arrived with the widespread revivals of the 1820s and 1830s. And many of the differences of opinion among these groups were reducible to the various interpretations of scriptural language in which their denominations' most characteristic doctrines were embedded, for they believed the direct word of God on these matters was stated in the Bible. If it were not, to what purpose was Scripture?

In this chapter I shall be considering only one of the

major controversies over scriptural exegesis, between the Unitarians, who championed an empirical, rational reading of the Bible, and the Trinitarians, who defended a more orthodox reading (supporting a triune God) by adopting a figurative view of its language.[8] The reason for my emphasis should be clear, for Ralph Waldo Emerson, Bronson Alcott, Theodore Parker, Elizabeth Peabody, and other transcendentalists who became concerned with the problem of language (albeit to various degrees) were nurtured within the cocoon of the Unitarian church. The dialogues about exegesis that occupied the older members of their generation and greatly influenced their own concerns provided the initial formulation of philological premises against which they later rebelled and which opened one door to new modes of symbolic perception. In a study that traced the entire history of biblical criticism among the various denominations in this period one could, I believe, find support for the claim that a culture-wide shift toward a more symbolic ordering or reality was under way.[9] Here, however, I am concerned more with the origins of the interest in metaphoric language in such writers as Thoreau, Hawthorne, and Melville, men whose tangible relationship to such groups as Methodists or Freewill Baptists was only marginal but who owed at least implicit debts to the better-known Unitarians and transcendentalists.

By the early nineteenth century, Unitarians, or "liberal Christians" as they first were called, had emerged as a separate and powerful denomination with a philosophical framework built on the empiricism of John Locke. Even though recent scholars of this movement—most notably Daniel Walker Howe—firmly establish the Scottish Common Sense philosophers as those who laid the "metaphysical foundations of Harvard Unitarianism," the testimony of some of the transcendentalists themselves identifies their philosophical straw man not as Dugald Stewart, Thomas Reid, or other apologists for the empirical tradition but as the figure of Locke himself.[10]

The reaction of Sampson Reed, the Swedenborgian author of *Observations on the Growth of the Mind* (1826), was an early premonition of dissent within the liberal ranks. In his "Oration on Genius," delivered in 1821 when he received his master's degree from Harvard College, he irreverently declared that Locke's mind would not always remain "the standard for metaphysics." Nurtured on the Common Sense empiricism while at Harvard, Reed, through the aid of Swedenborg's theology, already had begun to pierce the shallowness of that empirical philosophy. He reminded his listeners that, given the developments in philosophical idealism, "had we a description of [the mind] in its present state, it would make a very different book from 'Locke on the Understanding.'"[11]

Reed's tone was openly belligerent, and his judgment no exception: The next twenty years saw a major assault against the Unitarians stem precisely from his observation. As Cameron Thompson has written, as long as the debate over transcendentalism raged, "the name of John Locke" remained "integral to its philosophical history," "a symbol of commitments too diverse and too profoundly rooted to permit facile compromise."[12] From among the various constrictions of this Lockean mind, some young liberals discovered, as Reed himself had, a conception of language that simply did not square with their newly adopted philosophical idealism.

In many of the theological controversies of Reed's day the age-old argument of how the written or spoken word impressed its significance on men, of how language *makes* its meaning, had resurfaced. Interest in this topic had also been kept alive by research in other fields, such as Lord Monboddo's attempts to relate human linguistic development to his observations on the higher apes; but in America the question had most often been linked to its theological ramifications.[13] In the 1730s, for example, Jonathan Edwards had taken the then novel Lockean epistemology and refashioned Calvinism into a profoundly emotional, yet intellectually respectable system.[14] But with the shift in philosophical currents at the end of the eighteenth century, men began another reexamination of the relationship between words and the things they signified. The formulations in Locke's third book of the *Essay Concerning Human Understanding* seemed less appropriate as these scholars began to reinvestigate the intuitive basis of man's mind.

Although Locke's theory came under increased criticism during the early romantic period (at first from the German idealists but later from such American theologians as James Marsh and Horace Bushnell), such attacks did not immediately demolish his well-wrought edifice. Lockean empiricism remained the solid foundation of the Unitarian creed (indeed, of the entire evangelical movement) and, in particular, was used to buttress the Unitarians' interpretation of the scriptural doctrines that concerned the nature and personality of God. Locke's theory of language, then, formed one of the major hurdles to be passed if the Unitarian mind was to invigorate itself by exploring new thoughts concerning the nature of man.

Locke's declaration of the arbitrary nature of language appealed to the Unitarians. In the empirical system, words were perceived merely as external stimuli, and the "truth" of language consisted of its utility. The source of meaning was simply "rational usage derived from sensory perception." Words were a contrivance designed for human convenience, and if they came to be used by men as the "*Signs of their Ideas,*" this was not through "any natural connection, that there is between particular articulate sounds and certain *Ideas,*" but only through a "voluntary Imposition, whereby such a word is made arbitrarily the mark of such an *Idea.*" The languages of the world thus had no underlying unity, and words "*in their primary or immediate Signification*" stood for nothing universal, only for the ideas "*in the Mind of him that uses them.*"[15] If men employed terms for which they had not experienced the sensory analogue, they could not know the meaning of what they said. Conversely, words themselves were not universal symbols, for the truth of each idea was to be learned empirically by each man to whom the word-idea was expressed.

The implicit analogy between Locke's theories on government and language is evident and has been recognized.[16] Both were artificial constructs resting upon a contract "voluntarily" entered or, more precisely, upon a *contextual* ar-

marians than to philosophers," he recognized that in some cases philosophers "ought not to escape censure when they corrupt a language" by using words in a way that the "purity of the language will not admit."[23]

Reid never concerned himself with *how* or *why* words meant what they did; rather, he was fascinated by the precise vocabulary of such fields as mathematics and natural philosophy, in which sophistry never took root. If logical axioms and definitions were not apparent to man's common sense, men had to lay down "some general principles concerning definition," a term he described as "nothing else but an explication of the meaning of a word, by words whose meaning is already known." But he also admitted that, given this premise, some words never could be defined, for there were some terms that had to be relied on "in their common acceptation" if they were to be used fruitfully in communication. "We may easily be satisfied that words cannot be defined which signify things perfectly simple, and void of all composition."[24] This simplistic premise of relying on common sense to provide such definitions removed him from apparent ontological difficulty.

Reid's compatriot, Dugald Stewart, another influential Common Sense philosopher whose *Elements of the Philosophy of the Human Mind* was equally popular among Americans, shared this concern with precision of definition and stressed that figurative language, because it proved too ambiguous, had to be stricken from logical discourse before it proved too distracting.[25] The occupation of philosophers, he thought, was to inform and enlighten mankind, not to please them as "men of fancy" sought to in their use of extravagant imagery. Even though it might inspire admiration or faith, language that partook too much of eloquence or emotion became one of the most fruitful sources of error and disappointment.[26] To the Common Sense philosopher, verbal signs were to be as spare and precise as the algebraic figures in an equation. To invite embellishment—be it poetic or religious—merely contributed to logical imprecision, a thought unacceptable to the painfully proper Common Sense mind.

In the early nineteenth century in New England's cultural centers, then, language was thought to be purely *con-*

textual and best comprehended by the intellectual tools given men as rational creatures. To the Unitarian mind, philosophers of each age had agreed upon a certain precision of terms and any understanding of other peoples' conceptions of reality hinged on a historical awareness of the particular meaning given to language at that time.

When such an understanding was brought to bear on the question of words used in the Holy Scriptures, however, the issue grew more thorny. Could the word of God merely be *contextual* and not possess some further, or absolute, significance? According to Lockean premises, if the Bible was the word of God, it was also the word of God set down by men *in a particular place at a particular time* and so had been affected by the vagaries of historical circumstance. Language itself was not divinely inspired but was inspiration affected by the limitations of time and chance above which no human artifact could rise. Thus, the Unitarians' main interest was in the *reliability* of the empirical evidence surrounding scriptural testimony. It never occurred to them that words themselves could be viewed as vitally provocative symbols, which transported men to an awareness of universals that might be apprehended though sensory experience but that lay beyond it.

Some New Englanders—most notably Joseph Stevens Buckminster—now had become interested in the Higher Criticism of the Bible developed by such scholars as Herder, Eichhorn, and Griesbach, but these Americans did not realize how the recent biblical scholarship in the German universities depended upon the intellectual freedom granted by Kant's distinction between the real and phenomenal worlds.[27] Within a few years the corollaries to Kant's philosophical system opened a Pandora's box for American biblical commentators who failed to consider the epistemological consequences of Kantian idealism. Only the more resilient among them could adjust their beliefs to propositions suggesting that the key to man's spiritual existence was found in his "Reason." The controversy over scriptural testimony between the Unitarian Andrews Norton and the Trinitarian Moses Stuart illumi-

[24]

nates how such glaring philosophical oversight contributed to the Unitarians' already crabbed intellectual position. By the time such progressive theologians as James Marsh and Horace Bushnell entered the philological debates, the Unitarians' philosophy of language already was under sharp attack.

Norton, who subsequently achieved fame for his diatribes against Emerson's "infidelity," was the chief expositor of the Unitarian view of the Bible. He had read theology with Henry Ware, who in 1805 had been appointed to the Hollis Chair of Divinity at Harvard, assuring the Unitarian ascendency at that institution. Earlier, Norton had been under the tutelage of the great Buckminster himself, whose impressive library offered a solid introduction to contemporary European theology. Installed as Dexter Professor of Sacred Literature at Harvard's Divinity School, Norton had by 1819 read enough German criticism to begin his lifelong project of proving the "genuineness" of the Gospels.[28]

His chief opponent, Moses Stuart, an orthodox Trinitarian, held the chair of sacred literature at Andover Theological Seminary, the institution founded to counter Harvard's liberalism. Stuart was "probably the best-read scholar" in biblical criticism in New England, so profoundly saturated in the German scholarship that at one point the Andover trustees feared for his orthodoxy. They investigated his beliefs, but because they realized that their clergymen had to adopt similar methods of textual scholarship if they were to maintain the orthodox position against the Unitarians, Stuart escaped with a censure. When in 1819 William Ellery Channing delivered his famous sermon on Unitarian Christianity at the ordination of Jared Sparks in Baltimore, Stuart was presented with the opportunity to chastize the Unitarians for their apostasy.[29]

The heated exchange that began when Stuart attempted to refute the arguments Channing had advanced concerning the "unscriptural doctrine of the Trinity" revolved around the ultimate authority invested in scriptural language. For Stuart the question was, "What did the writers mean to convey" in the biblical passages? Once the textual scholar had treated the Bible with the same grammatical and literary tools

[25]

he brought to any other ancient book (that is, once he had ascertained the words' *meaning*), the text, as the word of God, was authoritative. "It is orthodoxy in the highest sense of the word," Stuart declared, and "everything which differs from it, which modifies it, which fritters it away, is *heterodoxy*, is heresy." His only query was what idea the language of this or that passage conveyed. When this was answered "philologically," a Christian "had to believe what is thought, or else to reject the claim of divine authority." Simply stated, scriptural studies were to be conducted by one's philology independent of one's philosophy. But after that investigation, the truth discerned was binding, for the Bible was an inspired text.[30]

Channing contended that, before any text could be considered as authoritative as the Trinitarians suggested, it had to agree with *the general sense* of the Bible and be part of the universal truth revealed by Christ and his disciples in the New Testament. The question he posed was not only what the original writer meant to convey but whether his text had validity for all ages. The underlying assumption was that the interpreter himself could distinguish between what Theodore Parker later called the "transient and permanent" in Christianity. Channing maintained that the Bible was in part composed of other than divine utterance and in many places dealt with subjects such as the "nature, passions, relations, and duties of man." Moreover (this was blasphemy to any Trinitarian), man was expected to "restrain and modify" scriptural language "by the known truths which observation and experience furnish."[31] Trinitarians like Stuart sharply rejected this idea of bestowing final authority in man's reason rather than in divine revelation. To their thinking no one had the authority to modify propositions to make them agree with man's limited experience. God's word had a divine significance that did not change over time. Truth remained constant, and to assert the contrary was only another display of man's inherently sinful nature.

In opposition to the Unitarian position, Stuart sought to establish the theological authority of the Bible by using exegetical scholarship within the tradition of orthodox Calvinism. Just as Edwards had adopted Lockean epistemology to his own theological purposes, Stuart read the German scholars to reinforce beliefs already held. The Unitarians argued that Christ was more human than divine and so not a part of the Godhead in the orthodox sense, a suggestion Stuart regarded as heretical arrogance, the rash judgment of men trying to ascertain too much through their limited faculties. In a crucial admission, Stuart stated that any Trinitarian who believed in the inscrutability of God never would undertake (as the Unitarians openly did) to "describe affirmatively the distinctions of the Godhead." Such terms as "proceeding from the Godhead" and "the Logos made Flesh" were merely "language of approximation," feeble efforts to describe the indescribable. Humble Christians made no claim to know the literal significance of such terminology; and though language expressed enough of the truth about God to "excite our highest interest and command our best obedience," its function was at best suggestive. The final truth at which language hinted emitted a constant light only partially disclosed through the medium of words.[32]

Channing was not an outstanding textual scholar and did not reply directly to Stuart's attack on his sermon, but the redoubtable Norton needed no prompting to enter the fray. As early as his installation to the Dexter Chair he had proclaimed a theory of language that aligned him strongly with the Common Sense rationalists. "Words, as well as coins," he declared, "change their value over time with the progress of society," thus making the philological scholar aware of their "intrinsic ambiguity and imperfection." Moreover, words "regarded in themselves alone" often proved inadequate to "convey one definite meaning," a stumbling block a biblical commentator could overcome only by "reference to extrinsic considerations." Therefore, the informed theologian, especially in that day and age, had to be "in the most comprehensive sense of the word, a philologist," a belief Norton himself took with high seriousness.[33] In the same year that Channing published his sermon on Unitarian Christianity, Norton brought out the first edition of his *Statement of Reasons for Not Believing the Doctrines of Trinitarians*, the *locus classicus* of the Unitarians' position on language.[34]

The part of this long work of most concern here is section

[27]

vii, "Of the Principles and Interpretation of Language," but even before reaching that point in his argument, Norton alerted his readers to the delicate and treacherous ground on which he was treading by his adoption of German critical principles. In his introduction he paid tribute to the foreign scholarship and noted that the Germans had thrown "much light upon the history, language, and contents of the books of the Old and New Testaments." What they had neglected, he maintained, was the preservation of "the authority and value" of Scripture. Not concerned with whether or not Christianity was divine revelation, they insisted on presenting it as a "system of doctrines and precepts for the most part probable and useful" but not as unassailable truth. "In many cases," Norton declared, they have "substituted for past errors the most extravagant speculations of their own," thus making Christianity merely "a popular name for a certain set of opinions." Even the liberal Norton could not agree with such a pragmatic assessment of the faith once delivered to the saints, and his primary purpose in composing his *Statement* was to "vindicate the true character of Christianity," which "must be presented to men as it is."[35]

Norton's arguments were patently simple. Supporting his position through German Higher Criticism, he restated Locke's principles of language and suggested that even biblical words were "human instruments for the expression of human ideas." It was impossible that words should express anything else but an "idea or aggregate of ideas which men have associated with certain sounds or letters." Thus, words had no "other" meaning and were not inherently symbolic: They always had to represent something that the "human understanding is capable of conceiving." All that had ever been written down (in Scripture and elsewhere) could be understood rationally by intelligent men, and as far as any words have meaning, he magisterially declared, "they are intelligible." Further, though Norton was generous enough to admit that there were some truths that finally were incomprehensible, he thought they were such as could not be expressed through verbal signs. It was not his purpose to speculate on such hypothetical matters: His research led him to grapple only with the "historical circumstances surrounding scriptural language, its peculiarities of idiom, and the prepossessions of writer and audience." *How* divine wisdom was transmitted to earthly creatures, especially when that wisdom contradicted common sense, was something he did not condescend to consider.[36]

Norton thought the art of interpreting the Bible derived mainly from what he termed the "intrinsic ambiguity of language." But, rather than maintaining (as Stuart did) that some theological concepts were approachable only through figurative or symbolic discourse, he resolved questions of ambiguity in a straightforward, unimaginative way, declaring that "when the words which compose a sentence are such that the sentence may be used to express more than one meaning, its meaning is to be determined SOLELY by a reference to EXTRINSIC CONSIDERATIONS." Stated more bluntly, this meant that one's intuition, or the flights of imagination during a state of inspiration, had nothing to do with understanding the "truth" of scriptural passages. Cultural differences (for example, what he termed the "Oriental and popular" style in which the "Hebrews" were wont to express themselves) accounted for most misrepresentations of language. "Figures and turns of expression familiar in one language are strange in another," and so proper interpretations of phrases that seem to "bear a Trinitarian sense" could be achieved definitively only through a consideration of "the character of the writer, his habits of thinking and feeling, his common state of expression . . . his settled opinions and beliefs . . . the general state of things during the time in which he lived [and] the particular local and temporary circumstances present to his mind and writing."[37] The main difficulty in the study of Scripture, then, resided in confusion over "figures" not currently vital in the culture. The phrase "I and my Father are one," Norton maintained, sounded strong and pointed—not to mention downright confusing! But, after a careful study of the biblical idiom, the phrase was decipherable as "I am fully empowered to act as His representative." The relationship between God and Christ was so much more "reasonable" when understood this way.

Similarly, Norton was outraged by the proposition that "the same being is both God and man" or that "the Father

[29]

is God, and the Son is God, and the Holy Ghost is God; and yet there are not three gods, but one God."[38] Such words were the result of a writer's social and historical context, his peculiar way of viewing reality, which in the Old Testament world was often emotional and figurative because the great majority of Jews "had scarcely the power of apprehending a truth presented to them as a philosophical abstraction, in its naked and literal form."[39] It never occurred to Norton that, in a transcendent moment, a man might be aware of things never before perceived or that such visions might become an unshakable part of his faith, Christian or otherwise, regardless of the time in which he lived. Intuitive principles (and symbolic representations), Norton believed, had no place in the life of a rational individual.

Norton's intellectual flaw was his profound inability to fathom how language, if understoood in a more figurative sense, extended the boundaries of the religious sensibility. If language were more than the fabrication of human minds, if it were also an image or shadow of divine things, could it not be that, through a wise submission to his intuition, man could discover new dimensions to his religious experience? Norton and other Unitarians would not accept this. They believed God's revelation to man did not extend to specific language. Revelation was conceptual rather than verbal, and the exegete's primary goal was the recovery of those concepts that could return men to the purity of the original churches. That this conceptual revelation was available to rational man and that language was of secondary importance and not within its very self the embodiment of truth were cardinal assumptions of the liberal Christians of that day.

It is difficult to overemphasize that the verbal wrangling of scholars like Norton and Stuart epitomized one of the main conflicts within American Christianity in the early nineteenth century, especially in New England.[40] The indexes of such denominational journals as the Unitarian *Christian Examiner* and the Trinitarian *Biblical Repository* are replete with articles by theologians grappling with the import of the Higher Criticism. To follow the intricacies of their arguments is to understand how the language of logical inquiry, so long a mainstay of the rational Christian mind, was eroded by the attacks of those who declared that the Bible was composed in languages not of logic and rationality but of eloquence and emotion and so was a document that had to be treated differently than it had been by most theologians to that time.

Moreover, in the late 1820s the debates within theological circles began to include philosophical propositions that declared that the communication between men was based on more than arbitrary imposition of meaning by man himself. Some biblical scholars, already taken with the idea that Scripture was best viewed as a kind of poetry of the human soul, advanced the notion that this poetry was couched most effectively in the imagery of nature, a concept they had absorbed from readings in European romantic literature and philosophy. Natural eloquence, they believed, stemmed from the imagery nature lent to men. If this were true, and if one also believed that all verbal signs originally stemmed from man's observations of the natural world, the issue was raised of a "natural" language analogous to the spiritual truths for which men had so long sought adequate expression. When some young ministers, dissatisfied with what they took to be the deadness of the theology they had inherited, had their eyes opened to this language of correspondence between nature and spirit, and to the concept of transcendent Reason, a very different theology developed.

But this story, with its various American and European strands, requires a chapter of its own. Such "Christian transcendentalists" as James Marsh and Horace Bushnell were quite literally the spiritual midwives of the symbolic consciousness in the New England Renaissance.

The books of Locke, Priestley, Hartley, and Belsham were in my grandfather Freeman's library, and the polemic of Locke against innate ideas was one of my earliest philosophical lessons. But something within me revolted at all such attempts to explain soul out of sense, deducing mind from matter, or tracing the origin of ideas to nerves, vibrations, and vibratiuncles. So I concluded I had no taste for metaphysics and gave it up, until Coleridge showed me from Kant that though knowledge begins with experience it does not come *from* experience. Then I discovered that I was a born Transcendentalist, and smiled when I afterwards read, in one of Jacobi's works, that he had gone through exactly the same experience.

James Freeman Clarke,
Autobiography (1891)

Chapter Two

Transcendental Logic
From James Marsh
to Horace Bushnell

In 1842 the New Thought among younger Unitarians was so much in the public eye that Charles Mayo Ellis, a minor figure in the liberal movements of the day but important as one of Theodore Parker's strongest lay supporters, anonymously published *An Essay on Transcendentalism*, one of the first systematic attempts to explain what had emerged under the rubric of transcendentalism.[1] Through its hundred-odd pages Ellis essayed an exposition of the major components of the revolt against Unitarian religious views prevalent in eastern Massachusetts.

Like Emerson, who in his more impressionistic essay, "The Transcendentalist" (1841), had explained the relationship of the New Thought to Unitarianism as a dichotomy between idealism and materialism, Ellis reminded his readers that the latest developments in American philosophy and theology were best comprehended as a reaction against the commonly accepted psychological view of man and his limitations; that is, as a criticism of the Lockean psychology that so severely restricted man's awareness of his true spiritual nature.[2] He regarded the empirical philosophy as purely "sensual" and thought its practitioners had erred in so strongly affirming that "all knowledge, the affections[,] and the religious sentiments," could be shown to have come "into the body through the senses." The philosophy toward which the keener young minds were reaching was far more spiritual and implied that man could be understood only if he acknowledged something besides the "body of flesh,"

[35]

that is, "a spiritual body, with senses to perceive what is true, and right, and beautiful."[3]

Although Ellis nowhere explicitly mentioned Locke, the point of his remarks could not be mistaken. He noted how the "old" philosophy, because it derived all its ideas "from sensations," led only to atheism, or at best to a religion "which is but self-interest." In rhetoric chosen to suggest the bestiality of adherents to the "sensational" school, he added that the empirical philosophy brought one to "an ethical code which makes right synonomous with indulgence and appetite" and justice "with expediency." Sounding somewhat like a latter-day Jonathan Edwards making distinctions between selfishness and disinterested benevolence, Ellis concluded that Lockean sensationalism bred only a limited and selfish vision, which could not bring its followers to any closer harmony with the universe: It reduced man's love for "what is good, beautiful, true, and divine" to a concern with mere "habit, association, or interest."[4]

Ellis's book suggests how greatly the philosophical thought of New England had changed in a twenty-year period. By the late 1830s one of the main topics of conversation among Boston's intellegentsia concerned just these new psychological dimensions the European romantics had long believed inherent in mankind. The empirical philosophy of Locke, so attractive to the Enlightenment mind, had ceased to satisfy many members of the younger generation, and in what to the Unitarians seemed frightening numbers Harvard students began to talk of the philosophy of Kant and Coleridge and uttered strange words about Reason and Understanding. "It is remarkable," noted the staunch Unitarian Francis Bowen in his preface to a volume of essays in which he defended the Unitarian epistemology, that the "authors most studied among us at present do not belong to the English school, but to the French and German." More importantly to one whose interests were represented by the conservatism of Harvard College and State Street, he added that the "general features of their speculations offer the strongest contrast to those traits which have always distinguished the writers of the same subject in our mother country." When he went on to complain that the foreign philosophers' writ-

[36]

ings were "exciting controversy on subjects of great import," he implicitly acknowledged the American mind's far-from-painless transition to the romantic age.[5]

German philosophy, then, was making itself felt. First brought to the attention of Americans through Madame de Staël's *De l'Allemagne* (1810) and later by such students as George Ticknor and George Bancroft, it allowed the fresher minds of New England to speculate anew on such important subjects as the origins of language and knowledge.[6] If empiricists suggested that all knowledge was derived through sensory experience, members of the new schools of thought, following such romantic distinctions as those between Reason and Understanding, and Imagination and Fancy, posited that man had a "knowledge of philosophical principles by an immediate beholding without the powers of reason or the aid of experience." Whereas empiricism subordinated man to nature, the new philosophy was disposed to "subordinate nature and experience to man," providing an emphasis away from the senses. As tradition has it, to call someone a "sensationalist" suggested that he was an intellectual and spiritual dullard.[7]

In the idealistic system "transcendental" knowledge was understood as "theoretical knowledge about the necessary principles of all knowledge." The way men encountered the world around them, the way they *saw* it, was necessarily founded upon a priori principles.[8] This, of course, was tantamount to maintaining that men were able to "see" differently than any Lockean imagined, for what was perceived was assimilated by principles that had to be regarded as "transcendent of experience." To define man in Lockean terms was to deny him any creative power over the constant sensual bombardment of the outside world. Conversely, spiritual idealists saw men possessing the divine ability to integrate the outside world through the powers of their minds: A person who understood the promptings of his Reason was bathing in an ether that provided divine inebriation.

In many ways such thoughts proved immensely liberating to thinkers dissatisfied with the then prevalent stress on rationalism. Emerson's characterization of the 1840s as a "saturnalia of faith" is perhaps the most succinct way of sug-

[37]

gesting the spiritual and emotional excitement of the period.[9] On one level, what occurred in New England was no less than a religious revival, a renewed sense of the spirit of God speaking to and through human beings who believed in the divine origins of their communications. There is no avoiding the fact that there was such a spiritual visitation around Boston during the period we are discussing: Shelves of books describing its magnitude are its ample testament. What needs to be reexamined is the compelling thought that, if men were seeing (that is, perceiving) differently from the way conservative Unitarians suggested, did this not also imply that those sights and insights were to be *communicated* differently as well? If there was a realm of knowledge preeminently *spiritual*, could it not be that a different kind of language was necessary to describe that knowledge to others? And, if some thoughts had their origin in that ineffable but ever-present sphere termed the oversoul, could not some parts of language have their roots in the same universal substance?

The present-day resurgence of interest in people like James Marsh and Horace Bushnell is partially explained by the fact that these men, while nominally remaining within the bosom of established churches, dealt, like many of their better-known counterparts among the transcendentalists, with just such questions. Both men were known for their liberalism, Marsh as an educational innovator in his capacity as president of the University of Vermont and Bushnell for his revolutionary treatises on the Trinity and other points of Christian doctrine. Equally important were their contributions to the development of a symbolic mode of discourse, formulations that, though made in a more strictly theological arena, ranked with Emerson's in their potential for liberating men to a new understanding of their spiritual and imaginative potential. Although separated widely in interests and accomplishments, viewed together these two men offer a sharp focus on the ways European romantic philosophy, especially as reinterpreted by Samuel Taylor Coleridge, affected both the American Christian tradition and the emergence of a poetic form of discourse in which the notion of ambiguity played a large role.[10]

The most recent assessment of Marsh's career is equally

applicable to Bushnell's. Marsh is now viewed as not so much a transcendentalist as a transitional figure astride two cultural eras, someone who worked "in all of his writings to hold together the divergent pietist and rationalist elements of American culture that had been delicately balanced during the seventeenth century." That Marsh was "more Romantic than Jonathan Edwards" and "more Puritan than Emerson" and sought in his theology a "middle ground between Orthodoxy and Transcendentalism" recalls Bushnell's comparable struggle with the writings of New England's greatest theologian while he flirted with Coleridge's *Aids to Reflection*.[11] Unable to unshackle themselves completely from Edwardsian thought, both ministers redefined its poetic essence in light of new epistemological theories and produced what in retrospect appears to be a transcendental "orthodoxy." Not wanting to sell their birthright as New England Congregationalists, they struggled with ideas so provocative that, often unknown to them, their theological formulations replaced the doctrinal elements of their theology with the *poetic*, thus revealing to their followers new dimensions of religious experience. And, most importantly, in both men's works language itself was the key to understanding what impact the new philosophy had on traditional Christian doctrines.

Born in Hartford, Vermont, in 1794, Marsh was raised in a staunchly orthodox household, and when in 1817 he decided to pursue a career in the ministry there was no question but that he should attend the new seminary at Andover, a fitting place for one already abreast the tide of doctrinal controversies.[12] Marsh, however, was not happy with Andover's academic regimen, and late in 1820, at the time Channing's Baltimore address was making such a stir, he thought the stimulation of the Divinity School in Cambridge might cure his unrest. Two months in Boston, though, convinced him of the Unitarians' moral and spiritual deficiencies and soon he reentered Andover, where he came under the influence of Moses Stuart and his contagious dedication to exegetical studies. By February of that year Marsh reported in his journal that under Stuart's guidance he felt as though he had "conquered" the German language, and he plunged into

[39]

biblical exegesis head on by undertaking a critical reevaluation of both Testaments.[13]

In 1824 he was ordained to the Congregational ministry at Hanover, New Hampshire, and in 1826 the University of Vermont, seeking intellectual leadership, called him to its presidency.[14] Throughout Marsh's association with this institution—he stepped down from his post in 1833 to pursue his scholarly interests, becoming professor of moral and intellectual philosophy—he worked to establish its curriculum on a Coleridegean foundation. Moreover, his own discovery of Coleridge and his subsequent publication of the first American edition of *Aids to Reflection* (termed by one historian of the transcendentalists the group's "Old Testament") called forth sympathetic responses from figures in the mainstream of the transcendental movement.[15] Though Marsh himself did not produce a major treatise on the philosophy of language, his examination and sponsorship of certain European ideas cleared long vistas for men like Alcott and Emerson, who considered the epistemological implications of language as then conceived one of the main stumbling blocks of the age. From the first, what was implicit in Marsh's work was his suggestion that the age demanded a renewed understanding of how religious experience could be discussed; that is, of what power *language* had to capture and make accessible the essence of the Christian pilgrimage.

This emphasis is visible in Marsh's work from his first published effort, which appeared in the *North American Review* in 1821, a few months before he completed his ministerial training at Andover.[16] Ostensibly a review of a recent book by Ludovico Gattinara di Breme defending modern romantic literature against its detractors, the essay provided Marsh an occasion to discuss many of the philosophical issues he had encountered in his eclectic education, especially those concerning the relationship between past and present understandings of the role of the artist in both secular and religious spheres. It was no small indication of his precocious intellectual gifts that his summary and discussion of di Breme's arguments so impressed readers that some of them believed the great Edward Everett himself had authored the piece. And Everett, the editor of the *Review*, told his friend

George Ticknor, who had recommended Marsh for the essay, the piece could only have been written by someone with a firsthand knowledge of Europe, high praise for a young man who had traveled only as far as Virginia.[17]

Marsh's essay engaged what proved one of the most significant intellectual problems of the day. As one recent commentator puts it, he attempted to answer the difficult question of "how an emerging modern sensibility resulted from a new relationship between faith, reason, and imagination."[18] The key word here, of course, is *imagination*, for Marsh and many of his Christian contemporaries were struggling to find a legitimate place for the romantically defined faculty in the creeds to which they adhered.

In the earliest days of the Church, Marsh thought, the faith required of all religious believers was implicitly based on an imaginative understanding of the natural world; but the Enlightenment's reliance on Newton and Locke had added the restrictive requirement of *rationality* to any view of nature. Marsh sensed that imagination had to be returned to the religious sensibility if old creeds were to be significant to his contemporaries. Because of their faith and imagination, the literature of ancient peoples, Marsh said, was "replete with the wonders of external nature." It was also evident that the minds of these writers were open to the "entire, or at least prevailing influence of the objects around them," thus producing states of mind dependent on the "predominant character of the scenes in which they were placed." Their imaginations clung to objects of nature, and the "earth teemed with new forms of ideal perfection."[19] In terms reminiscent of Emerson's when he reminded his readers of the close relationship between man's spirit and the colors nature wears (*W*, 1:10), Marsh proclaimed that he admired in the ancients the sense their poetry gave that "to them all things were real."[20] The seas and the sky "were filled with realities" because the ancients lived in a universe so charmed that they "trembled even before their own ideas and fantasies . . . with which they peopled both the visible and invisible worlds." The natural world offered these writers constant energy and inspiration, and, perhaps most important to the young Marsh who so assiduously sought reinforcement for his own

[41]

faith, it bred religious feelings that implied "faith was co-existent with the world of the imagination [and] had vastly more influence upon their feelings and actions." The ancients "had not learned to write their poetry," Marsh declared, "but they lived it."[21]

In contrast, the world of Lockean premises in which modern writers lived and worked was one of a constant skepticism debilitating to faith. "We of the present day stop to analyze, and call for proof," he declared. In contrast to the openly imaginative ancient writers, contemporary literature produced thoughts "disciplined and guarded on every side by the fixed laws of philosophical inquiry." No doubt recalling the spiritual frigidity he had found so endemic in Cambridge, Marsh lamented that to the moderns it seemed a virtue "to exclude the influence of feeling, and [to] reduce the operations of the whole soul to the measured movements of a machine under the control of our will," a situation that squelched any true religious or aesthetic emotion. If its objects have to be examined "philosophically," "our faith is at last but an imperfect one." People had to acknowledge how much in error men were who "love and hate by letters" and who seem to have no true feelings for what they express as part of their faith.[22] Anticipating Emerson's 1838 diatribe against the Unitarians, Marsh knew to his deepest nerve that the modern sensibility mistrusted feelings but that without such emotion (provided by an imaginative understanding of the world) faith could not be vital.

Marsh never became a member of the openly rebellious transcendentalist camp, but this review revealed a profound interest in romantic thought that marked him as a theological liberal who wished to use the new metaphysics to support a religious orthodoxy.[23] Stuart had trained him too well for him to leave the faith in which he had been raised; and in Marsh's next published work, a review of his mentor's *Commentary on St. Paul's Epistle to the Hebrews*, this desire to reconcile belief in an intuitive faith with Trinitarian Calvinist dogma was everywhere visible.[24] That even Stuart misunderstood his intention points to the intellectual confusion and the conservative reaction that by 1830 had set in against many Continental ideas.

[42]

In contrast to the aesthetic considerations of his earlier review, in this essay Marsh's subject matter was decidedly theological. He was entering a debate over the meaning of the doctrine of redemption that recently had been set in perspective by Nathaniel William Taylor of Yale, who attempted to argue against both the Unitarians at Harvard and the conservatives at Andover and for whose journal, the *Quarterly Christian Spectator*, Marsh undertook the review.[25] In arguing that the fragmented state of the churches of New England resulted from misconceptions of the *vocabulary* used by the different factions, Marsh anticipated the later formulations of Horace Bushnell. To Marsh's mind, the doctrine of redemption, contrary to Stuart's view, could be understood if one realized that a rational analysis of scriptural language yielded only something to be comprehended by what in the new philosophy was termed the "Understanding." To have a true sense of what the ancients meant by redemption, one had to consider the term *imaginatively* or *intuitively*, with the Reason, coming to know, as Marsh put it, "the inward and subjective nature of it."[26]

Following a line of argument he had begun in his earlier review, he stated that the terms used by the apostles in describing the doctrine of redemption once had been meaningful but that this meaning now could not be recaptured through analytical or rational language. "For those who have the whole of the New Testament in their heads, and read it aright, and feel its powers, the language of the Apostles ought to mean more, than these metaphorical representations, literally interpreted, could express."[27] His implication, heresy to any heir to the Lockean mind, was that some concepts could not be rationally understood and yet still had beauty and grandeur. Head and heart were reconcilable, and any Unitarian or Trinitarian who set out to "explain" the doctrines of his faith through logical analysis simply displayed a severe restriction of imagination.

What is clearly visible in these early works of Marsh, then, is a concern over the late Enlightenment mind's destruction of the vital spirit of religion. To attempt to solve denomi-

[43]

national controversies by an appeal to the powers of the mind alone seemed to Marsh insufficient, for the emotional substance of religion was grander than any logical conception of it.[28] A more imaginative understanding of faith was necessary, and Marsh thought this could be provided through careful study and application of the works of people who stressed the intuitive side of the religious experience. As he read more deeply in contemporary philosophy, Marsh became convinced that in particular Samuel Taylor Coleridge presented answers to many of the theological and epistemological questions of the day, and he actively solicited support to reprint his works on the American strand.[29]

Marsh's reputation among the transcendentalists clearly was based on this early sponsorship of Coleridge, especially on his edition of the *Aids to Reflection* published in 1829. More specifically, the long "Preliminary Essay" with which Marsh prefaced the volume attracted those who, like the Vermont theologian, were struggling with the inadequacies of their inherited faiths. Kenneth Cameron accurately describes the importance of this prefatory statement by claiming it was a "trumpet blast against the metaphysics of John Locke as well as a commentary on contemporary thought in the United States," for in it the author called attention to a "growing dissatisfaction with prevailing opinions of man and man's will [and] surveyed the shortcomings of Paley and Locke."[30] This summary is apt, for the young Marsh, obsessed by the concerns evidenced in his earlier essays, had set out to do nothing less than mend the fraying Christian fiber of an entire nation through his reading of Coleridge.

Marsh's success in spreading Coleridgean thought is worth noting. In 1847, when it was less daring to flaunt one's appreciation of European thinkers, Andover's venerable Noah Porter showered Marsh with praise by claiming that "Coleridge had the advantage of being introduced to our theological arena by one of the most distinguished of our scholars." More revealingly, Porter lauded Marsh for his contributions to a "wakeful, thorough, and scientific theology in which, let alarmists and inescapables say what they will, rests the hope of the church."[31] Such praise, however, came

belatedly; through the 1830s and early 1840s only the theologically avant-garde—people like transcendentalists and liberal Unitarians, and a few Congregationalists like Bushnell—
appreciated the magnitude of Coleridge's contribution toward healing a Christianity sick to its soul. And, as I have
noted, it is a further irony that Marsh did not intend to woo
Boston's liberal element through his sponsorship of Coleridge but sought instead a reconciliation between Unitarians
and orthodox Calvinists, much as Coleridge himself tried to
reinvigorate the failing body of the Church of England. That
the *Aids to Reflection* became, in Perry Miller's phrase, the
"book which was of the greatest single importance in the
forming of [the transcendentalists'] minds" was something
Marsh had not anticipated.[32]

Marsh's subject matter, however, could not help but be
suggestive to the transcendentalists, for the "Preliminary
Essay" focused on the split between reason and faith that
so occupied people like Bronson Alcott, Emerson, Theodore
Parker, and others.[33] To Marsh there seemed to be an almost
irreparable breach between the worlds of philosophy and
religion, and the main difficulty confronting nineteenth-century theologians and philosophers was how to combine these
two arenas of human discourse so that man could again possess a rational faith. A central problem, as Marsh perceived
it, was the Unitarians' insistence that any faith without a
rational principle supporting it was mere superstition, while
the equally stubborn orthodox maintained that reason was
incapable of providing the emotion needed to foster and
nourish a living faith. Coleridge, echoing the German idealists, suggested that the basis for this painful distinction
between man as a spiritual and as a rational being was based
on a division *within the mind* of man itself.

More specifically, this meant that in the nineteenth century the "natural" or rational mode of being and knowing
did not recognize the "spiritual" or intuitive one, knowledge
of which was gained only through persistent investigation
into man's emotional life, an activity not encouraged by the
empiricists, for whom outward reality was more important.
In Marsh's words,

So long as we hold the doctrines of Locke and the Scottish meta-physicians respecting power, cause and effect, motives and the freedom of the will, we not only can make and defend no essential distinctions between that which is *natural* and that which is *spiritual*, but we cannot even find rational grounds for the feeling of *moral obligation*, and the distinction between *regret* and *remorse*.[33]

The empiricists saw men's actions, both natural and spiritual, linked in a chain of cause and effect. But they did not understand that only the natural (if you will, the lower) part of man worked in a quasimechanical way, according to the laws established by Newton and Locke. The Understanding could not garner spiritual truths, which were available to the Reason alone.

In this psychological distinction between Reason and Understanding Marsh located the importance of Coleridge and, by extension, of Kant and Schelling.[35] If one could grasp the power of these two psychological concepts, he would have a new vision of the spiritual dimensions of man. To Marsh, Coleridge emerged as someone who used these concepts (and others) "with more precision" and adhered "more strictly to the fixed and permanent laws of language" than any other contemporary philosopher. No one wrote

with a more habitual and present apprehension of the precise import of every term . . . [and] the faults of his language, if faults they be, are such as might be expected from one who has been accustomed to think with unsparing effort, to mark with keen and philosophical discriminations the differences of things.[36]

The problems of religion and philosophy, then, had to do with a lack of precision in terminology. Marsh noted how the so-called "common language" of the day, "including even that of our own popular metaphysics," was but "the language of the market, too vague and ambiguous to satisfy a mind, that would think and reason in precise terms." In *Aids to Reflection* Coleridge helped his readers to discover and "distinctly apprehend" different meanings so that one could "appropriate to each a several word" and thus understand the words so appropriated by others, words as significant as Reason and Understanding.[37]

Thus, Marsh believed that the painful split between religion and philosophy could be healed only if men paid more attention to their spiritual nature and expressed that nature through an accurately formulated vocabulary. Hence there was a "necessity of associating the study of words with the study of morals and religion." Even while nurturing the minds of children, men had to recall that "the most effectual method of instruction [is that] which enables the teacher most successfully to fix the attention upon a definite meaning . . . to call it into distinct consciousness, and assign to it its proper name, so that the name shall henceforth for the learner have a distinct, definite, and intelligible sense."[38] The cry, then, was for a *specificity of language* that captured the essence of spiritual ideas; that is, for the theological precision of an Edwards developed within a philosophy that went beyond the constricting vision proposed by the empiricists and did justice to the religious imagination of mankind.

By the 1830s Marsh's edition of Coleridge was hard to keep in stock in bookstores in cultural centers like Andover; and, because his rendition of Coleridge's system in his "Preliminary Essay" was so broadly painted that his readers could, in one critic's judgment, "interpret it according to whatever lights they brought to it," Coleridgean thought gradually became more accepted in American intellectual circles.[39] Interestingly, Coleridge's success often was identified with the same concern for and use of language that Marsh had noted. In 1835 a critic in the *North American Review* examining Coleridge's *Friend* waxed eloquent as he mentioned the "accuracy and purity of the use of language," so unlike anything native philosophers produced. Coleridge's was prose without "mental waverings, or half-meanings, or indefinite phrases," writing so "severe and scientific, that nothing but original and strong thought can move in it." The reviewer also noted that Coleridge was "relinking the word to the thought, of which, in common usage, it had ceased to be the exponent." Then, in an anecdote that revealed what many Americans discovered in the prose of the British philosopher, he explained how Coleridge already had discovered the remedy for all the confusion in modern thought. It was "to be provided by a dictionary, constructed on the one only philosophical principle, which regarding words as

[47]

living growths, offsets, and organs of the human soul seeks to trace each historically, through all the periods of its natural growth and accidental modifications."[40]

Words as living growths of the human soul—an amazing thought, as though the secret to the power of language Coleridge possessed was found within the mind itself. Similarly, in his seminal book on Coleridge, I. A. Richards identifies another such revealing moment. In a letter the poet sent to his contemporary William Godwin, Coleridge urged the philosopher to write a book "on the power of the word, and the processes by which the human feelings form affinities with them."

Is *Logic* the *Essence* of thinking? In other words, is *Thinking* impossible without arbitrary signs? And how far is the word "arbitrary" a misnomer? . . . In something of this sort I would endeavor to destroy the old antithesis of Words and Things: elevating as it were Words into Things, and living Things, too.[41]

Coleridge and his American readers were focusing on language and its uses in a way that suggested that within words there was a potential energy of which their contemporaries knew little. "The value of the Science of Words" to which Coleridge sought to "direct the Reader's attention" was thought to be of key importance in the nineteenth century, so much so that, if words were not "THINGS," they were at least "LIVING POWERS, by which the things of most importance to mankind are actuated, combined [and] humanized."[42] Meaning simply would be lost if man did not pay closer attention to language.

Because it contained such sentiments, *Aids to Reflection* became a "rallying point for a constructive attack on both Locke and Scottish Common Sense," and its reputation in America, largely based on Marsh's edition, grew rapidly among theologians and philosophers who discovered within it an outline through which to revitalize piety in the American churches.[43] Marsh's friend Joseph Tracy, for example, wrote to him shortly after the book's publication suggesting that, once the *Aids to Reflection* had "the attention of thinking men fixed on [Coleridge's] distinction between Reason and Understanding," Marsh would have "done enough to reward the labors of a life."[44] The German scholar Dr. Charles Follen bestowed similar praise.

Your edition of Coleridge, with the excellent prefatory aids, has done and will do much to introduce and naturalize a better philosophy in this country and particularly to make men perceive that . . . there is still more in the depths of their minds that is worth exploring, and which cannot be cheap and handy in the works of Scotch and English dealers in philosophy.[45]

The American publication of Coleridge's *Aids to Reflection* thus heralded an era in which men began reexamining the premises of their belief in the way man's mind was structured and in how symbols were derived from it. The idealistic philosophy Marsh helped introduce through his sponsorship of Coleridge and the Cambridge Platonists lent itself to a variety of constructions in psychology and philology; and, because of this, Marsh went far toward providing his contemporaries with a new vocabulary for dealing with the philosophical and theological complexity of the nineteenth century, a vocabulary which, though "scientifically" precise, found a place for words that displayed man's capacity for dreaming.

Despite the fact that at the first meeting of the so-called Transcendental Club such luminaries as Emerson, Alcott, Brownson, Hedge, and Ripley discussed Marsh's "Preliminary Essay," Marsh himself never felt comfortable associated with that group of liberal thinkers. He had many friends in the Boston area and paid frequent visits to Channing, Ticknor, Bancroft, and others, "by all of whom he was received with honor"; but, as the transcendentalist movement gained strength, his relations with its participants and fellow travelers dropped off. In 1837, when George Ripley asked him to contribute a volume to his *Specimens of Standard Foreign Literature*, "to undertake the translation of such work in theology or philosophy . . . illustrated with an introduction and notes, similar to your valuable commentaries on Coleridge," Marsh politely refused. A later solicitation from Ripley's *Dial* prompted a similar reply.[46]

In such reactions to his transcendental brethren Marsh restated his allegiance to a world order still essentially Calvinistic. What he missed in those southern New Englanders

[49]

who had so quickly grasped the importance of his teachings was intellectual rigor in their manifestos. Such misgivings about the liberal movement in theology were aptly summarized when he described the "whole affair of Boston Transcendentalism" as "rather superficial," for the disaffected young Unitarians possessed "many of the prettinesses of the German writers" but not their "manly logic and strong systematizing tendency." "They pretend to no system of unity, but each utters, it seems, the inspiration of the moment, assuming that it all comes from the universal heart, while ten to one it comes from the stomach."[47]

Marsh was too much a Trinitarian to allow Reason as free a reign as the transcendentalists did; he feared that if the transcendentalists had their way the corner stones of civilization (including the orthodox interpretation of the Bible) would soon be destroyed. Like Moses Stuart, Marsh believed the new scholarship from Germany was best taken as a "religious guide-post" that would keep men from "straying into the revolutionary paths whereunto the Lockean 'sensuous philosophy' had tempted them."[48] He did not want to see any continuation of Emerson's "saturnalia of faith": "I very much fear," he confided, "that [the transcendentalists] mean nothing more than the opposite of sensualism and still have a wide space between them and the spiritualism of St. Paul."[49]

Marsh, then, holds a critical position as a transitional figure in the movement away from Lockean empiricism toward a renewed spiritual idealism. More than Stuart, who still was tightly bound to an exegetical tradition that demanded allegiance to the final authority of scriptural revelation, Marsh declared the importance of emotion in confirming the truths of Scripture. Moreover, Marsh's, and Coleridge's, stress on the need to reexamine the meanings of the terms used to describe man's religious experience— "to rescue words already existing and familiar, from the false and vague meanings imposed on them by callousness"— fueled the fires that already burned within the Unitarian camp.[50] If the human personality could not be understood because of the garbled condition of language, was there not reason to explore the promptings of intuition and to attempt a recovery of some more primitive accuracy to speech? It was

Marsh's self-imposed duty to introduce Coleridgean thought to America at a time when such questions began to be asked more frequently among its intellectuals.

By recovering a "sense" or "faculty"—the Reason—which had been displaced in the maze of empirical philosophy, Marsh prepared his readers to understand that there was something universal to all men, a mysterious source of intuition that at any moment could instruct man's beliefs, in theology as well as morality. From this premise it was not a great leap to the further suggestion that, before civilized life caused the dispersal of the human tribe into discrete nations, all men had derived their language from the same reservoir of intuition, one that taught them marvelous analogies between their minds and the outside world. But Marsh himself never followed through the implications of such thoughts, and neither did most of his contemporaries. What had most impressed them in Coleridge's thought was its emphasis on the role of the emotions in the religious life.

A decade or so later, however, another New England Congregationalist minister discovered in Coleridge what Marsh had only begun to explore. Horace Bushnell recognized the necessity for emotion in religious life as well as the equally important requisite of a language honest to that emotion, and the result of his concern became the basis for a conception of symbolic discourse that by its innovation shocked many of his contemporaries. As we shall see, the radical propositions Bushnell developed are closely related to Marsh's concern that the barren ground of theological speculation be watered with words vivid and precise enough to allow man's spiritual growth. Bushnell believed that the cardinal points of Christian doctrine were so profound and immediate that they could only be rendered through a poetic vocabulary. In his own way he was restating Marsh's belief that men had to conceive of themselves and their relationship to the universe through the same modes of discourse utilized by the ancients.

After the successive storms over his radical theological opinions had subsided, enabling him to reflect on the training of his earlier years, Horace Bushnell answered a query from

John T. Sewall, professor of homiletics at the Bangor Theological Seminary in Maine.[51] Sewall had asked if certain marked traits in Bushnell's style were the result of any particular mode of instruction. Bushnell's answer provides another example of how important Coleridge's philosophy was to young theologians in the early nineteenth century.

Bushnell recounted his rude country origins and his entry to Yale in 1823 as a young man from New Preston, Connecticut, who, instead of going to college immediately after his country schooling, had worked with his father in the family business of wool carding. Upon entering Yale he discovered "he had no language" in which to clothe his religious experiences. As he put it, if he chanced to have an idea, "nothing came to give it expression." He admitted to Sewall that "the problem was, in fact, from that point onward, how to get a language, and where," and he further explained that if he had any previous model in mind it was William Paley, whom the young student recognized as having a "certain beauty in his plain go-afoot style." "I thought I might hope," declared Bushnell, "with my poor vernacular outfit, to make some progress towards a standard thus pitched for pedestrian attainment."[52]

He did not stop his account there, for the true revelation was still to follow:

By and by it fell to me to begin the reading of Coleridge. For a whole half year I was buried under his *Aids to Reflection*, and trying vainly to look up through. . . . My habit was only landscape before; but now I saw enough to convince me of a whole other world somewhere overhead, a range of realities of a higher tier, that I must climb after, and, if possible, apprehend.

Thus, the transcendent nature of experience expressed so provocatively by Coleridge overturned Bushnell's youthful faith in the logic chopping of the theologians to whom he had been exposed, particularly of Nathaniel William Taylor, under whom he had been tutored at Yale. Given this glimpse of the sphere Coleridge termed the Reason, Bushnell began to consider how he could transform the subtle power of language into a theologically reinvigorating tool. "I discovered how language built on physical images is itself two stories

high, and is, in fact, an outfit for a double range of uses."
In the first sense it was literal, "naming so many roots, or
facts of form"; but in the other it was nothing less than "figure, figure on figure, clear beyond the dictionaries, for whatever it can properly signify."[53]

After his spiritual awakening Bushnell's theological
speculation was marked by an emotional intensity different
from that sanctioned by his Yale teachers. "Writing became,
in this manner, to a considerable extent, *the making of a language*, and not a going to the dictionaries" (italics mine). Feeling a new exhilaration in the choice and use of his vocabulary,
he became aware of how, as he put it, "the second, third,
the thirteenth sense of words—all but the physical first
sense—belong to the empyrean, and are given, as we see
in the prophets, to be inspired by."[54]

In his advocacy of a new stance toward religious language, Bushnell began to see how the creative use of religious
discourse could bring men into an emotional state that provided a more sincere attachment to the cardinal doctrines of
the Church than could any mere consent to dogma. And, as
we shall see, one of his distinct contributions to American
Protestantism stemmed from the same premise: He proclaimed the end of the age of uniformity in religious discourse, for only multiplicity, an acknowledgment of the infinite possibilities of one's faith, could do justice to the nature
of man's religious life. This same declaration would, of
course, reverberate profoundly in the realm of imaginative
literature.

With James Marsh, then, Bushnell joins the group of
"Christian Transcendentalists," men who chose to remain
within denominational boundaries but whose theological
positions owed much to the same philosophical developments that influenced the more heretical transcendentalists.[55] These men had in common an interest in certain aspects of romantic theology as preached by European luminaries
like Coleridge and Schleiermacher, whose tenets they believed had to be incorporated into American Protestantism
to prevent its becoming increasingly unattractive and meaningless.[56] Their renewed stress on what Jonathan Edwards
had termed a "sense of the heart" was offered to reinvigorate

[53]

a Protestant orthodoxy that had suffered greatly at the hands of the rationalists.

In addition, Bushnell emerges as one who offered a soothing poultice to the open sores that stung American Protestants. Besides warning his contemporaries of how much they overestimated the logical mode of reasoning at the expense of the intuitive, he criticized the clergy's slavish allegiance to a restrictive vocabulary when they needed a vivid language of inspiration with which to address parishioners alienated by their sterile sermons. Beginning where Marsh left off, Bushnell developed a philosophy of language more closely linked to the inspired speech Marsh had admired in the Hebrew prophets than to any contemporary religious discourse. At the same time, he became one of the first theorists of the symbolic mode in American intellectual history.[57]

When Bushnell was training for the ministry at Yale, the climate of its theological thought varied considerably from the rarefied atmosphere around Boston and Cambridge, for Yale exhibited little influence of the "liberal" Christianity that had so altered Harvard's Divinity School.[58] Yale's conservative stand had been assured ever since the ascendancy of President Timothy Dwight in 1795, and in time the theological authority he so long enjoyed was assumed by his brightest pupil, Nathaniel William Taylor, from whom Bushnell received the bulk of his religious training. Aligning himself with other Yale graduates—Lyman Beecher, Edward Dorr Griffin, and Asahel Nettleton, for example—Taylor agreed with the Congregationalists' after-the-fact rationalization that the disestablishment of religion in Connecticut was a positive event because it freed denominations from any insidious link with a government that might try to control them. Moreover, Taylor assured himself that if all religions had to compete for the support of the populace, the Congregational faith stood in a strong position because of its success in promoting so many spiritual awakenings.[59]

More importantly, Taylor's stress on the universality of moral obligation upon all true Christians proved a major contribution to the emergence of a new strain in the New England theology—the "New Divinity." Against such critics of Calvinism as the Unitarians, who considered it absurd to believe that God had allowed sin into the world, Taylor argued strongly that Christians should not be discouraged by the fact of their innate depravity. As one recent historian describes Taylor's assumption, all a preacher had to do was to appeal to the neutral self-love that marked the core of human personality and to "demonstrate to man that his true happiness lay in obedience to God's law."[60] Every sinner had *power to choose to the contrary of sin*; thus, his spiritual transformation could occur with a speed seemingly impossible to older Calvinists who considered regeneration a time-consuming, and primarily supernatural, process. The minister's obligation was to present the Gospel message in so convincing a manner that the sinner *instantly* would choose to come to Christ and so commence the reformation of his Christian life.

The problem for young Bushnell—and for countless other troubled ministers—was that Taylor and his supporters (especially Beecher, the field general of New England revivalists) were in effect perpetuating the line of barren theological argument developed by those who first interpreted Edwards's system of divinity. The later history of Calvinism in New England has been wittily described as the "transformation of Edwards's poetry into uninspired prose," and the subsequent clarifications—more *obfuscations*—of such people as Samuel Hopkins and Joseph Bellamy, as well as of Edwards's own son, more often than not proved incomprehensible logic chopping to any but the most tireless theologians.[61] What made it so was that neither Timothy Dwight nor Taylor had ever considered abandoning Edwards's basic *psychological* premises, which were grounded solidly in John Locke; thus, they were lured into the same attitudes toward language held by their Unitarian opponents. What the young divinity student of the 1840s needed was an escape from the "Christianity of Common Sense."[62]

Taylor's appeal to the ego principle was, then, a "rational" solution that provided additional support for the vision Americans had of themselves as a self-assertive people. It allowed them to answer their thorny questions and

[55]

nagging self-doubts through a reliance on their own will power. Taylor, disengaging himself from the majority of European romantic theologians, told generations of his students at Yale that one of the chief dangers to an understanding of true religion was "the unintelligible language" employed by such philosophers as Kant and Aristotle. What American Calvinists needed, he asserted in a letter to a friend, was "a sound, deep philosophy," yet one of "common sense . . . such as all the world can understand."[63] Unfortunately, in the hands of people like Taylor or Dwight, whose four-volume *Theology Explained and Defended* ranks as one of the most deadly treatises in the New England theology, this meant a philosophy that appealed to the authors' simplistic vision of how Edwardsian theology could be made more accessible. To read heavily in Dwight or Taylor, however, is to realize the difference between Edwards's genius and mere intelligence.

As we have seen, however, some ministers who were in sympathy with the latest Continental scholarship (especially of such theologians as Schleiermacher) came to believe that the Calvinist system could be salvaged more meaningfully, and efficiently, through an acknowledgment that the deepest springs of the religious sensibility flowed from the heart, not the head.[64] James Marsh had attempted to merge this romantic premise into his Congregational faith, but the New Divinity men at Yale gave his efforts little attention. It was Bushnell who, after he had discerned the secret of Coleridge's method, undertook nothing less than the "revision of American Protestantism in terms of the *Aid's* transcendentalism and American romanticism."[65]

As Bushnell himself noted, one of the most important problems confronting him was the search for a language that conveyed his understanding that religious certainty came not from rational assent to a body of dogma but through an individual's private emotional experience of the divine. Bushnell felt he had to recast the Christian message in a manner accessible to people who, though bristling under the sterile theology preached at them each week, still felt a profound need to understand the language and symbols in which the new dispensation had been revealed. In 1849 Bushnell pro-

[56]

vided his most detailed exposition of this emotive language when, after being asked to preach at such important institutions as Andover, Harvard, and Yale, he decided to publish his sermons and appended to them a drastic reinterpretation of the nature and function of language in theological discourse.[66]

The topic of language in theology to which he addressed himself in his "Preliminary Dissertation on Language" had been on his mind at least as early as 1839, when in a letter to his wife he admitted that in a recent lecture at Andover he said some things "very cautiously in regard to the Trinity which, perhaps, will make a little breeze." However, he believed the views aired at the seminary were well worth the trouble they might cause:

I have been thinking lately that I *must* write and publish the whole truth on these subjects as God has permitted me to see it. I have withheld till my views are matured; and to withhold any longer, I fear, is a want of that moral courage which animated Luther and every other man who has been a true soldier of Christ.[67]

God in Christ, the volume of sermons in which his thoughts on language were contained, certainly stirred his "little breeze" into a full gale. Writing to his lifelong friend Cyrus Bartol, a Unitarian minister who constantly flirted with the transcendentalist movement, Bushnell noted that his hope for the volume was not necessarily "to convert anybody to me and my ways" but rather to do something far more "dear" to him, to "start up inquiries of a different type, and lead to thoughts of a different character from those who have occupied the field of New England theology and so to revisions, recastings, new affinities, more faith and less dogma, and, above all, to a more catholic and fraternal spirit." He fully expected to be "set upon all round the circle" by his detractors; but (in an admission revealing his revolutionary insight into the problems of nineteenth-century Protestantism) he also believed that "a class of men who have heart enough to go into the *aesthetic* side of religion" soon would vindicate his efforts.[68]

By Bushnell's own admission, the year preceding the publication of *God in Christ* was one of the most important in his life. Early one February morning in 1848 he seemed to pass a "boundary" into faith, where he gained "a sense of the freeness of God and the ease of approach to Him."[69] All his recollections of that day emphasize this same *experience* of faith, the *emotion* of the religious life that had remained inaccessible to him while he remained a mere "legal" Christian. Inspired by the divine and supernatural light he had seen, he began to frame a theory of language by which he might share his joy with others as well as integrate his emotion into the dogmatic structures of the church he represented. Bushnell wanted his readers to pierce the rotten diction that clotted most religious controversies and to realize that the truest apprehensions of religion were those that consisted of an aesthetic understanding, not merely an assent to emotionally barren dogma.

In an "advertisement" to later editions of *God in Christ*, the publisher wished all readers to know that Bushnell "attached a special importance" to his "Preliminary Dissertation on Language," for it was so much "the key to his method of approaching truth, that it may almost be said to be impossible thoroughly to comprehend him, without having read it."[70] With his essay on language Bushnell wished to clear the air for a deeper understanding of his theology, for he, like Coleridge and Marsh, believed that a great part of his contemporaries' religious difficulties originated in misunderstandings of religious vocabulary.

Bushnell began his essay provocatively enough. He proclaimed that, after thinking for many years about the question of language, he found it such "an instrument, that I see not how anyone, who rightly conceives its nature, can hope any longer to produce in it a real and proper system of dogmatic truth," a shocking statement to those New Divinity schoolmen who constantly labored to square biblical language with the pragmatic demands of their contemporaries. Bushnell was, he quite bluntly stated, interested in language only "as regards its significancy, or the power and capacity of words, taken as vehicles of thought and spiritual truth," not in its ability to become a tool of impeccable and unquestionable logic (GC, pp. 10–11).

Taking his initial cue from Coleridge, and duplicating

to some extent what Marsh had suggested in his own "Preliminary Essay," Bushnell explained that he sought to ascertain just how words could "mean" something to those who used and heard them. Positing language to exist potentially in all men, he speculated that the first words uttered were descriptions of the sensations of the physical objects around men. All sights, sounds, smells, tastes, and touches were easily named, and their names came "into currency without difficulty, when sounded as representations of the objects" (GC, p. 19). For the moment relying on Lockean propositions that he later would modify significantly, Bushnell said that, except for a few words whose properties were onomatopoeic, the words associated with such physical sensations were arbitrarily designated. "No theory of sound, as connected with sense," he wrote, "will be found to hold extensively enough to give it any moment" (GC, p. 20).

Bushnell's true interest, however, lay not so much in the origins of language as in its later development into what he termed the "language of intelligence," which "under an outward form" carried "an inward sense" to serve the "uses of the mind." Here he located most of the confusion in speculative theology, for if any outward object was named, it supposedly was verifiable. But if one wished to speak of a thought or emotion, or of a "spiritual Being," *not* empirically verifiable, how was this possible? Bushnell's answer lay in what he felicitously termed the "mediation of things," that is, in "objects and acts in the sensible [i.e., verifiable] world" that answer to "the Logos or internal reason" of the concept to be expressed. The consistent logician had to insure that each party in any controversy had an adequate understanding of the "vast analogy in things, which prepares them, as forms, to be signs or figures of thoughts" (GC, p. 22).

Here Bushnell expounds what appears to be a standard "correspondential" theory, related to systems of religious typology in the Middle Ages and to the theology of people like Emanuel Swedenborg. Because Bushnell's notion of language goes beyond a mere one-to-one correspondence between object and thought, however, at this point suffice it to say that what he envisioned was a world of "forms" in the sensible world that connect to—or, if you will, are prepared for—any thought or emotion man seeks to express but that *do not operate as precisely* as words in logical discourse. The intellectual category of language was different from the physical; it never could be as precise as the language of "things" Swedenborg described.[71]

Expressing an idea that recurs in Emerson's writings, Bushnell declared "a Logos in the forms of things" by which they are "prepared to serve as types of images of what is inmost in our souls" (GC, p. 22). The outer world that envelops our being "is itself a language, the power of all language."

And if the outer world is the vast dictionary and grammar of thought we speak of, then it is also itself an organ throughout of intelligence. Whose intelligence? By this question we are set directly confronting God, the universal Author, no more to hunt for Him by curious arguments and subtle deductions, if haply we may find Him; but He stands EXPRESSED everywhere, so that turn whichsoever way we may please, we behold the authority of His intelligence. No series of Bridgewater treatises, piled even to the moon, could give a proof so immediate, complete, and conclusive. [GC, p. 24]

Known, then, to its deepest core, the world was "an amazing fount of inspiration elsewhere not to be found," which set man always in the presence of "Divine thoughts and meanings" and which made the words he uttered "luminous of Divinity" (GC, pp. 30, 32).[72]

Bushnell's reading of Coleridge thus had given him an idea that radically transformed his sense of the truth Christianity offered. For if the language of intellect was *at best* analogic, could man speak of divine matters in any vocabulary but that of metaphor? God was "EXPRESSED" everywhere, but what if one sought to describe that presence? Was it possible? Such considerations about the reliability of language, Bushnell thought, were enough to "make a thoughtful Christian stand in awe, even of his own words" (GC, p. 32).

In his essay the brunt of Bushnell's attack was aimed at those religious disputants who stubbornly refused to recognize how language was split into the literal and the intellectual or figurative. While in their "historical investigations of words" these men excavated "a subsoil of physical bases," they did not see that all words "relating to thought and spirit should be figures." The usual method of the nineteenth-century theologian was to

> assume that there is a literal terminology in religion as well as a figurative . . . and then it is only a part of the same mistake to accept words, not as signs or images, but as absolute measures and equivalents of truth; and so they run themselves, by their argumentations, with a perfectly unsuspecting confidence, into whatever conclusions the *logical forms* of the words will carry with them.

From such assumptions, Bushnell maintained, all the "distractions, the infinite mulitplications of opinion," and the errors and strife of the Christian world had their result. To comprehend the nature of religious truth and so end their confusion, men had to gain a new sense of the "nature, capacities, and incapacities of language" (GC, p. 40).[73]

Elaborating his sense of the inherent difficulty of presenting thoughts or emotions in a language of logical precision, Bushnell pointed his readers to the *Treatise on Language* of Alexander Bryan Johnson, a contemporary businessman-cum-philosopher who maintained that, because of the manifold variety of empirical objects named by words, even the language describing *physical* objects was hopelessly imprecise.[74] Paraphrasing Johnson's conclusions, Bushnell claimed that "in the physical department of language" no words were "exact representations of particular physical things," for words named only genera and not individuals. Words only represented what man's senses revealed to him and, because all the senses did not necessarily operate in providing an impression of some empirical fact, in language there was the opportunity "for endless mistakes and false reasonings" even in matters "purely physical" (GC, p. 43).

Bushnell thought the conclusion to this state of affairs was self-evident: If so great a margin of error existed in how man talked about what was physically verifiable, the possibility of misconstruing or misusing *figurative* language increased geometrically. Language used figuratively had an endless chain of associationist values that depended on an

[61]

individual's private stock of experiences; as such it was *inherently* ambiguous. It was absurdly arrogant for theologians to pretend that when arguing about biblical texts they worked within a logically closed system.

Words, then, had a different usage from what most people assumed. They were just *signs* of thoughts to be expressed and did not "literally convey, or pass over," thoughts from one mind to the next. They were "hints or images" to help one *toward* the comprehension of some fact or thought. Logicians erred in assuming everyone knew the meanings of such words as "God," "atonement," or "sin," when in reality it was just these types of words that expressed the very ambiguity of which language was capable. Words never truly contained an idea but were meant merely to suggest it. Using a trenchant metaphor, Bushnell explained how figurative words were "but a kind of painting in which the speaker, or writer, leads on through a gallery of pictures or forms, while we attend him," catching at the thoughts suggested by the forms. "In one view, they are all false; for there are no shapes in the truths they represent, and therefore we are to separate continually . . . between the husks of the forms and the pure truths of thought presented in them" (GC, p. 46).

Theological disputes of the kind that tore at the Unitarians and Trinitarians in the early years of that century occurred because the disputants never stopped to consider how "the mind and truth" continually take "new shapes or dresses—coming forth poetically, mystically, allegorically, dialectically, fluxing through definitions, symbols, changes of subject and object." Anyone who did not appreciate the shimmering nature of language as it was constructed in man's mind was a mere "opinionist," bound to be frustrated in attempts to convince others of the truth of the vision beyond his words (GC, pp. 49–54).

The cumulative force of this part of Bushnell's argument is overwhelming and caused one of Bushnell's contemporaries to remark caustically that if words were as vague as Bushnell declared he wondered how the man contrived to "hold conversation with his family."[75] But Bushnell's most controversial proposition was yet to come: For, taking into

[62]

account the imprecise nature of language, he suggested that language constantly mended its errors *"by multiplying its forms of representation"* (italics mine). The creative use of language involved a powerful dialectic process: "as form battles form, and one [word] neutralizes another, all [their] insufficiencies are filled out" and "the contrarieties liquidated," allowing the mind to "settle into a full and just apprehension of the pure spiritual truth." Man never comes as close to absolute truth, Bushnell declared, "as when it is offered paradoxically," under "contradictions"; that is, "under two or more dictions, which taken as dictions, are contrary one to the other" (*GC*, p. 55).

Here then was a remarkable proposition for theologians: To express the inexpressible, one must deal in paradox. The great poets operated thus; so, too, did the prophets. And the authors of the Four Gospels. Bushnell told people that what Christians had argued over for 1,850 years could not even be discussed in the ways they had chosen to set the problems. Participants in theological controversies had assumed that concepts like the Trinity or the Atonement could be analyzed logically when, in reality, they were terms that could not exist apart from contradiction and ambiguity. Truth was not two-dimensional but *spherical*, to be apprehended through a multiplicity of forms. Furthermore, the great Christian mysteries existed under the "same conditions and laws which pertain to language." Resorting to another painterly example to explain himself, Bushnell pointed out that, just as an artist would take a friend to different points of a landscape to give him a just conception of its full outline, so, too, a book like the Gospel of John, the most "contradictory" book (and so containing "more and loftier truths than any other" in the Bible), offered words not for men to apprehend as empirical facts but to make evident the multiplicity of forms necessary to embrace the truths Christ preached (*GC*, p. 56). To Bushnell as well as to Emerson, a foolish consistency was, indeed, the hobgoblin of little minds.

Bushnell also thought it obvious that no logical deduction could prove anything "not previously known by inspection or insight," a profoundly Coleridgean sentiment. Furthermore, Bushnell's exposure to European theology con-

[63]

vinced him that one of the most devastating errors made by his contemporaries was to think that the faculties of insight and intuition could be suspended once propositions were logically established. Logicians thought they could argue on the basis of the analogy words bore *to each other*, as though words themselves were the values under investigation, when in fact they were only their signification. Contrary to what one found, for example, in algebraic processes, in theological discourse there were no fixed quantities with which to work: To act as if there were was foolhardy and a waste of time. For all Nathaniel William Taylor's verbal scrambling to perpetuate what he thought the consistency of the Calvinist system, his, like Andrews Norton's, was finally a failure of religious imagination.

What needs to be stressed at this juncture—and we will have to investigate the notion more completely when we treat Emerson's views on language—is that Bushnell came preciously close to maintaining that the Christian religion was best understood as a *symbolic* system. Its truths, profound as they were, could be captured only through an appeal to the imagination, for they were figurative and often contradictory. Those authors to be most respected—here Bushnell had in mind primarily religious authors, but he did include Goethe—were the ones who most multiplied "antagonisms," offered "cross-views," and brought us "round the field" to show how truth looked from different perspectives (*GC*, pp. 58–59). The reader had to "pass round accordingly with him, catch a view of him here and another there" (*GC*, pp. 67–68). Ambiguity became the hallmark of "truth" in any great literature, a notion Bushnell's contemporaries Hawthorne and Melville would exploit to much more profound limits.[76]

Returning to the example of the Bible, Bushnell explained how a book like the Gospel of John was to be seen as "a vast compendium of symbols," all of which contributed to the apostle's sense of divine truth (*GC*, p. 69). Like other biblical expositors, of course, Bushnell acknowledged that one had to labor to know the *literal* meaning of John's phrases as far as a knowledge of ancient languages could reveal it; but such etymological studies were insufficient for an im-

aginative grasp of the intended message. Orthodox Trinitarians too often settled on *one* of his symbols "as the real
form of truth" and then compelled other people to submit
to it, contributing to the rancor among sects that so characterized the religious tone of the nineteenth century. And
the Unitarians had done no better; they merely "decocted
the whole mass of symbol" and drew off the extracts "into
nicely rounded pitchers" that could not contain the mysteries
of eternity (GC, p. 70). The Christian who would have the
"truth-world overhanging him," like the "empyrean of stars,
complex, multitudinous, striving antagonistically, yet comprehended . . . in a boundless score of harmony," had to
forgo logic and approach the Bible as the natural poetry it
was (GC, p. 71).

Again echoing Marsh when he had praised the language
in which the ancient writers recorded their poetry, Bushnell
proclaimed religion's "natural and profound alliance with
poetry." The teachings of Christ were "utterances of truth,"
not arguments over it; and Christ, himself the most divinely
inspired poet, brought his message "in living symbols, without definition, without proving it even as logicians speak."
His truths had to be discovered anew by Christians of each
generation; his words could not be logically assimilated, thus
leaving little hope for anyone who sought to develop "a sat-
isfactory and truly adequate system of scientific theology"
(GC, pp. 74–75). When set into words, man's comprehension
of divinity could only be composed of "analogies, signs [and]
shadows" of the "formless mysteries above us and within
us" (GC, p. 78).

At such times Bushnell sounded as though he wrote his
essay after reading such transcendentalist manifestos as
Theodore Parker's "Transient and Permanent in Christianity" or George Ripley's "Jesus Christ, the Same Yesterday,
Today, and Forever."[77] The Hartford theologian had an acute
sense of the basic immutability of truth; it was only the context in which the truth was found that ever changed. Still at
least partially relying on the principles of British empiricism
to which he had been rigorously introduced at Yale, he explained that "it is not the truth that changes, but that we
change." Men were different in different ages, "living as

[65]

parts in a different system of things and thinkings"; it was unrealistic for them to assume that the metaphors for spiritual truths were constant. Because men's "contents and antagonisms" were different, they could not see "the same truths in the same forms," making it necessary sometimes to "change the forms, to hold us in the same truths" (GC, p. 80).

Bushnell based his objections to the Unitarians on similar grounds. To his mind, the Unitarians' "abundant protesting" against all creeds missed the true mark. He himself never had felt any oppression or restraint under the various creeds with which he had come into contact but rather had acquired from them a more complete sense of Christianity. He had prepared himself "to accept as great a number" of creeds as fell his way, for when they were subjected to the "deepest chemistry of thought," they became so "elastic" and "ran so freely into each other, that one seldom need have any difficulty in accepting as many as are offered him" (GC, p. 82). Any truth sincerely offered had the value of drawing another tangent to the many-sided one: For the Unitarians to claim that through his rational faculties man could understand *all* that religion offered was a sign of their utter lack of imagination.

Language in theology, then—and here we begin to see the possibilities Bushnellian thought held out to writers of imaginative literature—could be seen only as "an instrument of suggestion" rather than as one of "absolute conveyance of thought." Thus, the main danger to which thoughtful men subjected themselves was to believe a dogmatic writer who, through a bit of "perverse effort expended on his words," tried to bring men logically to a point where any reliance on intuition was absurd (GC, p. 88).

Bushnell hoped his dissertation would alleviate such "dogmatic tendencies in religion" as people began to realize that true faith depended not upon the niceties of logical deduction "but principally on the more cultivated and nicer apprehension of symbol." Rather than striving to bend the rules of experience and intuition to fit the revelation of the Bible as most Calvinists had come to understand it, the teacher of religion had to stress the *aesthetic* qualities of the genuine faith. In particular, New Englanders had been too intent on developing a rationalistic faith, at the expense of understanding that there was a "PERCEPTIVE POWER in spiritual life, an unction of the Holy One . . . an immediate, experiential knowledge of God" that made the true Christian life possible (*GC*, pp. 91–93). Under Bushnell's assumptions, the study of the Bible and its messages would be less catechismal and didactic and so more truthful to the "plastic undefinable mystery of spiritual life," to its symbolic nature. Truth then would be comprehended as a vital force "incarnated in all fact and symbol around us—a vast, incomprehensible, mysterious power" more reminiscent of the early Protestants' awesome conception of the deity than to the later dilutions of it presented by those of less imagination. Through his theory of religious symbolism Bushnell offered man the possibility to become spiritually energized by the various strains of celestial music that jarred and buzzed around his contemporaries. If his doctrines were generally embraced, men would have, he thought, "more of union . . . and more of the true piety enlightened by the spirit of God," neither of which, he added politicly, involved "any harm or danger" (*GC*, pp. 95–97).

Suffice it to say that the views of the Incarnation and the Trinity he presented in the major portion of his book offered these concepts in terms that were not so much "reasonable" as *poetic*. Such points of dogma were to be addressed through the "perceptive and aesthetic" dimensions of man's faith. The truths of the Christian religion could be grasped by mortals only in symbolic terms; and yet, because belief in and about them did make a practical difference to man (in terms of his day-to-day behavior), these symbols were as "real" as anything else in the world. Man's task was simply to enlarge his conception of truth.[78]

In summary, then, Bushnell's contribution to the cultural dialogue on language (as well as to nineteenth-century Protestant theology), lay in his belief that language provided an important example of the inherent ambiguity of any *mental* conceptions. More significantly, his understanding of how language provided a symbolic structure through which men gained more of an aesthetic sense of Christian revelation

[67]

persuaded him to remain a practicing Christian. In the centrifugal world of the nineteenth century, religious truth could be appreciated only through the multiplicity of symbolic rituals like language and only with the understanding that God never could be contained within the scope of one man's, or one creed's, "logical" system. The world of the spirit always was more comprehensive than man's conception of it.

The religion Bushnell demanded, then, was one that encouraged not complacency but, instead, an endless search for truth in its multiple, imaginative dimensions. Such doctrines as the Trinity, he maintained, served men's purposes by keeping their minds straining incessantly after God. The infinity of the deity demanded paradox—if not, then God simply was not as grand a thing as the prophets had thought him to be.

Given this understanding of Bushnell's theological and linguistic system, at this point it is worth examining, at least briefly, his relationship to so important a figure as Emerson on questions of language and epistemology; for while these two men did not arrive at similar doctrinal positions, the ways in which they perceived the link between language and spirit have made such critics as Charles Feidelson equate the theories of symbolism developed by the two men. While acknowledging Emerson as more apt to stress the "undifferentiated whole of perception and speech," Feidelson finds Bushnell the one who most revealed the "fertility" of the Emersonian vision by understanding how "logical opposition, constantly renewed, was the occasion and the material of an endless effort towards symbolic unity."[79]

To be sure, Bushnell's emphasis on the primacy of the poetic form is linked to Emersonian views of the poet; but it is more significant to understand how Bushnell differed from Emerson and his contemporaries in his insistence (as Barbara Cross phrases it) that, "though the spirit shining through things" is a point of departure for the religious life, words, rituals, and symbols create emotions not otherwise found in nature that add to man's grasp of the infinite. In the face of a transcendentalist vision that found God impartially *everywhere*, Bushnell insisted on the transcendent value of culturally derived religious symbols. His, then, became an "ordered Christian symbolism" where words themselves "transmitted a reality the senses could never discover."[80] Transcendentalism, as Marsh had noted, proved too amorphous; in its place Bushnell posited a transcendent system controlled by the ritual, symbolically conceived, of orthodox Christian doctrine. He had done no less than find a way to maintain faith and meaning in a world too apt to disintegrate at its edges.

What Bushnell found insufficient in Emerson's transcendentalism was precisely what one disgruntled Boston clergyman, more than mildly outraged by the liberals' attacks on the city's churches, termed a "shallow naturalism."[81] It seemed that transcendentalism's main threat was that, like the geological and evolutionary theories that soon would shake the churches, it turned the Bible into a set of myths no more important than any other of man's metaphors for understanding the world. The burden of Bushnell's theology after the publication of *God in Christ* was to show that there was "a cosmological necessity of redemption by Christ" and that humanity needed sacred ritual, as well as experience and logic, to remain steadfast in its faith.[82] Committed to a belief in intuitive knowledge because of his appreciation of Coleridge, Bushnell knew that the issue between himself and the yet more liberal exponents of American religion rested on the question of the final significance of any specific theological structure.

What Bushnell saw in the 1850s and beyond was a Christianity in danger "from what might be called a bondage under the method of science,—as if nothing could be true save as it is proved by scientific method." The error of the transcendentalists and many others who lauded the advances of science—which, after all, was but another extension of the human reasoning faculty—in exposing the universal laws of nature and God was their failure to realize the three kinds of law by which the universe was ruled: the law of nature, the moral law, and the law that served the end for which God created the world. Bushnell held that one could not go just to nature to find God, for he is ever "more visibly, convincingly, and gloriously expressed in Christianity than He is in all the world."

Show Him at the head of the greatest kingdom of minds, compassionate to sin, conversant with sinners, a hearer of prayer, an illuminator of experience, a deliverer from the retributions of nature, the glorious new-creator of all the most glorious characters in the world. Display the self-evidencing tokens of His work, as the God supernatural—God in Christ, reconciling the world unto Himself. There is more convincing evidence for God, in the life and passion of Jesus, than in all the mechanical adaptation of the worlds. . . . This kind of evidence restores the equilibrium of the mere natural evidences.[83]

To be preoccupied with nature in the manner of Emerson, then, was to risk losing sight of the further meaning of the Gospel plan whose distant logic was known only to those who contemplated the depths of Christ's mystery as well as the woods and streams around Concord, Massachusetts.

For Bushnell the aesthetic pleasures of the symbolic imagination—and the meanings the symbols suggested— provided the only viable way to comprehend a world order that denied attempts at the imposition of one truth upon it. In this sense he firmly and openly accepted the multiplicity that characterized the nineteenth century. Most interesting to my argument, of course, is that he first arrived at his conclusions from a concern with language, the communication of thought from person to person and from generation to generation. Contrary to an Andrews Norton or a Nathaniel William Taylor, Bushnell realized that words did not *mean* in any absolute sense. They existed as forms that *suggested* concepts to the religious and artistic imagination. There might be a reason why a word expressing a conceptual thought sounded the way it did, but this did not prove that the word was the same as the meaning. God gave us "foxes" to connote "cunning," but the fox was not *the* type of that attribute, only one suggestion of it. If the meaning of any thought was to be made clear to others, the well-balanced mind had to use its powers of analogy with the utmost imagination. After Bushnell, the consequences of such a theory of language for theology were apparent; in art they had not yet been investigated with similar intensity. To explain how this transformation came about will be the burden of my later chapters.

Finally, before we proceed to individuals whose concern with theological language took them more strictly into the world of literature, we should recall that Bushnell's decision to remain within the orthodox fold forces us to regard him differently than Feidelson does, for Bushnell's heritage is not so much among American literary symbolists like Emerson or Melville as with men like James Marsh, whose wonder at the wisdom of words developed while they contemplated the profound Christian mysteries and the language in which they were couched. Bushnell warned that if the symbolic imagination were not doctrinally confined it would run wild and strike itself down against the barrier of human egotism.

Language was most important to him when it was considered in its theological dimension. The implications of both Bushnell's and Marsh's ideas concerning language, however, proved immensely liberating to men whose respect for a strict theological consistency was not as great as theirs; for, as we shall see, the darker moral visions of Hawthorne and Melville depended on a "symbolic" experience of religious truth comparable to Marsh's and Bushnell's. Both Marsh and Bushnell were, then, transitional figures, but transitional in the sense of translating a philosophy of language and communication from a strictly religious to a more aesthetic sphere. Their epistemology demanded a new awareness of the ancient poetry inherent in words; and, if their own works never displayed that same inspiration, these men offered encouragement to others similarly concerned with problems of moral value and aesthetic integrity. When in the late nineteenth century theology became even further removed from strict confinement within specific creeds, the imaginative vision of these Christian transcendentalists finally was appreciated. Its effect in imaginative literature, however, was felt earlier.

The world being thus put under the mind for verb and noun, the poet is he who can articulate it. For though life is great, and fascinates and absorbs; and though all men are intelligent of the symbols through which it is named; yet they cannot originally use them. We are symbols and inhabit symbols; workmen, work, and tools, words and things, birth and death, all are emblems; but we sympathize with the symbols, and being infatuated with the economical uses of things, we do not know that they are thoughts. The poet, by an ulterior intellectual perception, gives them a power which makes their old use forgotten, and puts eyes and a tongue into every dumb and inanimate object.

Ralph Waldo Emerson,
"The Poet" (1841)

Chapter Three

The Example of Emerson
From Theology to Literature

The figures discussed in my first chapters are only the most prominent of many theologians in the early nineteenth century who found themselves in a crisis of rhetoric similar to that which preceded the Great Awakening a century earlier. As we study them and other of their contemporaries, it is evident that, at least through the 1820s, the primary debates over language remained centered on the "authenticity" of words in the Bible. Their concern with language was founded on theological or philosophical rather than on aesthetic grounds. At the same time, it should be apparent that the manner in which some of these men conceived the problems of religious language could easily lend itself to application in a more aesthetic sphere. Before this cross-fertilization was possible, however, there had to occur a further secularization of the doctrines of Christianity, a transformation advanced by the transcendentalist revolt within the Unitarian church.

Some of the liberals who came to be called transcendentalists declared that, contrary to what both the Trinitarians and the Unitarians proclaimed, verbal communication among men was based on more than an arbitrary imposition of meaning upon sound by man himself. By the 1830s some of these men, many of whom adhered to an idealistic philosophy similar to that adopted by Marsh, came to believe that nature, more than the Bible, displayed the revealed will of God and that, as some European romantics had suggested, man had to respond to nature, as well as to Scripture, with his intuitive faculty. From the "higher" critics of the Bible like Herder and Strauss they had learned to read Scripture for its *conceptual*, not literal, truth. But, extending the hints provided by Coleridge and Marsh, they regarded the emotional response necessary for genuinely religious sentiments as closely linked to how the Reason assimilated the "language of nature," which they found to corroborate the truths of the Christian religion.

To be sure, there were many transcendentalists—Theodore Parker and George Ripley are prime examples—whose interest in language remained essentially theological. Their closely argued essays and reviews in the pages of the *Christian Examiner* and the *Biblical Repository* mirror the concerns stressed in the earlier chapters of this study.[1] But to trace the origins of the symbolist imagination in America more completely we have to understand how debates over scriptural exegesis often became secularized, allowing the premises of such people as Marsh and Bushnell to be applied to imaginative literature, a development that occurred through the efforts of some of the younger liberals who adopted the idea of a "language of nature" into their philosophical and theological discourse.

I do not claim that in 1835 any man read his Coleridge or Swedenborg primarily to discover a new way to structure his understanding of language. But once some Americans understood the new philosophical propositions that freely allowed them to embrace an emotional faith they also began to discover the implicit connections between their newly adopted epistemology and their difficulties with religious language. In short, nature came to serve as their mediator between heaven and earth, just as it had in the recorded wisdom of the Hebrew prophets.

The figure in whom we can best see this merger of concern between scriptural language and the language provided by nature is Ralph Waldo Emerson.[2] Raised in a staunchly Unitarian household, he himself became a Unitarian minister after theological preparation at Harvard during the very years of the Unitarian-Trinitarian controversy. More importantly, while still a young man Emerson resigned from his Unitarian church to devote his life to writing and lecturing about the spiritual world he had come to understand after his readings in the "New Thought" of European romanticism. Significantly, though, as he undertook his new vocation as man of letters, the theological argumentation to which he had been exposed was not lost to him. Because his own faith had evolved to a point where he no longer required strict association with a specific denomination, however, Emerson's ideas about language in theology developed more fruitfully than those of some of his friends who remained within Unitarianism, liberal as it was.[3] Like his contemporary James Marsh, Emerson became interested in language as a form of vatic inspiration; but, lacking Marsh's need to defend Congregationalism, Emerson came to see language as most important in its primitive, natural form, not just because it then best reflected the truths Christ had taught but because it allowed the poet himself *to speak like Christ*. And, like Bushnell but again not tethered to the demands of any church organization, Emerson saw how within the language of nature there was an infinite variability of forms available to express man's thoughts, religious or otherwise. The story of Emerson's early years, then, illustrates in miniature his culture's growing acknowledgment that the nineteenth-century world could be confined under no rubric but that of constant change or motion or, put in more literary terms, by nothing but ambiguity or paradox.[4]

There have been many attempts to discuss the background of Emerson's interest in language, especially as critics seek to comprehend the "Language" section of Emerson's manifesto, *Nature*.[5] What has not been stressed sufficiently, however, is how much this interest derived specifically from the dialogue over scriptural exegesis in the early part of the nineteenth century. To be sure, the influence of such factors as Emerson's study of Swedenborgian correspondence, his reading of Coleridge (via Marsh's edition), and his interest in Neoplatonic theory is important. But I suggest that we must turn to the matter of language in theology to find the source of Emerson's gradual development of the mode of symbolic discourse that critics like Feidelson have so capably described.

Emerson's sermon on the Lord's Supper, for example, offers compelling evidence of his concern with the word of God as read by New England Protestants; and, interestingly enough, the thoughts he presented in this sermon (delivered after he had decided he could no longer administer the sacrament in good faith) still display argumentation based upon the exegetical principles of the very Unitarians whose judgment in matters of *doctrine* he was beginning to question. This strongly suggests that at this point in his life Emerson still was tied to the premises of a theory of language derived from Lockean epistemology. It would not be until his European voyage in the mid-1830s that he wholeheartedly adopted the idealism that thenceforth would rule his philosophy.[6]

Emerson had agonized a good while over the prospect of resigning from his Unitarian pulpit; and as he explained it in this moving sermon delivered to his parishioners after he had made his decision, his rejection of a ministry in their church was based primarily on their request that he continue administering the Lord's Supper, not on any personal animosity between them. After a rational examination of the scriptural evidence for continuing that rite, Emerson had come to the heartfelt conclusion that "Jesus did not intend to establish an institution for perpetual observance when he ate the Passover with his disciples." Following a line of reasoning more indicative of an Andrews Norton than a theological maverick who had begun drinking at the wells of European romanticism, Emerson declared the ritual of the Supper to be based only on local, Hebraic custom: Christ's followers (especially Saint Paul) had erred in assuming Christ intended the institution to be maintained permanently after his death (*WC*, 11:4, 12–13).[7]

To Emerson, the historical evidence from the Evangelists suggested that men "ought to be cautious in taking even the best ascertained opinions and practice of the primitive church" for their own. Moreover (ironically displaying what were still deep-dyed Unitarian colors), Emerson warned his contemporaries that in doctrinal matters they should "form a judgment more in accordance with the spirit of Christianity than was the practice of the early ages." Of course, what Emerson was in fact doing here as he stressed the spirit above the letter of the law was turning the Unitarians' exegetical principles against their own (to him) insufficient creed: He

[78]

decided that their commonly accepted practice of Communion was not in line with the deeper, more intuitive truths of the Christian religion. Having outlined his objections to the rite on *exegetical* grounds, Emerson politicly retreated, saying that he would be content to let others observe the Supper until the end of the world but that, for his own part, he was simply "not interested in it" and so in good conscience could not continue in the capacity requested of him (*WC*, 11:16, 24).[8]

It is a forceful argument for his concern with scriptural language that one of the most significant acts of his intellectual maturity was based in large measure on its premises. Like Bushnell a few years later, Emerson, too, sought a language that squared with his understanding of the permanent vitality of Christianity and yet one that remained true to the words in which the Christian religion was expressed. Six years later, when he came to address the graduating class of the Divinity School, his reasoning on matters of scriptural language had already evolved in provocative new directions, marking a decisive break with the faith of his fathers. But to arrive at that point—and at the positions outlined in works like *Nature* and "The Poet"—Emerson had to replace his Lockean epistemology with one based on the newly imported romantic tenets.[9]

In Emerson's intellectual development, then, "The Lord's Supper" belongs more to the age of Andrews Norton and Moses Stuart than *Nature* and the "Divinity School Address" do. What we have to appreciate is how Emerson, starting from a position comparable to Marsh's, moved his theories of language and poetry into quite another realm. If Bushnell's *God in Christ*, another work directly related to Marsh's, later became the springboard to a new liberal theology, Emerson's early essays themselves would fuel the imaginative fires of writers like Thoreau, Hawthorne, and Melville.

Even though in 1832 Emerson still adhered to Lockean epistemology (at least as it pertained to scriptural interpretation), he already had been exposed to one of the formative influences on his language theory, the Swedenborgianism of Sampson Reed.[10] Literary historians have long been aware of the importance of Swedenborg's thought—for example, a number of years ago Perry Miller claimed the Swedish theologian was "as pervasive an influence upon New England Transcendentalism as Coleridge"—but the importance for Emerson of Swedenborg's American disciple, Sampson Reed, went beyond Swedenborg's elaboration of a theological system Emerson would find compelling.[11] Reed's work included the germ of a philosophy of language that profoundly changed Emerson's ways of thinking about the nature of poetic discourse.

Reed and others felt liberated by what Swedenborg termed the "correspondence" between the inner and outer worlds. More explicitly (as Kenneth Walter Cameron summarizes it), Swedenborg believed in "the microcosm and the macrocosm (i.e. the 'all in each' and the 'each in all'), the centrality of man in nature, in the unity running through all things, in the gravitation of like towards like . . . in the . . . doctrine that everyone builds his own spiritual state or house."[12]

Many of these points were complementary to those in the German idealism popularized by Coleridge and adopted by American scholars like Marsh, for one of the most important components of Swedenborg's world view was his sense that there existed worlds of both matter and spirit, whose connection (both actual and symbolic) needed further exploration if man were to understand divine law. In short, Swedenborg provided his eager American readers another way of understanding the critical distinction between the Understanding and the Reason.

Further, as Miller has shown, Swedenborg's thought announced that the "organic principle, if piously observed, cannot fail to achieve coherence by the method of surrender and receptivity, because the correspondence of idea and object, of word and thing, is inherent in the universe."[13] To Swedenborgians, then, nature did not remain the subject matter of the physical sciences, for Reed and others posited an inward, spiritual reason why outward nature was the way it was.

Swedenborg also extended his examination of correspondential relations to scriptural doctrine and in this regard became particularly important to the figures in this study.

[80]

In a manner reminiscent of the intricate systems of biblical typology worked out by sixteenth- and seventeenth-century Protestants better to comprehend their relation to the scheme of Christian history, Swedenborg had delved into the Bible and discovered that, as he put it, "in the Mosaic account of the creation . . . there is everywhere a double meaning of words."

Viz., a spiritual as well as a natural [one that] appears clearly to the apprehension of every man. . . . For . . . whatever orginated in the ultimate parts of nature, on account of receiving its origin from heaven, involves something celestial in what is terrestrial, or something spiritual in what is natural; and it does so on this ground, that everything that is represented in the divine mind cannot be carried out in reality in the ultimate parts of nature, and be formed there according to the idea of Heaven. There results then a correspondence of all things, which with divine permission, we shall follow out in its proper series.[14]

The world men perceive, then, is an "influx" of divinity, a pulsation from the godhead, an effect of the spiritual world's offering (if you will) hints of the final spiritual reality in partially metamorphosed form.

To Emerson and his contemporaries, Swedenborg's doctrine of correspondences represented yet another way of approaching scriptural language, one that might be termed allegorical or protometaphoric. But, considering the subsequent disillusionment of many transcendentalists with Swedenborg—and even the American Swedenborgian Sampson Reed's later disavowal of any links to *them*—it is important to note that the natural world perceived by the Swedish mystic was not filled with myriads of shifting symbols that each man could interpret in his own way. As Austin Warren puts it in his study of one of America's better-known Swedenborgians, the elder Henry James, Swedenborg believed that "within the letter of the Word there really exists a continuous inner meaning, dealing always not with history and geography and persons, but with spiritual states."[15] There was a *single* meaning to be read in Swedenborg's universe, and the truly blessed man never could mistake the wisdom of God's messages written for him.

In his revealing essay on Swedenborg included in *Rep-

[81]

resentative Men (1850), Emerson openly stated his criticism of this thinker. He noted that Swedenborg's perception of nature was "not human and universal" but "mystical and hebraic." Criticizing Swedenborg in terms that might just as well have been leveled at members of the quarreling sects in the New England states, Emerson noted Swedenborg's fault to be in his tethering "every symbol to a severe ecclesiastical sense." He did not realize that "the slippery Proteus is not so easily caught. In nature each individual symbol plays innumerable parts, as each particle of matter circulates in turn through every system. . . . Nature avenges herself speedily on the hard pedantry that would chain her waves. She is no literalist." If Nature was no "literalist," Swedenborg's "theological bias" fatally "narrowed" any interpretation he might give of it. "The dictionary of symbols is yet to be written," Emerson declared, and the "vice" of the Swedish master's mind was its "theological determinism," his assumption that he himself had cracked the universal code and thus could read Christian dogma everywhere in nature. With Swedenborg, Emerson complained, we seem "always in a church" (WC, 4:121–22). How much better for an eclectic philosopher to use the *example* of Swedenborg's method to read the book of nature, but with an imagination free from the restrictions of dogma.

In the 1820s, however, Emerson's disenchantment with Swedenborg and his disciples was still many years away. His first introduction to the idea of these correspondences so central to the Church of the New Jerusalem, an introduction he enthusiastically welcomed, came from Sampson Reed, who graduated from Harvard College in 1818 and then attended the Divinity School.[16] Reed had no notions of going the way of so many of his classmates—that is, into the Unitarian pulpit—and, stepping to the beat of his own drummer, he became an apothecary while he continued to study the tenets of Boston's newest faith.

Reed's taste for literary matters—he contributed scores of essays to the *New Jerusalem Magazine*—was evident as early as 1821, when at the Harvard commencement he delivered an "Oration on Genius" that won the praise of both William

Ellery Channing the elder and Emerson himself, who received his own bachelor of arts degree that same day. Although not printed until 1849 when the astute Elizabeth Peabody included it in her literary journal, *Aesthetic Papers*, Emerson was so taken by it that he borrowed Reed's manuscript, made notes from it, and "kept it as a treasure for years." Peabody herself noted that Reed's essay was handed about in manuscript among other of the literati as well, and she further reported that when she took a copy to Dr. Channing, for whom she was serving as amanuensis, he related how "extremely pleased" he had been to have heard it as he sat on the commencement platform when it was delivered in 1821.[17]

Reed's open indictment of John Locke is what most attracted Emerson. Reed urged his classmates to leave behind Locke's shallow empiricism and to turn their minds to the relationship between mind and nature to find new springs of inspiration for their religious faith. Then, after describing the restorative powers of nature as he understood them, Reed went on to define the new "eloquence" of the age as a joyful union of "spirit and nature" in which the genius of the mind "would descend, and unite with the genius of the rivers, the lakes and the woods." In words that must have sounded decidedly strange to a generation contemplating the more "productive" uses of nature, Reed suggested that, as men learned of the wisdom reflected in their spiritual relationship to the outer world, "thoughts would fall to the earth with power, and make a language out of nature."[18]

Reed completed the oration with a description of his prelapsarian vision, a world in which "Adam and Eve knew no language but their Garden" and in which they had "nothing to communicate by words" because of the wonderful expressiveness of their surroundings. "The sun of the spiritual world shone bright on their hearts," and their senses were open "with delight to natural objects." Therefore, Reed argued, "what had they to say?"[19] He was implying, then, that they knew a language *beyond* mere words. In the new dawn that he hoped to see, man would return to an Edenic state in which his communication would be apparent through references to the outward objects of creation and where outward verbal forms thus would be charged with new meaning.

Emerson enthusiastically received Reed's next public effort, his *Observations on the Growth of the Mind* (1826). The young minister joyfully reported to his brother that in his own "poor" judgment Reed's publication was "the best thing since Plato of Plato's kind, for novelty and wealth of truth."[20] The Unitarians Parker and Channing, too, admired the work, and even the young agnostic Thoreau came to read it. All of these men were beginning to understand the mind much as Reed himself did. Moreover, the aesthetic theory implicit in the pamphlet (even if it could be construed as mere Neoplatonism) met their ears with a sympathetic ring.

Rather than seeing the mind as a vacant receptacle to be filled by sensations from man's nerve endings, Reed described it as a "delicate germ, whose husk is the body," which was put into the world so that "the light and heat of heaven may fall upon it with a gentle radiance, and call forth its energies." To Reed the Lockeans' conception of man as a creature formed wholly from outside sources was the height of insult. "The mind must grow, not from external accretion," the youthful Swedenborgian declared, "but from an internal principle."[21]

Of most interest to us, though, is Reed's belief that the "growth of the mind" was closely linked to a proper perception and interpretation of the natural world. He thought, for example, that children should not study the marvelous pathways of science just to acquire an understanding of the physical workings of God's Creation. Like Bronson Alcott, who may well have acquired this idea from Reed, he saw how a close understanding of nature benefited as well the aesthetic and moral sensibilities of children. It would teach them "poetry," a term by which Reed meant nothing less than "all those illustrations of the truth by natural imagery, which sprang from the fact that this world is the mirror of Him who made it."[22]

Echoing Swedenborg, Reed believed that at the Creation God had impressed into the fabric of nature a set of correlatives, or symbols, which man, after discovering the creative

[84]

power of his mind, could read with a new and ever-increasing clarity. But before this could occur the poetic imagination had to be refined into a "chaste and sober view of unveiled nature" and had to find "a resting place in every created object." When man reached this profound state of meditative revelation in which he discerned the relation of the natural object to man's mind (as well as "to its creator"), he would discover, in Reed's felicitous phrase, a language "not of words, but of things."[23]

"A language not of words, but of things": a suggestion so different from the Unitarians' belief that the only language men possessed had been imposed on them by arbitrary conventions originally based on mere human contrivance. Reed proclaimed a universal set of symbols surrounding men, one that, when made apparent, allowed a more profound comprehension of their Creator than was possible within the constrictions of humanly derived dogma. To Reed's mind the genius of the age would be he who recognized that "everything which is, whether animal or vegetable, is full of the expression of that for which it is designed." If men but understood nature's language, Reed prophesied, what could they add to its meaning? It was because men were "unwilling to hear" that they found it "necessary to say so much," and they drowned "the voice of nature with the discordant jargon of ten thousand dialects." "The very stones cry out," Reed pleaded, "and we do well to listen to them."[24]

What Reed thus injected into the increasingly rarefied theological atmosphere of New England was the heady suggestion that if men wished to regain their proper relationship to nature (and, by extension, to their Creator) they had to stop their petty bickering over matters of grammar and syntax and pay more attention to the visible proofs of God and his truth, which often were not restricted by the formalism of man-made logic. Of course, Reed's message was similar to the arguments of some of his contemporaries—like James Marsh—who believed that the most eloquent language (embodied in its highest form in Scripture) was the language of *natural metaphor*. From entirely different vantage points Marsh and Reed wanted men to regard language more metaphorically, drawing on the wealth of God's Creation to an-

[85]

imate their descriptions of truth as the prophets before them had known it.

Reed's pamphlet was most appealing to Emerson because Reed colored his imagery with very few *explicitly* Swedenborgian terms. Because he did not obscure his statements in a haze of impenetrable dogma, Reed also did not seem to be limiting to an explicitly Christian scheme the meanings placed on objects of sense. Thus, he could fire the energies of men who saw the world of nature not in terms of an intricate Christian allegory but as revelation of a new kind, one proclaiming the divinity of divinity that flowed through all segments of Creation without exception, a suggestion beyond even a pantheistic sense of the immanence of God.

The impact of Reed's work on Emerson and others was undeniable. Even James Freeman Clarke, ministering to a small Unitarian congregation in the wilds of Louisville, Kentucky, had learned of Reed's book through Emerson and spoke favorably of the doctrine of correspondences. Bronson Alcott obtained his own copy of the *Observations*, and Emerson read regularly in the *New Jerusalem Magazine*, to which Reed contributed numerous pieces.[25] It is no exaggeration to claim that ten years after the publication of the *Observations* the doctrine of natural-spiritual correspondence permeated the transcendentalist imagination, both in literature and epistemology.

Emerson also knew of another New Church figure who demands our attention: Guillaume Oegger, a French Catholic priest who was known to the Boston liberals through an early translation of a segment of his major work, *Le vrai Messie; ou, l'Ancien et le Nouveau Testamen[t]s, examinés d'après les Principes de la nature* (Paris, 1829).[26] In 1842, ever alert to foreign thinkers who might illuminate America's peculiar philosophical condition, Elizabeth Palmer Peabody published the first sixty pages of this work as *The True Messiah; or, The Old and New Testaments Examined According to the Principles of the Language of Nature*, in her own translation, which had circulated in manuscript seven years earlier, in time to be available to Emerson as he was formulating his seminal book, *Nature*.[27]

Emerson explicitly mentioned this "French philosopher" in the "Language" section of *Nature*, where he is particularly

[86]

indebted to Oegger's ideas (*W*, 1:22–23). This Swedenborgian treatise was much more avowedly theological than Reed's—indeed, Oegger's very title suggests the limited range of his work. Because God never acted from mere whim, Oegger thought, but rather with a premeditated divine purpose, the visible Creation could not be anything but "the exterior circumference of the invisible and metaphysical world" and as such spoke to man of what was behind its natural facade. Once the world was regarded as the perimeter of divine Creation, an extension of Logos, it became apparent that "material objects [were] necessarily *scoriae* of the substantive thoughts of the Creator, *scoriae* which . . . always preserve[d] an exact relation to their first origin." In Oegger's mind, once this fact became apparent, man's task was to understand how "visible nature must have a spiritual and moral side"; that is, he had to "read" its messages to him.[28]

Oegger pointed to the same difficulty that prompted Marsh's investigations into religious language and troubled Emerson and other transcendentalists: Religion and philosophy, especially "natural" philosophy, had been unfortunately separated into exclusive spheres. Unconsciously aligning himself with Marsh and Coleridge, Oegger maintained that the division of truth into a "Christian" sphere and a "philosophical" one was "an absurdity which should never have entered any well-organized mind," for the natural and spiritual worlds were directly related, *correspondentially*. Oegger maintained that "no fibre in the animal, no blade of grass in the vegetable kindgdom, no form of crystallization in inanimate matter" was without its "clear and well-determined correspondence in the moral and metaphysical world," a theory Emerson himself would try to substantiate. Once man overcame his inability to put together the two spheres, nature became like "a book in which we may read the perfections of God," permitting men to "dart into the moral and metaphysical world."[29]

As Oegger applied such principles to the Bible, he echoed an argument Marsh had made in his essay on ancient and modern poetry, an argument that Emerson found persuasive. To understand the inspired language of the ancient texts, Oegger declared, one had to understand that the prophets spoke in *emblematic* terms. If the deepest language was, after all, "nothing but the perception of the emblems of life and intelligence" contained in nature's bosom, why should not man realize it was in *this* language that Christ spoke to his disciples in the parables? For Oegger, the secret to reading the Bible was to study its emblematic similarities, following them through all their "branches." The result would be a "real" language "inwoven with the ordinary discourse," which conveyed a "consistent sense, higher than natural sense, though parallel with it."[30]

Providing Emerson with an idea that he would develop fruitfully in "The Poet," Oegger insisted that Christ always addressed himself to "his whole creation, by weaving into that [conventional language] another language which was universal." But after Christ's death the two manners of speaking—by "natural emblems" and by "articulate sounds"—became mixed, resulting in a language that was "poetic or extatic, in which conventional words are used only to recall the more significant emblems of nature."[31] The true poets of any age resorted to this vocabulary to communicate their deepest wisdom, just as it was used by Christ and his apostles.

But Emerson became aware that Oegger, like his mentor Swedenborg, persisted in making nature speak as a "literalist." The natural world at which Oegger raptly stared was seamless and led him to its appreciation only as another exemplum of the dogmatic system described in Swedenborgian treatises. Oegger's (and Reed's) basic importance to Emerson, then, was in offering a compelling alternative to the language of rational discourse in which Emerson and other of Boston's clergy had outlined their spiritual aspirations. These Swedenborgians spoke of words in a way that suggested that there was more meaning to them than was readily apparent and, more importantly, that a new understanding of the truths of the Bible could be acquired through a proper regard for the relationship of words to nature.

If their notion of the language of nature was restricted by an adherence to a strict theological system, these thinkers still proved to their readers that man could be sincerely religious without being a mere "sensationalist" in philosophy; for to claim that God could be understood better through nature's objects than through logical language was an acknowledgment that the mind itself was the integral shaping force within man. Nature did not exist merely to be absorbed by man's multiple nerve endings but was to be interpreted by his Reason, in acts that allowed him to move—to transcend, if you will—to a higher spiritual plane. The Swedenborgians in whom Emerson read thus reinforced a conviction that the mind itself was the chief force in altering man's consciousness of the religious elements of his existence. If one felt its force in brooks and forests, as well as in the parables of Christ, religion would have a new vitality.

As Emerson's ears were opened to this new conception of language in religious discourse, he rethought his Christian belief even more deeply. Then, with the publication of *Nature* in 1836, he announced to the world that he had discovered an alternative way to view what many had come to see as the mere "commodity" of nature and, more importantly, that many of the perplexing problems of language that so animated contemporary philosophical and theological circles could be resolved through this new vision. It is not too much to claim that with *Nature*'s publication America's bondage to Lockean epistemology was symbolically broken, freeing thinkers to reconsider both religion and philosophy in profoundly new ways.

At this point it is good to keep in mind that Emerson's resignation from his Boston pulpit did not imply his intention of totally departing from Christianity: His quarrel remained with the outward forms of the churches, with the distinction between what his friend Theodore Parker called the "transient and permanent" in Christianity. For example, Emerson's continued appreciation of such writers as Coleridge and the Cambridge Platonists stemmed from the fact that these men dealt with similar theological distinctions and had sought to marry—as many transcendentalists did—idealistic philosophy to the concerns of the church. Even as Emerson readied his first book for publication he could write to his brother William that *Nature* was but a preliminary effort toward a more thoroughgoing reform; his design was to "follow it by and with another essay, 'Spirit,' and the two shall make a decent volume."[32] That the sequel never appeared under that title testifies to the thoroughness with which Emerson had combined the two concepts of nature and spirit in his brief essay. For the next decade his lectures and addresses would continue to emerge as distillations of the mystical essence he had confined in the 1836 work.

Kenneth Burke, in a salient essay on Emerson's *Nature*, provides us with a particularly useful key to that book. He suggests that Emerson's theory of correspondence enshrined therein is best understood as "the building of a *terministic bridge* whereby one realm is *transcended* by being viewed *in terms of* a realm beyond it" and, further, that this "pontification" or bridging of two worlds can best be served in the realm of aesthetics by "stylistic procedures designed to serve as *bridges* (or intermediaries) between Nature and Supernature." Burke provides as the most obvious example of this kind of symbolic "bridging" the terms "man" and "God"; to close the gap between the two, humanity posits Christ, the "god-man."[33]

Burke's schematic introduction to Emerson's system grows in importance when we realize that in later works like "The Poet" Emerson strongly suggests an equation between the poet and Christ, a concept I will subsequently explore in more detail. Emerson, who had rejected the conventional historical Jesus as mediator, placed his mantle on all men who recognized and used the correspondential keys strewn throughout the natural world. *Nature*, then, is an early attempt to work out a profoundly new definition of the mediation between this world and the supernal. Or, put another way, Emerson therein sought a method through which the Me and Not-Me, the soul and nature, could be brought into a relationship that culminated in spiritual transcendence for the individual soul. This was to be accomplished through language.

Reconsidering the theological quarrels that had surrounded his youth, by 1836 Emerson had decided that nature suggested theological "uses" which, if properly assimilated, provided a means for man's ascension to another sphere of consciousness. Moreover, that one of his key chapters spoke

[90]

explicitly to the problem of language suggests how, in the world he envisioned, the man aware of the vibrancy of natural language could move spiritually upward to a state of particular exhilaration. And if the idea of correspondence was at the center of the transcendental metaphysic, we do well to read *Nature* with the recognition that its author believed that the hinge of correspondential relations significantly turned on a dialectic between *word* and *thing*.[34] Any philosopher who still used words merely as logical counters could not meet Emerson on his own ground.

In an early review of *Nature* the stalwart Unitarian Francis Bowen encountered just this difficulty. Assessing the work for the Unitarian *Christian Examiner*, Bowen admitted that the book held "beautiful writing and sound philosphy," but he also noted his distress over what he termed "a certain vagueness of expression" and a "vein of mysticism that pervades the writer's whole course of thought." Evidently these flaws troubled him enough for him finally to dismiss the book, for, as he read further, its perusal became nothing less than "painful," its thoughts "frequently bewildering."[35]

Bowen's review-essay displays how the conservative Unitarian mind struggled to resist the philosophical currents washing the barren shores of New England theology. He was astute enough to recognize the novelty of the work, which arose, as he put it, "not from the choice or distribution of subject," nature still being a rational enough topic of discussion among intelligent theologians, but rather from Emerson's "manner of treatment"—so unlike the method of Paley—which remained for Bowen "cloud-cap't phraseology" indecipherable to any but those sympathetic to the ravings of the German idealists. To Bowen, the results of Emerson's forays into Continental metaphysics were nil: "instead of comparing truths and testing propositions," *Nature*'s readers had to "busy themselves in hunting after meaning, and investigating the significance of terms."[36]

This is precisely what Emerson, following the lead of Marsh and Reed, wanted. He believed the terminology used to assess man's spiritual capacities had to be reexamined and extended to include the provocative insights of the contemporary European philosophers. If the phraseology in which he couched his argument seemed affected, it was not from any desire to confuse his readers but rather in order to shock them into what he termed "an original relation to the universe." What Bowen thought a silly infatuation with the "formation of a large class of abstract nouns and adjectives" from the German language involved Emerson's attempt to free his contemporaries from the constrictions of a vocabulary inadequate to describe their profound religious experience.[37] "We are now so far from the road to truth," Emerson declared, "that religious teachers dispute and hate one another, and speculative men are esteemed unsound and frivolous" (W, 1:8). That cry echoed, and would continue to resound, throughout New England, at least until the time when the vision of Emersonians and Bushnellians alike was more generally accepted. *Nature* was Emerson's announcement that the mediation between God and Man—Nature and Spirit—was not something experienced only by the historical Christ. The machinery of transcendence, Burke's "bridging," was available to all men, if only they could accept a vocabulary, as well as a theology, based on their intuitive insight into the natural world.

Nature has been explicated frequently and at great length, but the section on language, the linchpin in Emerson's conception of language in its symbolic as well as theological applications, still needs elucidation, if only to enable us later to consider Emerson's most thorough reworking of theological language and dogma into the poetic, his essay "The Poet." The reader of the 1836 manifesto misses much if he neglects to recall that *Nature* had a dual purpose: It was as much cultural critique as philosophical position paper. In it, Emerson was asking his readers just how fulfilled a nation could be if it defined as the highest uses to which nature could be put such economic enterprises as the Erie Canal or the development of hundreds of miles of iron-railed roads. The corruption of man was followed, as Emerson wryly noted, by the corruption of his language, and in the American nation both these declensions were highly visible (W, 1:20).

Emerson's pronouncement on his nation's inherent rottenness was explicit. All around him he saw "simplicity of character and sovereignty of ideas" broken by the prevalence of "secondary desires, the desire of riches, of pleasure, of power and praise." Duplicity and falsehood everywhere were spreading, and man's "power over nature as an interpreter of the will" was being lost:

New imagery ceases to be created, and old words are perverted to stand for things which are not; a paper currency is employed, when there is no bullion in the vaults. In due time the fraud is manifest, and words lose all power to stimulate the understanding or the affections. [W, 1:20]

With an implicit nod in the direction of the magisterial Jonathan Edwards, who in the mid–eighteenth century had been able to awaken the religious affections with his reinvigorated vocabulary, Emerson declared the spiritual bankruptcy of his contemporaries' words and deeds. The words they used to describe their religious lives no longer *meant* as they had before. Their meanings were blurred, and so valueless, with men no longer willing to act on them. Emerson suggested that this sad state of affairs had occurred at least partially because his countrymen had strayed from the higher purposes once present to them in the fabulous book of nature's revelation.[38]

The chief glory of his essay is Emerson's open declaration of this moral and epistemological failure that, once so acknowledged, had to be rectified if religious faith was to be restored. And the remedy Emerson brought to this cancerous situation was the spiritual idealism he had adopted from Marsh, Reed, Oegger, and others. Emerson's answer to his contemporaries' theological and ethical crisis lay in his recognition that man had to use nature upwardly to move through the "subtle chain of countless rings" to the world of spirit, an ascension that had at its vital center the whole question of language.

This must be underscored, for Emerson had begun translating what a few years earlier had been primarily a theological concern into the realms of *ethics* and *aesthetics*. Like Coleridge, whose writings had the same wide applicability, Emerson's criticism of his contemporaries' epistemology was useful for far more than a remedy to the problems among

[93]

differing Christian denominations.[39] He declared that the language used by men in the 1830s did not do adequate justice to the range of their imaginations and that this affected how they saw the world ethically as well as doctrinally. To aid this situation, the language of religion had to be "naturalized." If that task could be accomplished, both a spiritual and a secular awakening would occur.

In his essay Emerson saw nature as the vehicle of thought in three ways:

1. Words are signs of natural facts.
2. Particular natural facts are signs of particular spiritual facts.
3. Nature is the symbol of spirit. [*W*, 1:17]

There was an ascending order of importance to these propositions, but Emerson believed each of them had to be carefully and, to use an Edwardsian term, "affectionately" assimilated before the individual comprehended the strength and meaning of the "terministic bridge" the author was constructing. For example, the idea that words were signs of natural facts appears patently obvious but has behind it much of the thought of Reed and Oegger and the Neoplatonists, and perhaps even some tidbits culled from the arguments of Norton, Stuart, and other of Emerson's contemporaries among the Unitarians and Trinitarians. As Emerson saw it, this proposition was the first in a series of links in the chain of correspondence whose purpose was to make men aware of the almost occult relationship between their minds and the natural world.

If words were based on the mind's relation to natural facts, this relationship was made even more significant by Emerson's supposition of a unique linkage between the worlds of matter and spirit. "The use of natural history," he confidently declared, "is to give us aid in supernatural history." That is, if understood aright, nature yielded a vocabulary that explained man's relationship to the spiritual realm: "The use of outer creation [is] to give us language for the beings and changes of inward creation." The language in which man expressed thoughts and emotions was only "borrowed from sensible things" to raise his mind to higher thoughts; but, in a line of argument that reveals his concern over what had become a critical problem within his own intellectual community—the loss of vital piety in the Unitarian faith—he also lamented that most of the "processes" by which these transformations from matter to spirit were made now were "hidden away from us in a remote time when language was framed" (W, 1:18). As man drifted further from his moorings in the natural world, the result for religion (as well as for philosophy) was a vocabulary progressively more removed from the inspiration and wisdom of the ancient texts.[40]

Nature, then, provided words that conveyed a "spiritual import" and unlocked another world of experience to man. "It is not only words that are emblematic; it is things which are emblematic," he proclaimed. Man had to see himself— that is, in the thoughts and emotions that best defined his spirit—reflected in the world of everyday experience. Further, man's spiritual dimension, the extent to which he touched the Not-Me, was defined through a relation to the visible, natural world. "Every appearance in nature," Emerson suggested, "correspond[s] to some state of mind . . . [that] can only be described by presenting that natural appearance as its picture." An enraged man was fittingly named a lion, a cunning man a fox, a lamb innocence, a snake subtle spite (W, 1:18).

Leaning heavily on the almost allegorical understanding of nature and spirit he discerned in Swedenborg and his disciples, Emerson contended that there was "nothing lucky or capricious in these analogies." They most emphatically were not the "dreams of a few poets here and there" but constantly pervaded all nature. Man, especially when he spoke of spiritual matters, was an "analogist" and studied relations "in all objects." Intuiting what later thinkers discovered to be one of the definitive traits of the human race, that men are symbol-making animals, Emerson believed that the innumerable "rays of relation" man discerned provided meaning to his existence. "Neither can man be understood without these objects," nor "these objects without man." In a metaphor startling for its candor, Emerson declared the facts of natural history, or conversely, of human consciousness, by themselves "barren, like a single sex" (*W*, 1:19). For fruition they had to be joined to their other half, at which point symbolic expression of the spiritual world became possible for anyone.

Emerson was astonished—here we wish for proof that he had read the early essays of James Marsh in the *North American Review*—that the "same symbols are found to make the original elements in all languages." The more he studied the "ecstatic" pieces of literature, the more it was apparent that the idioms of all languages "approach each other in passages of the greatest eloquence and power." And here his dependence on Oegger obviously surfaces, for in that Swedenborgian's work Emerson perused a chart of what Oegger thought the predominant symbols used in all religious discourse; to Emerson this suggested that "this immediate dependence of language upon nature, this conversion of an outward phenomenon into a type somewhat of human life, never loses its power to affect us" (*W*, 1:19–20).

Content that he had shown men thus to be "assisted by natural objects in the expression of particular meanings," Emerson proclaimed the deeper import of the language of nature. It was not to convey "pepper-corn informations," merely expediting "the affairs of our pot and kettle." The language of nature presented nothing less than the essence of God. The "grand cipher" of the world did not just serve men's particularly petty uses but provided an illustration of the spirit as it became translated into the outer world. "Parts of speech are metaphors," Emerson declared, "because the whole of nature is a metaphor of the human mind." And if nature always stood ready to "clothe" what man said and to provide him with the imagery necessary to convey complex thoughts and feelings, he simply could not avoid "the question of whether the characters are not significant of themselves" (*W*, 1:21).

May I declare explicitly what should now be apparent? In *Nature* Emerson, though eschewing explicit references to the theological debates over the origin and meaning of language, still addressed the issues raised by such people as Marsh, Stuart, Norton, and others. He advanced the proposition that all men could be instructed in proper moral, spiritual, and, as we shall see, aesthetic teachings through observation of natural laws and the language to which they give rise. "A life in harmony with nature, the love of truth and virtue," Emerson believed, would "purge the eyes to understand the text." With enough patience and insight, man would discover that "the laws of moral nature answer to those of matter as face to face in a glass." The very axioms of physics translated the "laws of ethics" as he discovered, for example, that in both the physical and moral spheres "the whole is greater than the part" and "reaction is equal to action." "These propositions," continued Emerson, "have a much more extensive and universal sense when applied to human life, than when confined to technical use" (W, 1:23). The more man understood his position in nature, the higher his soul was lifted.

Emerson anticipated an argument Horace Bushnell later made in his *Nature and the Supernatural*, for Emerson implied that religious men have nothing to fear from the new advances of science.[41] Science was a threat to faith only when it was *improperly* understood. If science was defined as the accurate study of nature, it could do nothing but further an understanding of the relationship between matter and spirit. Its symbols, new though they might seem, aided in the "bridging" between the Me and the Not-Me. Moreover, scientific laws, properly regarded, made the universe more "transparent" and allowed the "light of higher laws than its own" to shine through the material veil. For Emerson, as for Edwards before him, "the visible creation [was] the terminus or the circumference of the visible world" and facts the "end, or last issue of spirit" (W, 1:22).

We gain another insight into Emerson's involvement in the philological controversies of his day when we consider the imagery of his concluding paragraph in his section on language. There he claimed that what before had been unconscious truth locked in the oversoul became, when "interpreted and defined in an object, a part of the domain of knowledge—a new weapon in the magazine of power."[42] To the enlightened Christian every object was luminous, a stimulant to arouse individuals from the spiritual lethargy that paralyzed the age. The words theologians used had been flogged into drivel, while, at the same time, the manifold objects of the world lay everywhere about, wired to spiritual meanings, waiting for the electrifying moment of vision. Words, things, and Spirit united in a potential force field, which could burst into an apocalypse of inspired language of a kind man had not known since his days in Eden. If this relation "between mind and matter" were known "by all men," Reed's prognostication of a language not of words but of things would be realized. Emerson believed it would do no less than usher in the kingdom of God among men.[43]

In his recent biography of Emerson, Joel Porte (following Jonathan Bishop's lead) convincingly argues that in Emerson's address before the graduating class of the Divinity School in 1838 he was consciously, and quite pointedly, parodying both the religious language and the dogma of many of the conservative Unitarians in the audience.[44] I would argue further that, at this point in his career, Emerson had formulated the kind of demythologized Christianity that allowed him to explore the heuristic value of symbols that for him hitherto had been confined to use in a more strictly theological realm. With a performance like the "Divinity School Address" behind him, Emerson could begin to express to his contemporaries the rather startling fact that they could best understand the dimensions of their religious belief if they accepted the fact that not only had Christ walked among them more as a man than as the Son of God but also that his highest service to them resided in the poetic or ecstatic language in which his heavenly vision was expressed.

In the "Divinity School Address" Emerson at times made it sound as though his understanding of Christ had transformed that figure into a type of the artist, a man who (like Jonathan Edwards in his "Personal Narrative") explained how he had seen "further" than others with more limited vision—An example is Emerson's statement of how Christ recognized "that God incarnates himself in man, and evermore goes forth anew to take possession of his World," a statement closely followed by Emerson's lament that his contemporaries do not understand that "there is no doctrine of the Reason which will bear to be taught by the Understanding." Emerson knew full well that it was the Understanding that "caught this high chant from the poet's lips" and perverted it into a mere "Mythus" (W, 1:81). But it is in his later essay "The Poet," one of the few optimistic pieces published in his *Essays: Second Series* (1844), after the death of his five-year-old son Waldo, where we best can see the transformation from religious to aesthetic symbol that characterizes Emerson's later work and forms one of his enduring contributions to America's intellectual development.

When the reader understands how early efforts like "The Lord's Supper," *Nature*, and the "Divinity School Address" are scarcely disguised struggles with questions of language and theology bequeathed Emerson by contemporary theologians, every page of "The Poet" reveals a man moving those questions into a much larger arena. Here Emerson provides answers that have less and less to do with those questions' doctrinal or dogmatic implications, which prior to 1830 had been the exclusive concern of anyone engaged in theological controversy. We need only think back to Emerson's earlier soul-searching about the historical accuracy of the Scriptures (just prior to his delivering "The Lord's Supper") to appreciate how far he had come—via Coleridge, Reed, and others—when in "The Poet" he lambasted contemporary theologians for thinking it "a pretty air-castle to talk of the spiritual meaning of a ship or a cloud, of a city or a contract." Such men prefer, he noted sardonically, "to come again to the solid ground of historical evidence," not realizing "the highest minds of the world have never ceased to explore the double meaning, or shall I say the quadruple or centuple or much more manifold meaning, of every sensuous fact" (WC, 3:4). If his friends were to be faulted for any religious shortcomings, then, it was because they, like Emerson's acquaintance, the Reverend Barzillai Frost (whom he had parodied in the "Divinity School Address"), did not perceive the *literal* presence of the miraculous in nature's commonplace facts.

One of Emerson's most revealing paragraphs in this essay deals specifically with his sense of the poet as a universal Christ-figure, a passage that has not received the emphasis it demands, particularly in the context established in this study. Early in the essay Emerson provided his readers with a radically transformed understanding of the Blessed Trinity as he proclaimed that

the universe has three children, which reappear under different names in every system of thought, whether they be called cause, operation, and effect; or, more poetically, Jove, Pluto, Neptune; or, theologically, the Father, the Spirit, and the Son; but which we will call here the Knower, the Doer, and the Sayer.

"These," he continued, "stand respectively for the love of truth, for the love of good, and for the love of beauty," and it is, he reminds us, the poet who is the "Sayer, the Namer, and [who] represents beauty" (WC, 3:6). To be sure, Emerson had mentioned this triad of truth, goodness, and beauty in his 1842 lecture "The Transcendentalist" at the Masonic Temple in Boston; but there the analogy to Christ was not explicitly made. In "The Poet" Emerson thought it important to suggest how much his contemporaries needed another redeemer, one whose grasp of language and symbol, as well as of divine truth, was comparable to Christ's, or at least to others among the world's great prophets.[45]

Throughout the essay Emerson elaborates the intended equation between Christ and the poet. Like Christ, who stood as ransom before his Father for the entire human race, so, too, the poet is "representative" and "stands among partial men for the complete man." Further, like the Christ who freed mankind again to the possiblity of entering heaven, so the poet is a liberator who "unlocks our chains and admits us to a new thought." When men are exposed to the truths the poet expresses, they recognize how "the use of his symbols has a certain power of emancipation for all men." And like the Savior who called all unto him as children, when the poet speaks men "seem to be touched by a wand which makes [them] dance and run about happily, like children." "Poets," Emerson brazenly declares, "are thus liberating gods" (WC, 3:5, 30).

Indeed, throughout the essay Emerson intends to make his readers aware that he means no deception when he equates the work of the Sayer with a process of salvation, for the poet provides a feeling akin to what those of an earlier generation (and, indeed, what some evangelicals of Emerson's own day) would have called a conversion experience. As he continues in this vein, Emerson sounds as though he were making a narration of the influence of saving grace upon his soul. "With what joy," he exclaims, "I begin to read a poem which I confide in as an inspiration! And now my chains are to be broken; I shall mount above these clouds and opaque airs in which I live . . . and from the heaven of truth I shall see and comprehend my relations." The "new birth" is complete, for at such moments, Emerson announces confidently, he becomes "reconcile[d]" to live, while all nature becomes "renovate[d]." "Life will no more be a noise" to him who has experienced the effects of the poet's vision; and, as self-righteously as any of his seventeenth-century New England ancestors, Emerson claims that then is he able to "see men and women and know the signs by which they may be discerned fools and satans." The rebirth of his soul is complete, for "this day [when the poet's message is heard] shall be better than my birthday: then I became an animal; now I am invited into the science of the real" (WC, 3:12).

This remarkable reworking of the morphology of conversion into an aesthetic experience takes on more significance when the reader is aware of how closely the older forms of religious vocabulary have been melded with terms from the idealistic philosophy to which Emerson had been exposed: He details this dream-vision of transcendence with reference to an explicitly Coleridgean term. "This insight," Emerson declares, "expresses itself by what is called Imagination" and is best understood not by reference to any religious terminology but as "a very high sort of seeing, which does not come by study, but by the intellect being where and what it sees . . . by sharing the path or circuit of things through forms . . ." (WC, 3:26). In the presence of the poet wielding his liberating symbols, man stands, Emerson mystically suggests, "before the secret of the world, there where Being passes into Appearance and Unity into Variety" (WC, 3:14).

But it is imperative that the poet also become the "Sayer or Namer" and openly declare what has been hidden from his contemporaries because of their imperfect nature and limited vision. "The world being thus put under the mind for verb and noun, the poet is he who can articulate it." The secret of the universe, to paraphrase Robert Frost, literally sits in the middle of men, and the poet must do all in his power to make the secret apparent.

For through that better perception he stands one step nearer to things, and sees the flowing or metamorphosis; perceives that . . . within the form of every creature is a force impelling it to ascend into a higher form; and following with his eyes the life, uses the form which expresses that life, and so his speech flows with the flowings of nature. [WC, 3:20]

For the poet the world becomes "a temple whose walls are covered with emblems, pictures and commandments of the Deity," and it becomes his job to convey the meaning behind those emblems as evocatively as he can. Emerson's sometimes facetious contemporary Christopher Cranch may have thought such a statement extravagant, but Emerson indeed believed that "Nothing walks, or creeps, or grows, or exists, which must not in turn arise and walk before him [the poet] as an exponent of his meaning" (WC, 3:17).[46] Thus, the lessons from men like Reed and Oegger were assimilated, but along with the important corollary that man must not, like the self-centered mystic, "nail a symbol to one sense, which was a true sense for a moment, but soon becomes old and false." The poet is he who knows that "all symbols are fluxional; all language is vehicular and transitive, and is good, as ferries and horses are, for conveyance, not as farms and houses are, for homestead" (WC, 3:34). When man reads the true poet's works, Emerson believes, he finds himself on a version of Jacob's ladder, the rungs of which are assembled from the world's natural facts and by which he is to climb to view the world of spirit.

More could be said about this important essay, which suggests how in Emerson one sees the gradual change from an interest in the language of religious discourse to the more universal language of symbol, but by now the obvious point has been made. Over the period from 1832 to 1844 Emerson had come to see how the theological quarreling and epistemological confusion that had so shaken his faith in his native creed would not be eliminated through further hair splitting of theological terms. Like Horace Bushnell, Emerson came to believe in the efficacy of, almost in *salvation by*, recourse to a more "poetic" vocabulary for the expression of man's profoundly religious emotions.

For him the Higher Criticism of the Bible—an occupation that also troubled the faith of his good friend Theodore Parker, who was more deeply immersed in the German critical scholarship—did not lead to stringent testing of the historicity of particular biblical passages or events or even to a mere acceptance of the mythological content of the Old and New Testaments.[47] By the time he came to write "The Poet," Emerson, I would claim, had moved beyond both these positions, to a belief that what was most significant about the Bible was the lesson it proffered man concerning the inherent *poetry*, the very *divinity*, of his everyday existence. Emerson also intended to make his readers aware that the saving grace offered by the poet-figure was available to all men. "Hence the necessity of speech and songs," he declared; "hence these throbs and heart-beatings in the orator," all "to the end namely that thought may be ejaculated as Logos, or Word" (WC, 3:40). The world *itself*, Emerson believed, was this Logos, a wonderful cipher to be read and then incorporated into man's desire for spiritual transcendence. One word was as good as another, in the sense that all words pointed men back to the picture-language of nature. The various languages' later accretions of vocabulary did nothing to clarify the final meaning man sought, for the answer lay only in the simplicity, and in the very luminosity, of the world's manifold objects.

After 1836 Emerson became more and more interested in the language of nature and in the men who could read it. It was this skill in the young Henry David Thoreau that drew Emerson to his young townsman, and it was to this same gift that Emerson attributed the power of Walt Whitman's *Leaves of Grass*. But in attempting to understand his appreciation for such men we should always keep in mind how profound a revolution had to have been wrought for this disgruntled Unitarian finally to accept the substitute of a language of nature—and a *symbolic* one at that—for the authority of scriptural revelation. Here I have merely outlined a few of the turning points toward that final revolution, but other essays of this period, especially "The Method of Nature" (1841) and "The Transcendentalist" (1842), as well as the earlier lectures in the series "The Present Age" (c.1839) and later ones like "Nature" (1844) make this development even more explicit.[48]

For Emerson, then, the heuristic nature of language made all things possible; and, whereas in 1832 he had regarded speech in an almost Lockean, commonsensical way, by the later part of that decade he knew that such a conception was but a prison house to man's imagination and immortal spirit. Language had to be felt again as a liberating force. Further—and this fact gains importance when we come to study Henry David Thoreau's adoption of new philological theories—the implication of the Emersonian theory of language suggested that the world itself is an *emblem* of God, with the proper usage of words demonstrating a constant and universal analogy. Language was, indeed, "fossil poetry," and "every word . . . once a poem." But it was equally important to Emerson that every "new relation is a new poem," too (*WC*, 3:18). Thus, the poet is he who sets man on a continually ascending spiral toward spirituality. He liberates his auditors for further motion or transcendence, using the varied symbols of the natural world to point to the realm of eternal truth beyond. His job finally is not to provide that truth but to allow an approach toward it through the analogies perceivable in words and their derivations in natural facts. Here Emerson remains very much the mystic, finally denying the intrinsic value of the things of this world and seeking instead a transcendent relation to his surroundings. The true poet, the mediating figure who assumes the role of a liberating god, illustrates how reality may be *used* in the process of transcendence. As all words are vehicular and transitive, so, too, is the poet.

The critic Charles Feidelson thinks that, given Emerson's writings on language and poetry, what that writer "tried to render as metaphysical doctrine, and expressed more adequately by his very ambiguity of statement, was the resurgent capacity for symbolic experience, based on a sense of the inherent power of language."[49] What Feidelson does not note, however, is that earlier in Emerson's career the notion of symbolic literature was *not* Emerson's main concern. He was less interested in man's ability to comprehend "symbolic" experience than he was in reaffirming his belief that there did, indeed, exist a realm of spirit approachable in moments of illumination. By the 1840s, however, Emerson's reading in the varied offerings of European romantics, especially in the theology of the Swedenborgians, made him more aware of the "transitive" value of words, their inherent ability to *convey* spiritual experience. But at first he was not particularly interested in their shimmering or mutant power per se, as someone like Melville was. Emerson rarely doubted that there was something beyond the confines of this material plane toward which the things of this world pointed him.

Although Emerson appreciated how any word—or any natural fact, for that matter—could become a different "symbol" to different people, he had no hesitation in declaring that, finally, a word or object served a higher purpose, the unveiling of an unambiguous spiritual or moral truth. But others among his contemporaries began calling into question the existence of the higher sphere itself, and their conclusions about the relationships among words, things, and the Spirit were much more tenuous. Men like Thoreau, Hawthorne, and Melville were more removed from the infighting of New England's theological circles than Emerson was, and it is in their works that we see the most important resolution of those questions of theology and aesthetics that had become clearly discernible in Emerson's writings.[50] If their moral universe appeared considerably more complex than Emerson's, it was not only because they lacked his streak of "cosmic optimism." A good deal of their anxiety over the final meaning of the "spiritual" world and the values embodied in it sprang from their differing solutions to the equations between the worlds of matter and spirit that Emerson found so linear. To express this newfound complexity they turned to a symbolic discourse that brought them to the threshold of a modern consciousness about the use of literary symbol and its ability to represent the ambiguities found in the deepest truths of God and man.

[105]

In all the dissertations on language, men forget the language that is, that is really universal, the inexpressible meaning that is in all things and everywhere, with which the morning and evening teem. . . . With a more copious learning or understanding of what is published, the present languages, and all that they express, will be forgotten.

Henry David Thoreau,
Journal, 23 August 1845

Chapter Four

Farther Afield

Henry Thoreau's Philological Explorations

Emerson's eloquent funeral oration aside, the first biography of Thoreau was undertaken by someone who at the time of the Concord saunterer's death knew him even better than Emerson himself. In 1873 William Ellery Channing, nephew and namesake of the great minister who unconsciously had done so much to provoke the succeeding generation's rebellion against the wisdom of its fathers, published *Thoreau: The Poet-Naturalist*, a fitting memorial to the friend with whom Ellery had spent so many hours.[1] The young Channing was among the few men privileged to tramp about with Thoreau; their outings in the woods and fields of Concord, and their longer excursions to such distant (for Thoreau) places as Cape Cod, had given him as much insight as anyone into the strategies behind Thoreau's life and art.

Among the many salient hints to Thoreau's character strewn through Channing's pages is the revealing statement that any intelligent reader encountering Thoreau's well-honed literary productions should realize that "in much that Mr. Thoreau wrote, there was a philological side,—this needs to be thoughtfully considered."[2] Given this early assessment by one of Thoreau's closest companions, it is surprising how long it has taken critics to appreciate how the complex web of language in his mature works is related to a profound interest in contemporary philological theories. Of course, scholars have not overlooked the constant punning in *A Week on the Concord and Merrimack Rivers* and *Walden*, but what has been neglected until recently is the importance of language *theory* to Thoreau's conception of both his art

[109]

and the universe in which the artist functioned.[3] In a very visible way Thoreau's interest in and gradual assimilation of the philological theories current in New England's intellectual circles reinforced and provided new direction for his aesthetic achievement.

Like his onetime mentor, Emerson, Thoreau quickly escaped the restrictions of the Unitarian mind's empirical view of language and discovered from such far-flung characters as Charles Kraitsir, Richard Trench, and the Penobscot Indian guide Joe Polis how within the very structure of language was recorded an answer to what comprised the universe as far as man could know it. As he read the language of nature and fused philology with eschatology, Thoreau was able to understand his relationship to the Spirit more profoundly than many theologians of his day who never deciphered the inner, or (if you will) the genetic, code of the languages they studied. Moreover, as Thoreau transferred his philological knowledge to the craft of literature he demonstrated (from empirical observation as rigorous as any Lockean's) that language was not an arbitrary imposition of sound upon object but stemmed organically from the very core of the empirical objects themselves, thus offering men profound clues to the organization of the universe. Thoreau proved that Locke and his followers had not looked deeply enough into the nature of *things* to observe the truths he everywhere discerned, truths of literature as well as of life. In Thoreau, then, we find fulfilled the promise of Sampson Reed, for as the very stones cried out their message, Thoreau (like the ancient prophets) took the time to listen.

We should keep in mind, however, that, while during Thoreau's term at Harvard in the mid-1830s he had known firsthand some of the denominational infighting among the Unitarians, his interest in Christian dogma was not strong enough to engage him in the scriptural and doctrinal controversies that initially had provoked the philological speculations of Emerson and others. Thoreau's religious imagination turned more toward what we might for convenience term religious *mythologies*—hence, for example, his interest in the sacred scriptures of the Eastern religions.[4] Equally important, this preoccupation still brought him face to face with questions about the relationship of inspired speech to divine revelation and of human language to the natural world, topics that also concerned (albeit in more explicitly Christian terms) men like Emerson and, of course, Marsh, whose appreciation of Herder's work on Hebrew poetry had determined the range of his own philological interests. As Thoreau read more widely in Hindu and Persian texts, all the while considering the theories of philologists whose works he admired, his notion of what animated speech at the deepest levels took provocative shape. By the time he came to write *Walden* in the 1850s, his philological imagination had become one of the most sophisticated of its day, and his religious temperament, as Emerson aptly described it, one of the most "protestant."

More than with Marsh, Bushnell, or even Emerson, though, the origin of Thoreau's interest in philology is found in his concern with writing per se, a subject to which he was introduced by Edward Tyrell Channing, brother of the Unitarian divine. Beginning in 1819 Channing was professor of rhetoric at Harvard and during his career instructed most of the men (including Thoreau) who became prominent in the transcendentalist movement of the 1830s and 1840s.[5]

Channing thought contemporary writing displayed what he harshly called as great "a lack of reverence for the old rules of grammar as for the old forms of verbal purity," a situation that could be remedied only by a resurgence of activity among "critics and philologists" who might reverse this verbal corruption. Indeed, Channing was so upset by this abuse of language he even suggested that "the profound investigations into our language" that then were just beginning to attract "so much attention" should immediately be included among the "studies of advanced classes" at Harvard.[6]

He made this recommendation because, though he believed himself a rhetoritician and not a philologist, he had read enough about the philological work of Horne Tooke and others to know that the chief difficulty of anyone seeking to use language was his having to deal with its intrinsic "uncertainty." If they carefully considered language, Channing told his students, they would see that

it is not quite so mutable as running water, yet we know enough of its progress and retrogressions never to expect it to be stationary, while there remains any considerable amount of literary zeal, activity and freedom, or while we are constantly exposed to literary epidemics of languor and vicious taste.[7]

Regarding the study of belles lettres, then, Channing counseled his charges to trace intently the shifting meanings of language in different literary productions they studied and to take as their indexes to the definitions of significant words those authors' works in which the written expression most embodied the intellectual life of an entire culture, namely, the literature of Shakespeare, Spenser, and Milton. But because Channing supported the Unitarians' empirical view of language even as he enjoyed the rich and varied styles of the great authors, he did not search for *preternatural* correspondences between words and things, or things and ideas. If such analogies ever had been explicitly apparent, he thought, they too often were lost to succeeding generations whose new arbiters of style determined the standards of eloquence. Regarding the proper interpretation of scriptural language, Channing fell back upon the by then standard Unitarian response: Its imagery was the result of individuals' having lived in particular historical cultures, making scriptural interpretation dependent on the philologists' extensive knowledge of the Bible's context.[8]

I do not intend to make too much of Channing's influence on Thoreau, but it is worth suggesting that some of Thoreau's peculiar tastes in literature—for example, for the spicy exploration narratives of the seventeenth-century American settlers—may have derived in part from Channing's injunctions on style. More importantly, Channing often emphasized the need to understand a word's etymology before using it in one's writing. A successful writer, he proposed, had to accustom himself to an "analysis of terms, and follow them down their history from their primitive use through the changes they have experienced and the various purposes to which they have been applied."[9] Through such verbal archaeology one's own language would be sharpened and "an habitual force and vigor of expression" prompted. The study of word origins had its place, Channing maintained, if not to return people (as Emerson thought) to a radically proper relationship to the Spirit, then at least to reinforce one's capacity to phrase ideas in a compelling way.

Further, any hints about literary style and its relation to etymology that Thoreau received at Harvard College from Channing were reinforced by his consuming interest in those classical languages he studied, which offered etymological keys to so many English words. As Ethel Seybold reminds us, Thoreau's interest in classical philology was always "scholarly." "He made charts of the language families; he collected dictionaries of foreign languages, even Rasle's dictionary of the Abenaki tongue; he spoke often of the value of language training; his writing is full of speculation about word derivation and meaning: classical, Anglo-Saxon, French, Indian."[10]

More importantly, and corroborating William Ellery Channing's suggestion with which I began this chapter, Seybold concludes that, for all Thoreau's seemingly playful fascination with words, his interest never remained just etymological but instead was decidedly "semantic." Thoreau always sought to know the *practical* difference it made if one regarded words in light of their most primitive references. As he himself phrased it: "Talk about learning our *letters* and being *literate*! Why the roots of *letters* are *things*. Natural objects and phenomena are the original symbols or types which express our thoughts and feelings" (*Wr*, 18:389–90). Here, of course, another early influence on Thoreau's philological interests is strongly evident, for as he began to read Emerson in the late 1830s Thoreau saw that language was not only an expressive force that conveyed men's thoughts from one to another (that is, that language concerned *style*) but also a symbol of what he later would identify as "higher laws." This, of course, was not a proposition Unitarians like Channing or Norton would have announced to him, for it involved questions about language whose ramifications were more moral than historical. But Emerson's early essays were filled with just such important suggestions.

[113]

In Thoreau's published writings and journals it is easy to find examples of this Emersonian emphasis on the moral significance of language. In "Walking" (published in 1862 but delivered as a lecture throughout the previous decade), for example, he echoed Emerson's statement that words were "signs of natural facts." The true poet, Thoreau claimed, not only could "impress the winds and streams into his service to speak for him" but "nailed words to their primitive senses" and made his speech so "fresh and natural" that it would appear "to expand like buds at the approach of Spring" (*Wr*, 5:232). Concomitantly, just as the most evocative vocabulary stemmed from an appreciation of how man's words have their origin in the observable phenomena of nature, Thoreau's poet had to realize that all nature was a metaphor for the spiritual life. "All perception of truth," Thoreau remarked, "is the detection of analogy" (*Wr*, 8:463). "How indispensable to a correct study of nature," he maintained, "is the perception of her true meaning." Becoming an interpreter of supranatural analogies as well as a natural historian, Thoreau reminded himself not to underestimate the value of any simple fact, for it would "one day flower into a truth" (*Wr*, 7:18).[11]

If at points Thoreau's philosophy of language reflected Emerson's, his sensibility toward language and nature diverged at critical points from his older friend's.[12] If natural facts flowered into *words* as well as into truths, what did this mean to a man who came so close to those natural facts that they revealed to him secrets of nature that declared a meaning not hitherto understood by Emerson and that certainly were neither Christian nor Platonic? Emerson had instructed Thoreau to go to nature to discover higher laws. But what if these laws were not the ones Emerson expected to pervade the universe? Could Emerson understand what Thoreau meant when he declared that "most words in the English language do not mean for me what they do to my neighbors" (*Wr*, 15:121)? "My friend," Thoreau hoped, "will be bold to conjecture"; but would he "guess bravely at the significance" of Thoreau's words (*Wr*, 9:83)?

As it emerged, then, Thoreau's philological project was twofold: first, to uncover in nature those truths that to the patient observer blossomed from its every nook and cranny; and, second, to learn enough about the origin and meaning of language and its relation to nature to be able to use it to convey these truths. As Thoreau earlier had noted in his *Journal*, the problems men encountered were both cognitive and epistemological. "How copious and precise is the botanical language to describe leaves," he observed; but why is there no comparable vocabulary to describe man's moral state?

It is wonderful how much pains has been taken to describe a flower's leaf, compared for instance with the care that is taken in describing a psychological fact. Suppose as much ingenuity . . . in making a language to express the sentiments! We are armed with a language adequate to describe each leaf in the field . . . but not to describe a human character. [*Wr*, 8:409–10]

Throughout his life Thoreau took with profound earnestness his self-assigned task of trying to understand the human condition more profoundly through an investigation of the language of nature. "My profession," he declared, "is to be always on the alert to find God in nature, to know his lurking places, to attend all the oratorios, the operas, in nature" (*Wr*, 8:472). And if the music he heard from these delightful spheres eventually caused a reassessment of his allegiance to Neoplatonic theory as Emerson represented it, the artistic achievement of *Walden* proved the importance of this intellectual estrangement from his Concord neighbor.

As I have noted, Thoreau had a strong inclination toward etymology, as witnessed by his ownership of no fewer than seventeen dictionaries. But if Thoreau's delight in noting the similarities among languages fed a voracious philological appetite, this fascination with what words meant and what powers they held within them was augmented further by his literary excursions among writers who demonstrated to him the startling unities that lay beneath individual languages and who challenged him to develop a prose style congruent to the philological wisdom they unveiled to him.

One man who spoke to Thoreau's philological imagination was Richard Trench, whose *On the Study of Words*

[115]

(1851) enjoyed great popularity in England and America and was read by Thoreau in its second (1852) edition. What first attracted Thoreau to Trench's book was the author's indebtedness to Emerson's own sense of language, particularly as it was expressed in the important essay "The Poet." In the first edition of *On the Study of Words*, for example, Trench had referred to a "popular author of our own day [who] has somewhere characterized language as a 'fossil poetry.'"[13] Discovering in Trench's book a wealth of specific examples that displayed the author's essential agreement with Emerson's belief in the evocative power locked within words, Thoreau was moved to record in his *Journal* some of Trench's more Emersonian suggestions.

For example, on 23 January 1853, Thoreau noted that Trench explained that a "wild" man is a "willed" man, a fact that appealed to Thoreau's own love of wordplay. Extending Trench's discussion, Thoreau noted that

a man of will [is one] who does what he wills or wishes, a man of hope and future tense, for not only the obstinate is willed, but far more the constant and persevering. The obstinate man, properly speaking, is one who will not. The perseverance of the saints is positive willedness, not a mere passive willingness. The fates are wild, for they *will*; and the Almighty is wild above all, as fate is. [*Wr*, 10:482]

Such an entry certainly informs our understanding of the nature of Thoreau's obsession with "wildness," especially in his essay "Walking." Moreover, it explains the added bite of his satire when he derives the etymology of "village" from "the Latin *villa*, which together with *via*, a way, or more anciently *ved* and *vella*, Varro derives from veho, to carry, because the villa is the place to and from which things are carried." "Hence, too," Thoreau continued, "the Latin word *vilis* and our vile, also *villain*." This suggests, he concluded, "what kind of degeneracy villagers are liable to," for the village implicitly destroyed what Trench expressed to him about the will (*Wr*, 5:213).

Moreover, Thoreau could not have missed what Trench said in his preface as he paid his respects to previous purveyors of language like Coleridge and Horne Tooke, in whose

Diversions of Purley Trench had discovered a number of serious shortcomings. Trench suggested that a young man's "first discovery that words are living powers, [is] like the dropping of scales from his eyes, like the acquiring of another sense, or the introduction into a new world," a sentiment echoing the religious dimensions of Emerson's "The Poet" and bringing to mind Thoreau's notion (expressed in the "Reading" chapter of *Walden*) that, before we can understand the "significant" expression of the "heroic" books, "we must be born again." Later, he approvingly noted Trench's sentiment that such words as "transport, rapture, ravishment, [and] ecstasy" were the "true" words. "These are words I want," Thoreau exclaimed; "these are truly poetic words. I am inspired, elevated, expanded. I am on the mount" (*Wr*, 10:466–67). Then, too, Thoreau could admire Trench's claim that when someone takes the care to examine a commonly used word "it will be found to rest upon some deep analogy to things natural and things spiritual; bringing those to illustrate and to give an abiding form and a body to these."[14] The British philologist was supremely confident that words were nothing less than a witness "for great moral truths," which were to be revealed by writers whose language was based in nature's primal power.

If such Emersonian lines (indeed, they could as well have been written by Sampson Reed) remained vivid in Thoreau's mind, Trench's additional claim that God "had pressed such a seal of truth upon language" that men were "continually uttering deeper truths than they know" resonated more deeply. For, as we shall see shortly, Thoreau came to believe not only that men uttered deeper truths than they knew but that utterance itself reflected the deepest truth about the human condition. Such a suggestive statement from Trench—which Thoreau read as he was revising *Walden*—both illuminates the secrets in the final chapters of Thoreau's masterpiece and suggests the complicated intellectual background to that entire work.

Through his education and private reading then, Thoreau had developed what we might term a propensity toward the kinds of philological ideas he would explore further in his own prose; for example, Trench's suggestion (again echoing Reed and Emerson) that language developed from man in a revealingly *organic* way. From Creation, Trench claimed, man had been given the power of naming: Each word was "but [man's] reason, coming forth that it might behold itself." Moreover, Trench was sure that once this latent germ of expression was vitalized, it was like the "growth of a tree springing out of, and unfolding itself from a root, and *according to a necessary law*" (italics mine). This organic process, as Trench explained it, should not be compared to "the rearing of a house, which a man should slowly and painfully fashion for himself" but rather be understood as "the result of an innate and divine capacity for speech stemming from the Reason with which man was endowed."[15] And just as this "organic" aspect of language came to rule Thoreau's conception of inspired speech and of the world it described, Emerson's awareness of how words contained not only fossil poetry but fossil *ethics* and *history* as well was corroborated by Thoreau's surveying what we might term the "epistemological etymology" performed by Trench in the body of his book.

Thoreau's inclination toward such an organic renovation of his language was stirred by other readings as well; for example, after studying the Swedenborgian J. J. G. Wilkinson's *Human Body and Its Connexion to Man*, Thoreau confided to his *Journal* that it always had been his dream "to return to the primitive analogical and derivative sense of words," as Wilkinson, too, wished to do. With this in mind, Thoreau wrote that what he most admired in the book was the faith Wilkinson placed in "old and current expressions" as having sprung from "an instinct wider than science" (*Wr*, 8:462–63).

Then, too, Thoreau's essay "Thomas Carlyle and His Works" reveals an interest in that writer's "eminently colloquial style" that carries "all its load, and never breaks down nor staggers," and that prefigures Thoreau's later fascination with the speech of his Concord neighbors. Carlyle's books had this power, Thoreau thought, because in them one saw how "Nature is ransacked, and all the resorts and purlieus of humanity are taxed, to furnish the fittest symbol for his thought." Carlyle does not go to the dictionary, Thoreau exclaimed, "but to the word-manufactory itself" to express his many ideas.[16]

It is through such revelations, I think, that we can best understand Thoreau's high appreciation for such an often neglected form of literature as the exploration accounts surrounding the settlement of America. Such hints explain as well his pervasive interest in the Penobscot Indian language, which, like the "ancient" speech Marsh admired, Thoreau found particularly moving. It seemed to him that these "languages"—the swarthy Elizabethan and the native American—brought men closer to the primitive sense of things than the affected jargon of his contemporaries. Moreover, they offered a rigorous standard against which to measure his own stylistic achievement.

F. O. Matthiessen was the first to note that Thoreau did not read the early settlement literature merely for "stories" as, say, Hawthorne did.[17] Rather, as Thoreau himself phrased it when discussing his admiration for the Virginia histories of Captain John Smith, such pages let him think himself "in a wilder country and a little nearer to primitive times." Sounding at times like Sampson Reed praising the inspired language of natural man, Thoreau lauded those Elizabethan explorers who existed in a more primitive relationship to the land and its generative powers and who used a vocabulary that, because it was grounded firmly in first-hand experience, proved more vital than that of men whose literary creations came from the realm of "Fancy." Citing William Bradford's magnificent passage upon the landing of the Pilgrims at Plymouth, Thoreau warned readers to look for "standard English" only in the vocabulary of men like Bradford, who had undergone the experiences about which they wrote, and not in the works of those who titillated their imaginations from behind the protection of glass windows (*Wr*, 10:494). The most vital and enduring language came from men who had known to the marrow the natural facts that animated their narratives.

Thoreau's references to John Josselyn, an Englishman who published two accounts of his trips to America in the seventeenth century, further reveal this intersection of Thoreau's thoughts on language and style. In his *Journal* he noted that early American writers like Josselyn had a "strong and healthy, but reckless, hit-or-miss style," as if "they spoke with a relish, smacking their lips like a coach-whip, caring more to speak heartily than scientifically true," a description reminiscent of Thoreau's praise for Carlyle's "emphatic, natural, lively, stirring tones, muttering, rattling, exploding like shells and shot, and with like execution."[18] Such men as Josselyn were not to be "caught napping by the wonders of Nature in a new country" but were always alert to record just what they saw and to integrate it vividly into their prose (*Wr*, 13:108–9). Studying what Thoreau then recorded from Josselyn's two books and noting how he used the lessons learned from Josselyn in his own work, one discovers that, even apart from his more formal study of philology, Thoreau's literary endeavors always were marked by a desire to transform his own style into that "strong and healthy" prose he discovered among these early New Englanders whose works served as vivid reminders of the truth of Emerson's notion of a natural language.

Note, for example, his references to Josselyn in *A Week on the Concord and Merrimack Rivers*, a volume in which Thoreau also included excerpts from more contemporary historians or gazetteer makers. Comparing the early New England historians with their pallid descendants, Thoreau noted that Josselyn's generation had "stood nearer to the facts, than this, and hence their books have more life to them." By standing nearer to the facts, he told his readers, a "scholar may be sure that he writes the tougher truth for the calluses on his palms," creating sentences "tough, like hardened things, the sinews of deer, or the roots of the pine"; or, as he noted elsewhere, the public should demand of writers a style so precise that it reads "as if its author, had he held a plow instead of a pen, could have drawn a furrow deep and straight to the end."[19]

With such suggestions in mind, what else could explain his decision to include in *A Week on the Concord and Merrimack Rivers* the stark figures he once discovered in a "Fisherman's Account Current" of 1805: "one cod line," "one brown mug," and "a line for the seine"? "Hard, but unquestionable history," explained Thoreau, who had become finely tuned enough to record the evocative quality of such firsthand sources (*Week*, p. 35). He was beginning to read both books and nature with such creative imagination, and his appreciation of men like Josselyn and William Wood (another seventeenth-century New England author) was based on the fact that these were men to whom vocabulary, as well as history, was never just the immediate crudity of what happened but (to paraphrase Henry James) the much finer complexity of what one thought of in connection with it.

Writers like Josselyn, Thoreau noted, also were to be respected because they "use a strange, coarse, homely speech which cannot always be found in the dictionary, nor sometimes be heard in polite society, but which brings you very near to the thing itself described (*Wr*, 13:108–9). Certainly he had the words of Carlyle in mind at that point; and again, perhaps even more vividly (if unconsciously), a few paragraphs later, when answering his own call for sentences "verdurous and blooming, as evergreen and flowers, because they are rooted in fact and experience" (*Week*, p. 104), Thoreau brings the reader close to the essence of a fish he is trying to describe. The "Horned Pout, *Pimelodus nebulosus*, sometimes called Minister, from the peculiar squeaking noise it makes when drawn out of the water, . . . [is] a dull, blundering fellow, like an eel vespertinal in its habits, and fond of the mud" (*Week*, p. 31). Here the natural and moral worlds are indeed brought closely together, even if at the expense of Thoreau's acquaintances among the Concord and Boston ministries! As Thoreau noted later in the same book, "all the moral laws are readily translated into natural philosophy, for often we have only to restore the primitive meaning of words, or to attend to their literal instead of their metaphorical sense" to frame the most apt descriptions (*Week*, p. 362).

It was a similar vividness of expression, a sense that writing, whether about seventeenth-century exploration or nineteenth-century economy, should contain "pure discoveries, glimpses of *terra firma*, though by ship-wrecked mariners, and not the navigations of those who had never been out of sight of land," that Thoreau discovered in the

[121]

American Indian vocabulary he so loved to study and hear (*Week*, p. 98).

While making his trips to the Maine wilderness, for instance, he more than once inquired of his Penobscot guides the meaning of the native name for his beloved Concord River, "Musketicook," and was pleased to learn it had a significance verifiable in natural fact. It was, they told him, "the Dead-Water Stream," or the "Grass-Ground River." As with so many other Penobscot Indian words—for example, "Ktaadn," which meant "highest land"—here was a language that was, indeed, fossil poetry, "a purely wild and primitive American sound, as much as the barking of the Chickaree." The Penobscot language indicated that these native Americans were themselves still organically rooted to nature. Hearing that tongue spoken by men like his guide, Joe Polis, reinforced Thoreau's belief in the English language's corruption, while concomitantly proving to him that aboriginal speech was still so evocative that with few exceptions "the language of [the Indians'] forefathers was still copious enough for them."[20]

Thoreau's contact with the expressive Indian tongue intensely focused his concern with language and style, for while conversing with the native Americans he learned how familiar they were with natural phenomena, their vocabulary proof of "all that intimacy" with the environment they inhabited (*Wr*, 16:294). It was a revelation to him, he admitted, when Joe Polis gave him the Indian names "for things I had only scientific names for before." In proportion as he understood the aboriginal language, Thoreau saw things "from a new point of view," whereas most of the American scholars he knew, "having little or no root in the soil," strove "with all their might to confine themselves to imported symbols alone," which did not embrace the essence of what it was they wished to describe. Thoreau recognized that "a more intimate knowledge, a deeper experience, will surely originate a word," and those who considered such a search not worth the effort only committed again "the old error, which the church, the state, the school, ever commit, choosing darkness rather than light" (*Wr*, 18:389–90).

From his interest in the ideas of such people as Channing, Emerson, Trench, Wilkinson, and Carlyle, then, Thoreau gained a just appreciation of a certain *style* of language that reflected what he termed the "first requisite and rule" in expression, that it shall be "vital and natural, as much as the voice of a brute or an interjection; first of all mother-tongue; and last of all, artificial or father-tongue" (*Wr*, 17:386). Thoreau wanted sentences constructed so truly that they were "as free and natural as a lamb's bleat" and words chosen so precisely that they conveyed startling knowledge garnered from everyday experience. He could note, for instance, that "Evelyn and others wrote when the language was in a tender and nascent state and could be molded to express the shades of meaning." Like Emerson, Thoreau knew that even though some of these men's words "were long since cut and apparently drawn to the mill" they still could put forth a fringe of "green sprouts here and there in the angles of their rugged bark." These tough and well-seasoned words, even if they had been split into shingles and lath over the years, still could supply the building materials for poets "for ages to come" (*Wr*, 11:43).

What makes Thoreau's interest in language and symbol most important, however, and links him to the other subjects of this study is that for all his philological integrity—for all his talk of knowing *how* the word came to represent the thing—he was as profoundly concerned with the meaning of *things themselves* as any of the nineteenth-century figures I already have discussed. His schooling at Emerson's knee through such texts as *Nature* forced him to examine words and things for metaphysical certainty and imbued his punning with a deep seriousness, as though he were turning over each word for some hidden secret to his own existential condition. As Thoreau developed a more profound appreciation of language he assembled hints toward a startling proposition. If in its deepest core language reflected the natural world, then the extraordinary similarities among languages themselves might reveal the final meaning of the Logos as expressed through both them and the world they reflected, a meaning equally far removed from the Neoplatonic vision of Emerson and the Christian transcendentalism of Marsh and Bushnell. *Walden* was written to contain a truth

[123]

of this magnitude, and a large degree of the aesthetic and philosophical satisfaction we derive from Thoreau's masterpiece depends on our understanding the full range of its linguistic splendor.

Thoreau's philological and aesthetic achievement in *Walden* is clarified by an understanding of how he incorporated into his book the theories of yet another philologist, Charles Kraitsir, a Hungarian immigrant who arrived in Boston in 1844 and who, with the strong support of Elizabeth Peabody, began proselytizing his novel manner of teaching foreign languages.[21]

Peabody herself was one of the premier purveyors of philological theories in New England and was instrumental in bringing to contemporary theological and philological debates the best of recent European criticism.[22] As early as 1834 (in a review of Herder's *Spirit of Hebrew Poetry*) she displayed a concern with the authenticity of scriptural texts that showed her to be—as one might expect, given her closeness to William Ellery Channing—an adherent to the Lockean view of language. But even by that date her writing displayed some evidence of wider reading in philology and suggests why she later thought so highly of Kraitsir. In her review, for example, she discussed the *poetry* of the Scriptures, by which she meant "the expression of abstract spiritual truths by sensible objects, by the forms, colors, sounds, changes [and] combinations of external nature." This poetic language, she thought, existed because the human mind "in its original principles, and the natural creation, in its simplicity," were but different images "of the same creator, who linked them for the reciprocal development of their mutual treasures."[23] What she found of most interest in Herder, then, was what had so fascinated James Marsh—his description of the Hebrew poets' use of a "natural" language.

In this review Peabody also expressed a concern with the evocative power of language that dovetailed perfectly with Thoreau's interest in the vocabulary of such indigenously American cultures as Maine's Penobscot Indians. Primitive peoples, she thought, were "naturally poetic," but

[124]

as a society "ramified" and people talked more by imitation and custom and not from their primitive firsthand experiences, a thousand arbitrary and accidental associations "connected themselves with words and deadened the impressions" they naturally made on people. Suggesting a theory of the development of language similar to the one advanced in 1836 by Rowland G. Hazard (whose work she later republished), she saw language as moving to a level of "analytical" (today we would call it *technical*) expression in which words were no longer pictures of the natural world but merely social conventions. This language was commonly known as *prose*; and, while it provided a more precise expression of the differences among things, it sacrificed what Peabody called the "force, impressiveness, and exciting power" of poetry. The most poetic expression of all thought existed in the earlier stages of human civilization, but since poetry once had formed the basis for the first language, "it must always exist as a part of all [subsequent] languages."[24]

Peabody regarded "primitive man"—as he was discussed by Herder, Marsh, and others—as an original poet who named everything around him through the interaction of his speech instinct and the natural environment. Further, she believed that originally there was a reason (explained by her through the common origin of all things in the oversoul) why *such* a word meant *such* a thing, a premise that linked here temperamentally to philosophers like Emerson. For Peabody, a chief lesson of Herder's book was his suggestion that, if man went far enough back in his study of language, he not only would find the original roots of a tongue but could ascertain how these roots themselves were derived from "external and internal" nature. This theory—and here is the linchpin of the meaning of language for her and many transcendentalists—implied a universality to the oldest roots of language which, if understood, revealed what Peabody's friend Bronson Alcott once called a "Universal Grammar."[25] This grammar, in addition to providing a key to the more economic assimilation of the various modern languages, demonstrated the common origin of all men's thoughts in nature's reflections of the oversoul. And if all language was derived from a common source—the interaction of Reason with Nature—it declared a brotherhood of man far more inclusive than any defined by the arbitrary claimers of American political democracy.

Though Peabody's early forays into language study epitomized this concern with a natural language whose parts were intimately connected to the objects of the exterior world and which was available to all men, she had to wait a decade before she discovered someone whose writings provided "sound" evidence for such a theory. That man was Charles Kraitsir, who came to exert an important influence over the mature writings of both Elizabeth Peabody and Henry Thoreau because of the way he addressed their separate interests in the relationship between language and nature. We do not know if under Peabody's prompting Thoreau attended any of the Hungarian's lectures in Boston, but shortly after Peabody published Kraitsir's *Significance of the Alphabet* (1846) from her West Street bookstore, Thoreau owned a copy. He later extended his knowledge of Kraitsir's philology by reading his *Glossology: Being a Treatise on the Nature of Language and on the Language of Nature* (1852), a book he encountered while making revisions in *Walden* and whose influence permeates that masterpiece.[26]

Kraitsir's *Glossology* was an expanded version of the system on which he had lectured in Boston and which Peabody assembled into pamphlet form from notes taken at those performances. His purpose in presenting this larger study was to add further proof to his assumption that at the roots of all languages was a unity of meaning and symbol that stemmed from the fact that all men, "however diverse they might become by conflicting passions and interests, have yet the same reason, and the same organs of speech."[27] He claimed that the sounds man could produce through his vocal organs were limited in number and the explanation for the underlying unity of all tongues was a *physiological* one. Language was the relationship between a man's consciousness and his organs of speech.

Even though Kraitsir avowed that the main benefit of his theory would be an increased facility in the study of foreign languages, he also declared that his book was a tool designed for people who wished "to employ language for its divine ends, as a pole, so to say, whereon the tendrils of clear reason, benign humanity, and of chaste taste, climb up, in the direction of man's posture, towards the Source of Light." Still caught at least partially in the webs of religious controversy that dictated that any investigation of language had to be squared with the "facts" of biblical revelation, Kraitsir assured his readers that his study tended toward "an approximation of the various races and nations to that union into *one mankind*, which is admitted to have existed, by all earnest inquirers into language, and which is attested to by Gen., XI, 1."[28] What Peabody found so compelling in Kraitsir's system—and what made him so significant to Thoreau—was his search for and discovery of nothing other than that phantom of uniformity for which the nineteenth century yearned, a unity that demonstrated how, beneath their temperamental differences, all men were one in the oversoul.

In a passage useful in our attempt to distinguish Emerson's philosophical position on language from Thoreau's, Kraitsir elaborated his contention, seemingly conventional enough for the age, that words originated with a perception of the exterior world. Language, he explained,

was a symbol, a paradigm, an index, a finger-board, pointing in one direction to what is brought in and how it is brought within us; in another direction, to what is uttered and how it is to strike the minds of our fellow men. Man is a mirror of, but also a mediator between, all objects felt without and within himself, as well as between these objects and his own spirit on the one side, and between his spirit and that of his neighbors on the other.

Some impression, then, strikes a man. As important as what it does to him internally, thought Kraitsir, is what he does to make it external again, how through verbal forms he *reflects* or *expresses* it to other beings. The complexity of this process of "reflection," as well as the mediation between reason and vocal sound that occurred when a piece of language was formed, fascinated both Kraitsir and his Concord admirer but was a point about which Emerson offered no particular speculation. His own interest in language never extended to the physical manifestations of speech, wherein Kraitsir located the true unity of the race and which Thoreau found instrumental in understanding his own position in the natural world.[29]

To explicate further this idea of "reflection," Kraitsir distinguished between "speech" and "languages." The former was a "necessary function of man's sensations" and arose "instinctively, involuntarily, yet in keeping with the divine harmony of the universe." The latter, in their multiplicity, were what eventually had happened to speech—that is, it was brought under the influence of local and personal circumstance, multiplying its forms and thus permitting the kind of rational, historical study the Unitarian critics sanctioned. But the essentials of human speech, the way outer impressions were reflected back to the world, were always and everywhere the same. "Each people's genetic power of speech, peculiar in each, amalgamates the phonetic (sound) elements with the feelings and mental conceptions into an organic unity." Speech became, in Kraitsir's memorable phrase, "the explosion of reason," and the word itself—that is, the series of sounds of which the word was composed—became a "new outward object, linking the world with man and man with man." The sounds men uttered were conditioned as much by how they were made—by the vocal organs—as by what caused them, making the complex physiological *and* psychological relation that occurred when reason sought to explode into articulation the factor that provided an underlying unity to all human utterance. To Kraitsir, then, there was a law as to why "spirit" broke into the atmosphere the way it did. While languages now appear so different, in reality there was only one way words *originally* could be formed, "according to the triad" of the interaction of mind, object, and vocal organs. The "germs" of all languages were the same, and this fact argued for the final unity of man's spirit in the oversoul.[30]

Continuing a discussion begun in his earlier pamphlet, Kraitsir also elaborated the relationship among the "gutterals," "labials," and "dentals" he had discovered in his research into the Indo-European languages. These various types of sounds were the "strings" upon which the reason "performed" language. His description of their uses is worth quoting at length:

Henry Thoreau's Philological Explorations

To excite in other men something to be guarded and cherished like our heart, we gutteralize; to indicate wind, wool, wood, water, or any other moving object, we lap with our lips; to denote fleeting, flea-like, free lively butter (flutter)-flies on a level prairie, we combine labials with linguals; when speaking about steady, staring, indurated, enduring objects, we make a din at our teeth.[31]

One has to have a tin ear not to realize the seductive flavor of this kind of concentrated poetic argument, but Kraitsir was well aware that "the symbolism of sounds" had decreased by degrees "in consequence of the fading of the primordial poetry of the human mind." In words reminiscent of Sampson Reed's, he lamented that sounds themselves no longer were symbols with readily apparent meanings, for this loss of "intuitiveness and liveliness" in language had been balanced only slightly by a "greater compenetration of sound and thought."[32] Communication had moved to a more abstract level; and if before the word had "painted vividly the idea man had of the nature of the object," now it was more likely to bring to mind "the total of its characters and relations, not unlike a spiritual tableau."[33] The theoretical implication of Kraitsir's work, then, suggested that men had forgotten how a sound itself might symbolize something greater than the word in which it was embedded.

If knowing what sounds symbolized allowed a man to write a "true" sentence, could the glossological principle be extended to an *entire* work of art, one that embodied in its metaphors as well as in its words the divine truth, as far as man could know it? I surmise that Thoreau became deeply involved with the "science" of glossology as Kraitsir defined it not only for its practical application in making known the similarities among seemingly diverse languages but also because its concepts suggested that the enterprise on which he had long since set his mind, of returning to the "primitive analogical and derivative sources of words," was a philosophically important one, allowing the writer to integrate art and reality in a way hitherto impossible.

The linguistic ideas of Kraitsir, as well as of other philologists in whom Thoreau had read, permeate the structure and imagery of *Walden*, a book in which Thoreau warns the reader that "the volatile truth of our words should continually betray the inadequacy of the residual statement" (WP, p. 325). If we are successfully to read any heroic book—including Thoreau's own—"we must laboriously seek the meaning of each word and line, conjecturing a larger sense than common use permits" (WP, p. 100). Nature, Thoreau maintained, can support more than "one order of understandings" (WP, p. 324), and his book on that subject had to be read as "deliberately and reservedly" as it was written, with a keen eye (and ear) to that language of nature that informed his personal style and vision.

In his own etymological explorations, for example, Thoreau enjoyed discovering the original meaning of words, so that the archaeological treasure within a word would flower into a truth that radiated meaning all the more because of its proximity to the time when it first was created. "I desire," he once boasted, "to speak somewhere without bounds, like a man in a waking moment, to men in their waking moments." He was convinced, he added, that he could not "exaggerate enough to lay the foundation of a true expression." To exaggerate one's language meant to go beyond the common bounds understood for each sound-symbol, a project involving the verbal excavation Thoreau had come to love as he struggled to get the better of words. "It is," he maintained, "a ridiculous demand which England and America make, that you shall speak so they can understand you" (WP, p. 324). Thoreau knew that to record the natural wisdom he had discovered around Concord he had to use a powerfully evocative language, which, like the classics so admired by Marsh, Herder, and Peabody, was "dead to degenerate times."

Taking his initial hints from the correspondential theory of Emerson and the Swedenborgians, Thoreau attempted to weave into his prose not only the imagery but the very glossological meaning of the natural language; for, as he noted at the beginning of his chapter on sounds, men everywhere "are in danger of forgetting the language which all things and events speak without metaphor, which alone is copious and standard" (WP, p. 111). With this in mind, he then illustrates Kraitsir's method by describing the cries of owls "as the most melancholy sound in Nature" and relates how, whenever he tries to capture in words the owl's hooting, he finds himself "beginning with the letters gl," expressive of a mind "which has reached the gelatinous mildewy stage in the mortification of all healthy and courageous thought" (WP, p. 125). The "ancient u-lu-lu" of these birds, this "gurgling melodiousness," was best expressed by the same vowel *u* which, Kraitsir noted, implied a "hair-raising shudder" or dull pain.[34]

Through such simple glossological references Thoreau wished to make it apparent that he was prepared "not so much for contemplation, as for forceful expression" (*Wr*, 8:467), and to this end in *Walden* he often wrung from words the primal meaning that burned at their very core. Hence, for example, in "The Bean-Field" he declared his intention in raising beans to be much more than economic, for his agricultural work also was "for the sake of trope and expression, to serve a parable-maker one day" (WP, p. 162). As he planted, hoed, harvested, threshed, and picked—as he was determined to "know" beans—he also sowed the seeds of (as he put it) "sincerity, truth, simplicity, faith, innocence and the like" through the verbal inspiration his labors provided as he assembled his *Walden* (WP, p. 164). His concluding paragraph in that chapter reveals the true depth of this commitment to the broadcasting of thoughts, for, Thoreau philologically declared, "the ear of wheat, (in Latin *spica*, obsoletely *speca*, from *spe*, hope,) should not be the only hope of the husbandman; its kernel or grain (*granum*, from *gerendo*, bearing,) is not all that it bears." Like the vegetables and grains Thoreau raises, words themselves bear hope for all the desperate men of Concord. "How, then," Thoreau asks, "can our harvest fail?" (WP, p. 166).

The most bountiful "harvest" of Thoreau's philological sowing occurs in the "Spring" chapter of *Walden*, in which he finally made explicit a profound philosophical separation from most transcendentalists. I do not believe I exaggerate when I say that through his interest in the philosophy of language Thoreau finally struck as powerfully as Melville through the "pasteboard mask" of appearances, for by this point in his career Thoreau believed that the presence of a transcendent or spiritual realm might well be a mere Emersonian fiction. More importantly, after reading the lessons of the "Spring" chapter, we must acknowledge that the more religiously oriented among his contemporaries—Hawthorne and Melville, for example—were thrown into a spiritual darkness Thoreau never knew, primarily because of their inability to accept an essentially naturalistic vision, as he did, and to acknowledge their place in God's earthly Creation. If Melville's Pierre was tortured by the thought of Enceladus struggling against the gods in heaven, by 1854 Thoreau was content to see himself as Antaeus, drawing all his personal and artistic strength from the very earth Emerson, Melville, and others wished to put beneath them. Reading the "Spring" chapter, alert to Thoreau's philological wisdom, we gain a more powerful leverage over the entire aesthetic and philosophical weight of his masterpiece.

After he has moved his readers through the seasons of the year and again has arrived at spring, Thoreau notes how from the promptings of the sun the land around Walden Pond shows signs of metamorphosis. After reporting rather matter-of-factly on the condition of the ice as it begins to break in the pond, Thoreau shifts his attention to the thawing earth. "Few phenomena," he relates, gave him more delight "than to observe the forms which thawing sand and clay assume in flowing down the sides of a steep cut in the railroad."

When the frost comes out in spring . . . the sand begins to flow down the slopes like lava, sometimes bursting out through the snow and overflowing it where no sand was to be seen before. Innumerable little streams overlap and interlace one with another, exhibiting a sort of hybrid product, which obeys half way the law of currents, and half way that of vegetation. As it flows it takes the form of sappy leaves or vines, making heaps of pulpy sprays a foot or more in depth, and resembling, as you look down on them, the laciniated lobed and imbricated thalluses of some lichens; or you are reminded of coral, of leopards' paws or birds' feet, of brains or lungs or bowels, and excrements of all kinds. It is a truly *grotesque* vegetation . . . a sort of architectural foliage more ancient and typical than acanthus, chiccory, ivy, vine, or any vegetable leaves. . . . The whole cut impressed me as if it were a cave with its stalactites laid open to the light.

The whole bank, which is from twenty to forty feet high, is sometimes overlaid with a mass of this kind of foliage, or sandy rupture, for a quarter of a mile on one or both sides, the produce of one spring day. What makes this sand foliage remarkable is its springing into existence thus suddenly. When I see on the one side the inert bank,—for the sun acts on one side first,—and on the other this luxuriant foliage, the creation of an hour, I am affected as if in a peculiar sense I stood in the laboratory of the Artist who made the world and me,—had come to where he was still at work, sporting on this bank, and with excess of energy strewing his fresh designs about. I feel as if I were nearer to the vitals of the globe, for this sandy overflow is something such a foliaceous mass as the vitals of the animal body. You find thus in the very sands an anticipation of the vegetable leaf. No wonder that the earth expresses itself outwardly in leaves, it so labors with the idea inwardly. The atoms have already learned this law, and are pregnant by it. The overhanging leaf sees here its prototype. *Internally*, whether in the globe or animal body, it is a moist thick *lobe*, a word especially applicable to the liver and lungs and the *leaves* of fat, (λείβω, *labor*, *lapsus*, to flow or slip downward, a lapsing; λόβος, *globus*, lobe, globe; also lap, flap, and many other words,) *externally*, a dry thin *leaf*, even as the *f* and *v* are a pressed and dried *b*. The radicals of lobe are *lb*, the soft mass of the *b* (single lobed, or B, double lobed,) with the liquid *l* be hind it pressing it forward. In globe, *glb*, the gutteral *g* adds to the meaning the capacity of the throat. The feathers and wings of birds are still drier and thinner leaves. Thus, also, you pass from the lumpish grub in the earth to the airy and fluttering butterfly. The very globe continually transcends and translates itself, and becomes winged in its orbit. Even ice begins with delicate crystal leaves, as if it had flowed into moulds which the fronds of water plants have impressed on the watery mirror. The whole tree itself is but one leaf, and rivers are still vaster leaves whose pulp is intervening earth, and towns and cities are the ova of insects in their axils. [*WP*, p. 305–7]

Seen in light of glossological theory, a passage like this, so long inadequately understood, offers clear proof of an engagement with language that differed significantly from Emerson's, Bushnell's, and others' but still demonstrated a concern for language's final value in providing access to divine truth. As secular as Kraitsir's glossological theories may seem, we must realize how his formulation of language and its relationship to nature related to the exegetical controversies that at the time were fueled by such books as Bushnell's *God in Christ*. What Thoreau had done here was to show—through an elaborate hermeneutical exercise—how all words, derived from the basic "germs" of sound as described by Kraitsir, are reflections of the grand purpose of nature. If understood aright, then, the "language of nature" became "the True Messiah" that Oegger earlier described and Reed elaborated. Man's verbal expression, the "explosion of [his] reason," which often was muffled by the baggage of civilized life, reflected the great and eternal processes of birth, life, and death; that is, it displayed the inevitable change of which all life is made. What Thoreau offered as his most important "lesson" from the worlds of matter and spirit was that words were not merely steps to a higher reality but themselves embodied and reflected the reality, a thought intially suggested to him by Kraitsir.[35] For Kraitsir viewed language not just as Norton and the Unitarians had—as an index to the stages of human progress—but as a complex living organism partaking of the same divine spirit as the men who used it. The very etymology of "spirit" reinforced the insight, for "the spirit is spread-ing, sprout-ing, go-ing; gas-like, a ghost (*germ.* geist, self-acting), gush-ing, God's highest manifestation so far as it can be felt by us, in our spirit, especially in our mental faculties."[36] Because language itself was formed through those faculties, it was one of the most important links to God.

The most obvious metaphoric construct in Thoreau's philological image of spring's resurrection is the equation of the thawing sand, the raw earth itself, with an organic vegetative force. The *sand*—here the reader must be alert to the dental, fricative sounds of which the word is made—represents what Kraitsir would have called "dormant" effect; it begins to flow like *lava*. Streams *interlace* until the reader does not know if he is looking at a *living* stream or a *live* plant. Sappy *leaves* and *vines* appear as the thaw progresses; lichens are evoked, with their laciniated, lobed, imbricated thalluses. The dominant sounds become the liquid labials, and one sees a *living* organism that before was dead: Leopards' paws, birds' feet, lungs and bowels emerge as the earth stirs to life.

But to Thoreau the sand foliage conjures yet another image, of the *innards* or bowels of the earth. He feels as though he stands in a cave flooded with light and later comments on the vast size of the "sandy rupture." He thinks himself in the workshop of God as he *overflowed* himself, "strewing his fresh designs about" through an excess of energy. Here the reader witnesses nothing less than Thoreau's visionary metaphor for Creation: individual life struggling to put itself forth and, inevitably, fading again into the thin dentals and fricatives that denote death. The earth Thoreau sees is filled with living, flowing, running, moving energy and so labors with the idea of its streaming forms of life that it must everywhere project itself through the imagery of living things, in this case, *leaves*. The overhanging boughs become archetypal and are "pregnant" with the laws that all atoms contain within themselves.

Here Thoreau reads his "leaf" with every philological lens Kraitsir bequeathed him. All begins internally (with the gutterals) as a lobe, thick and moist in its womblike position in the earth (and in man's vocal organs), which then *slips* and *slides* outward, delivered finally to the *liquid labials*, and concludes in a leaflike sound, *dry* and *thin* when finally *externalized*. The liquids press it forward, as they do over the entire globe, but all ends in those dental sounds—"the symbols of death" as Kraitsir called them: l-e-a-f, g-l-o-b-e, l-i-f-e.

The wordplay continues complex as Thoreau moves from a lumpish *grub* in the *earth* to the airy and fluttering butterfly. Cause—gutteral; effect—labial; death—dental: all metaphors in the passage follow this pattern; and, before the reader is aware of it, the philological sleight-of-hand has brought him from an insect to the entire globe. The world is but a "leaf" and subject to the same laws. Towns and cities are but the "ova of insects" in the axils of this organism— an image calling to mind both *Walden*'s last page, when the dormant grub emerges triumphant from the table after lying entombed for decades, and Kraitsir's injunction to the religious man, who must make it his ambition to "trace the papillon of language, from the egg, through all the metamorphoses," until he reaches knowledge of the spirit.[37] The railroad cut becomes nothing less than a parable of man's entire existence, and Thoreau makes the lesson explicit: "this one hillside illustrated the principle of all the operations of nature." The Creator of the world "but patented a leaf" (WP, p. 308).

"What Champollion will decipher this hieroglyphic for us, that we may turn over a new leaf at last?" What Champollion, indeed, if not the curious Hungarian Charles Kraitsir and a handful of his New England disciples? In "The Poet" Emerson had maintained that "nature has a higher end, in the production of individuals, than security, namely ascension, or the passage of the soul into higher forms."[38] But could Thoreau hold this tenet, especially after discerning and describing this parable of the law of God's Creation, a hieroglyph verifiable as well in the very structure of language? This revelation in the flowing sand was so exhilarating that Thoreau turned to scatalogical puns to contain his wonder at it:

True, it is somewhat excrementitious in its character, and there is no end to the heaps of liver lights and bowels, as if the globe were turned wrong side outward; but this suggests at least that Nature has some bowels, and there again is mother of humanity. This is the frost coming out of the ground; this is Spring. . . . It convinces me that Earth is still in her swaddling clothes, and stretches forth baby fingers on every side. Fresh curls spring from the baldest brow. There is nothing inorganic. [WP, p. 308]

The hieroglyph repeated throughout nature and language not only displays the fact that (as Emerson and Reed had noted) words are coextensive with natural facts but, more importantly, that these natural facts are themselves the reality men have been chasing. The world of birth, change, and death is the ultimate secret to be read in organic nature, as well as in the highest mental activity of man, his language. Thoreau's insight was that life goes on and on in an unending cycle of constant change and that, while the individual organisms die, throughout nature the totality of existence is ever in the finest health. "We are surrounded by a rich and fertile mystery," Thoreau elsewhere proclaimed. "May we not probe it, pry into it, employ ourselves about it a little?" (*Wr*, 8:471). By the time he wrote *Walden*, Thoreau had done just that and discovered the true Logos God had contained in the very nature of things.

Viewed in light of language theory and natural history, the earth was not a "mere fragment of dead history, stratum upon stratum like the leaves of a book," but rather "living poetry, like the leaves of a tree which preceded flower and fruit." Gallows humor presiding even at the sacred moment when Thoreau describes the end of all his wisdom, he reminds his readers to recall how the earth's ever-vital throes will heave "exuviae from their graves" (*WP*, p. 309). The only thing sacred will be the motion, the great cyclical pattern of life that outlives us man-insects.

The sections of *Walden* that rehearse such philological speculation are legion and now are receiving extended attention from Thoreau scholars, especially Michael West, who already has published several important essays on the subject. Rather than rehearsing the specifics of his discoveries, it is more important to my own arguments to understand how Thoreau's interest in language reflects the concerns of other figures in this study and informs the aesthetic and philosophical structure of *Walden*.[39]

It is most important, for example, to understand that, while Thoreau's notion of the relationship between language and nature can hardly be termed "transcendental" in the Emersonian or "correspondential" in the Swedenborgian sense, he arrived at his philosophical and imaginative conception of language by working through the linguistic premises of such theories. The significant difference, of course, resided in his belief that the foundation for the "spiritual" life for which he prayed (and which he described in *Walden*) did not lie so much in the fact of transcendence to another sphere as in the permanence of the physical world in which he, as well as his language, was rooted.[40] Thoreau believed that man did not have to get anywhere; he was there already, surrounded by the literal ground of being from which he sprang and to which he would return. The analogies between words and things taught him that what correspondence they possessed was not to be understood as raising man to a higher realm of truth but served rather to alert him to the wonder of his sensuous worldly existence.

Hence, even an ostensibly transcendental chapter like "Higher Laws" presents the reader with evidence that, for all Thoreau's interest in a spirit that "can for the time pervade and control every member and function of the body, and transmute what in form is the grossest sensuality into purity and devotion," he knew to his core that man sometimes could withdraw from his bestiality but could "never change [his] nature" (WP, p. 219). Earlier in the book he similarly had noted how in his self-consciousness he was "sensible of a certain doubleness" by which he could "stand as remote from [himself] as from another"; yet when the "play" of life was over this outside "spectator goes his way" (WP, p. 135). The "glorious existence" to which man was entitled rested solidly upon the world of matter, properly perceived; and only when man acknowledged his "doubleness," the fact that (as Emerson said) he was "a god in ruins," could he comprehend the limitations placed on him by the very nature of which he was a part.

Walden, then, tells the tale of Thoreau's reimmersion in the oldest fount of man's inspiration, nature's original language, and the lesson plans he read there made his verbal posturing as "extravagant" as it was. Because of most men's "remoteness from [nature's] symbols" the "very language of our parlors" lost "all its nerve and degenerate[d] into *palaver* wholly." But if people regained the natural man's insight into language and nature, they would understand why nature's "metaphors and tropes are necessarily so far-fetched" (WP, pp. 244–45). Thus, Thoreau elsewhere noted, "it is salutary to deal with the surface of things," if the surface is properly understood. As he so beautifully put it in his *Journal*:

There is something invigorating in the air which I am peculiarly sensible is a real wind, blowing from over the surface of the planet. I look out at my eyes, I come to my windows, and I feel and breathe the fresh air. It is a fact equally glorious with the most inward experience. [Wr, 10:312]

With "breath" and "wind" derived from the same root-word for "spirit," Thoreau's point is even more apparent. All around man a spiritual ether flows; he only has to plunge into it to save himself and has no sane reason to rise above it.

Besides acknowledging Thoreau's specific references to the secrets the language of nature reveals, we also should understand that his truly "naturalistic" vision accounts for the larger imaginative impression *Walden* leaves upon the reader. If we attend too carefully to the infinite variety of Thoreau's world, we forget that "if we knew all the laws of Nature, we should need only one fact, or the description of one actual phenomenon, to infer all the particular results at that point" (WP, p. 290). Again the railroad cut passage comes to our aid, for in that one epiphany Thoreau makes the reader aware of how important a single fact can be. For Thoreau, the "coming in" of every spring is like "the creation of Cosmos out of Chaos and the realization of the Golden Age" (WP, p. 313). The whole of *Walden* presses us forward to just such moments when, after Thoreau has sufficiently examined himself in Walden Pond's reflection, he is able to understand how every spring (and our every reading of *Walden*'s own vernal prose) seals the knowledge of man's immortality as part of the eternal elements of which nature is made.

To Thoreau, then, the natural world and its startling language offer more than sufficient inspiration to mankind. As he already had said in his first book, *A Week on the Concord and Merrimack Rivers*:

We need pray for no higher heaven than the pure senses can furnish, a *purely* sensuous life. Our present senses are but the rudiments of what they are destined to become. We are comparatively deaf, dumb, and blind, and without smell or taste or feeling. Every generation makes the discovery that the divine vigor has been dissipated, and each sense and faculty misapplied and debauched. The ears were made, not for such trivial uses as men are wont to suppose, but to hear celestial sounds. The eyes were not made for such grovelling uses as they are now worn out by, but to behold beauty now invisible. May we not *see* God? [*Week*, p. 382]

The plea Thoreau raises in *Walden* is simply that man approach the sacrament of existence in the purest frame of mind possible, one of celebration. Nature and language both

[139]

taught him that God was everywhere visible. "Remember thy Creator in the days of thy youth," Thoreau warned. "Lay up a store of natural influences. . . . See, hear, smell, taste, etc., while these senses are fresh and pure" (*Wr*, 8:330).

One last example from the verbal splendor of *Walden* will suffice. Though we might choose many other moments in that book when Thoreau's vision of the universal language can be inferred from particular natural facts, his description of the merlin or pigeon hawk with which he concludes the important "Spring" chapter perfectly expresses the lessons Thoreau had learned about the language of nature, and the nature of language as it could be used aesthetically.

Thoreau was alerted to the bird's presence, he tells us, by "a singular rattling sound, something like that of the sticks which boys play with their fingers," and as he looked upward he saw a hawk "alternately soaring like a ripple and tumbling a rod or two over and over, showing the underside of its wings, which gleamed like a satin ribbon in the sun, or like the pearly inside of a shell."

It was the most ethereal flight I had ever witnessed. It did not simply flutter like a butterfly, nor soar like the larger hawks, but it sported with proud reliance in the fields of the air; mounting again and again with its strange chuckle, it repeated its free and beautiful fall, turning over and over like a kite, and then recovering from its lofty tumbling, as if it had never set its foot on *terra firma*. It appeared to have no companion in the universe,—sporting there alone,—and to need none but the morning and the ether with which it played. It was not lonely, but made all the earth lonely beneath it.

Like Wallace Stevens's jar on a hill in Tennessee, the sporting hawk serves as a point of reference, almost of definition, for Thoreau's own spirit, equally independent and sane in its aloneness. Linked both to the "airy and fluttering butterfly" described in the railroad cut passage and to the "strong and beautiful bug" whose "beautiful and winged life" had long gone unnoticed until Thoreau recorded its resurrection in *Walden*'s conclusion, the hawk fittingly represents the knowledge and freedom of—man's very identification with—nature's manifold language. The bird's "native nest" might well have been "woven of the rainbow's trimming and the sunset sky," Thoreau mused, and "lined with some soft midsummer haze caught up from the earth" (*WP*, p. 317). So it was with Thoreau's own "nest" in Concord, where, he noted, "God himself culminates in the present moment, and never will be more divine in the lapse of all the ages" (*WP*, p. 97).

One might say, then, as a recent critic has, that "the search for derivations in the texture of language provided [Thoreau] with a method and contributed to a style." But a more important fact is how such a search brought him to an appreciation of personal or individual mortality in the face of nature's perpetual "sanity" or good health.[41] By writing *Walden* Thoreau learned that "we are able to apprehend at all what is sublime and noble only by the perpetual instilling and drenching of the reality that surrounds us" (*WP*, p. 97). Thoreau himself often was "drenched" in that reality and was content with the effects of such exposure because he had learned that the accurate observer of natural facts—Louis Agassiz, for example—always discerned and accepted the frightfully close connection between life and death. And the accurate student of the language of nature discerned a similar fact in the glossological reading of "life" itself, the word l-i-f-e, growing and swelling, yet ending in that shrill and final sharpness of itself, like the vegetable l-e-a-f that epitomized it.

In this chapter I have tried to show how the study of language, an interest that initially was stylistic and etymological, contributed to Thoreau's mature artistic and philosophical vision and so links him importantly to the other men discussed in this study. I am not naive enough to think that by studying his philology alone we are somehow treated to all the secret springs of *Walden* or to the deepest recesses of Thoreau's mind. But I do mean to suggest that Thoreau's serious pursuit of a philosophy of language left irrevocable marks on the style and content of his works. Although his philological exploration might seem far removed from those of the biblical scholars whom I first explored, his study and adaptation of contemporary theories regarding the origin and function of language significantly extended those earlier figures' interest in the subject, particularly their investigations of the relationship of language to nature. Lacking the personal need to examine scriptural language for its ability to convey the literal, Christian words of God, Thoreau still regarded language itself as one of the keys to understanding man's postion in the universe. In his typically idiosyncratic way, Thoreau was as concerned with God's Logos as any practicing Christian.

Let me clarify this statement. Thoreau was interested in language's confirmation of certain universal laws because of his belief, transcendental enough, that all mankind had a common origin; hence his interest in the bizarre correspondential schemes of Wilkinson and Kraitsir. But because Thoreau was not just a philosopher or theologian but also an *artist* whose chosen medium was words, he became interested in language as more than a tool for polemic or dogmatic warfare. As Emerson suggested, somehow words are related to things, and things to truth, and the task of the artist is to capture as best he can the equation that makes those relations accessible to others. But for Thoreau what words were a symbol *of*—that is, of the natural world itself—assumed primary importance in his writing. If his study of language and nature brought him back to earth, to the things of this world, rather than to a shadow universe of transcendental ethics, it also meant that the true art had to be based on a close relation to a naturalistic universe.[42]

The chief significance of Thoreau's own philological explorations, then, was in how they reassured him that his world was not fragmented beyond repair but rather was unified in a powerful way in the cyclical nature of existence. In this regard he still was very much an Emersonian who sought to discover universal truths by which he could stave off existential confusion. Unlike Horace Bushnell, who was not arrogant enough to declare divine law comprehensible in all its intricacy and who counseled a generous, wide-ranging respect for the various symbols by which truth was to be suggested, Thoreau fully embraced his personal revelations (as he did so memorably in *Walden*) and declared them full of a saving grace akin to that professed by previous New Englanders who had fiercely defended their Puritan tenets.

Thoreau escaped the "blackness of darkness" that embraced some of his contemporaries. For him ambiguity did not become the dominant mode of artistic expression.[43] Like well-wrought mosaics, his books and essays bespeak a man who, while accepting his own insecure mortality, does so knowingly, and approvingly. As he said in *Walden*, he wanted to live "deliberately," "to cut a broad swath and shave close." By living "deep" and sucking out "all the marrow of life," he had come to know the unity of nature and his place in it (*WP*, pp. 90–91). His link—at least as far as language and teleology are concerned—is more to men like Emerson, or even Andrews Norton, than to Bushnell or Hawthorne and Melville. In saying this I do not so much intend to denigrate his complexity as an author or philosopher as to make readers aware that in the development of nineteenth-century American symbolism he was more important for returning his successors to the largest and most manifold symbol of all—the natural world—than for developing a new philosophy of language.

There are ironies to Thoreau's philological achievement, too, for while it is arguable that in his way Thoreau took the word of God as seriously as any minister of his age, this highly trained empiricist discovered that words contained a message no conventional Christian could avow. For Thoreau language offered a profound clue to the meaning of existence itself; and his study of language, from whatever amalgams it was made, pointed to and confirmed what he took to be the inescapable conditions of human existence. In an odd way, then—and I mean the analogy only suggestively—Thoreau was true to the severe Calvinist dictum that every man must look on his God—on the very nature and mystery of the universe—without any intermediary. And such courage, Thoreau implied, can lead to an experience so overwhelming that it restructures a man's whole inner life. Nature *is* the Spirit, Thoreau declared, and there is no particular moment when we are transported to another field. These are the fields of the Lord, and ecstasy is the experience of moving outside oneself by the sheer joy of being. The exploration of language in the common verbal symbols men used procured such a vision, a certainty in the face of which many other men would have trembled.

Thoreau's "modernism" and his contribution to the symbolist mentality through his study of language lie as much in the philosophical example of his life and art as in his conscious deployment of language and symbol. But, in a sense, this statement became as important as Emerson's or Bushnell's more formal pronouncements because it forced men to reassess the epistemological and ontological premises under which they as artists labored. I find it exciting that Thoreau remains in our imagination most vividly because of what he learned through the study of language, for this declares an important fruition of the labors begun by the American biblical scholars of the early nineteenth century. Thoreau's works offer vivid proof that to nineteenth-century writers language mattered even more profoundly than critics hitherto have thought. If Thoreau did not locate for his contemporaries the irrevocable word of God, he did provide an understanding of their true home as artists.

Melville, as he always does, began to reason of Providence and futurity, and of everything else that lies beyond human ken, and informed me that he had "pretty much made up his mind to be annihilated"; but still he does not seem to rest in that anticipation; and, I think, will never rest until he gets hold of a definite belief. It is strange how he persists—and has persisted ever since I knew him, and probably long before—in wandering to-and-fro over these deserts, as dismal and monotonous as the sand hills amid which we were sitting.

Nathaniel Hawthorne, *English Notebooks,*
20 November 1856

Say what some poets will, Nature is not so much her own ever-sweet interpreter, as the mere supplier of that cunning alphabet, whereby selecting and combining as he pleases, each man reads his own peculiar lesson according to his own peculiar mind and mood.

Herman Melville,
Pierre; or, The Ambiguities (1852)

Chapter Five

Ambiguity and Its Fruits
Toward Hawthorne and Melville

In Henry Thoreau's writings the study of language in its relation to art and religion reached a sophistication unrivaled
among his contemporaries in New England's intellectual circles. Examining his complex adoption of philology, we also
witness his most enduring achievement: the rediscovery of
that language of nature he called the "mother-tongue."
When the study of language entered the realm of art, as it
did in *Walden* and other of Thoreau's writings, it ceased to
be accessible apart from its aesthetic dimension and became
an inextricable component of Thoreau's *style*, and its analysis
demands literary rather than historical or philological tools.
For Thoreau the study of language had provided both epistemological and aesthetic keys with which to open the door
to a fuller comprehension and communication of nature's
secrets. Thus, besides offering a virtual *passe-partout* to the
shaded corridors of the natural world, the words of *Walden*
combined to form one of the most intricate works of literature
America has yet produced.

Thoreau's redemptive vision, as compelling as it was to
him, remained, however, a private, aesthetic formulation
that did not necessarily provide a coherent and consistent
world for others. With his profound respect for the sensuous
reality of experience, Thoreau (who, after all, was as accurate
and detailed an observer of fact as America has ever had),
like Emerson before him, came to believe unequivocally in
the final signification of all that he saw. He patiently assimilated the disparate facts of natural existence and accepted
the presence of life's manifold challenges more deliberately

than many of his contemporaries who had not looked so unblinkingly and untiringly on the natural world. As he returned readers to an appreciation of the things of this world, Thoreau refused ever to admit to being overwhelmed by the sheer complexity of the natural phenomena he studied: He was frightened by neither ambiguity nor multiplicity. This confidence in what he called the world's essential "sanity" marks his allegiance to a vision that, though based on a profoundly held naturalism, still was primarily optimistic. For Thoreau the study of language had secured an assurance that, given a wise perception of the disparate events around which man's life was organized, the world he inhabited always was meaningful.

But other men weaned of their transcendentalist ethics did not follow the same philological and philosophical paths to the serenity Thoreau had discovered. Though Hawthorne and Melville, for example, both had widely ranging intellectual interests, there is no evidence that either man perused the works of language theorists like Kraitsir and Peabody, Trench and Bushnell, or that they enjoyed whatever philosophical comforts Thoreau offered them in his writings.[1] However, they were acutely aware that their contemporaries constantly felt a moral uneasiness brought on by their living in an age in which the possibility of religious faith seemed to be ever decreasing. In their lives and art, both Hawthorne and Melville had to struggle with the philosophical bogey of Emerson's transcendentalism, for they felt compelled to question the seemingly blind optimism of a system that did so little to account for the contradictions men daily confronted. Both of these men came to see that the world was not constructed as simply as Emerson thought. To them, the facts of "correspondence" reported ambiguously about what man had to know of ethical behavior.

What is the price of man's spiritual redemption? Does original sin exist in all men? Has man any free will? Is the Bible the true word of God? What is the spiritual function of man's conscience? Such preoccupations crowd the pages of their stories and novels and betray how deeply Hawthorne and Melville were affected by the contemporary debates over language and epistemology that their more doctrinally inclined countrymen had raised in the theological arena.[2] Lacking the explicitly exegetical concerns of Norton or Stuart, and the philological imagination of Emerson or Thoreau, instead they investigated the moral consequences of the degeneration of theological language and doctrine, while at the same time incorporating into their works the concept of symbolic ambiguity that some of their contemporaries had raised.[3] On one level, then, the fiction of these two writers provided their readers with an aesthetic exploration of the dialogue concerning the final significance of religious terminology. In a world where religious certainty was more and more chimerical, they pioneered a rhetoric of ambiguity—later it would be called literary symbolism—that made possible discussion of man's spiritual condition in an anthropomorphic and pluralistic universe.

In part Hawthorne and (more particularly) Melville became the most prominent practitioners of the symbolic mode in American letters before the Civil War because of their ability to translate the widespread concern over the crisis in religious language and doctrine into the realm of imaginative fiction, where its implications could be explored more fully and, perhaps, honestly than in the philosophical essays of Emerson and Thoreau or through the liberal Protestant theology of Marsh and Bushnell. Hawthorne's and Melville's interests in the origin and development of language certainly were not as great as Emerson's or Thoreau's, but for the literary historian the lesson to be learned is that both novelists undertook investigations of language and meaning at a point where the more strictly theological and/or philosophical writers concluded, having left their readers virtually in a state of semantic exhaustion. To discuss the question of meaning inherent in language, these men developed a literary style similar to what Horace Bushnell termed a "poetic theology." Lacking that minister's faith in the final accuracy and truth of Christianity, though, both men plumbed the deepest religious and ethical concerns of their countrymen without guaranteeing that the answers they provided would be at all "ethical" in any accepted definition of the term. If, as Bushnell had suggested, religious truth was so immensely complicated and amorphous that it could be only approached

[149]

and never wholly embraced by any one individual's conception of it, thoughtful men were left with the dilemma of having constantly to ascertain how they might maintain meaning in the religiously fragmented nineteenth-century world. In the art of Hawthorne and Melville, the use of symbolic representation yielded not the joyful ecumenical embrace Bushnell had foreseen but rather a constant moral challenge to men's established standards of behavior.

In this brief chapter I intend to offer the example of Hawthorne's and, more particularly, Melville's art as an epilogue to the study of language I have detailed. Witness, for example, the haunting universe of Melville's *Confidence Man*. Written in the turmoil and depression following the critical failure of *Pierre* (1852), in *The Confidence Man* Melville directly attacks the problem of meaning in a world in which language is manipulated primarily toward selfish ends and not to express the timeless truths of the natural and moral worlds, as Emerson and others had suggested it could.[4] Set in the geographical center of America—on the Mississippi River—on board one of the century's technological wonders—a steamboat mockingly called the *Fidèle*—on April Fool's Day, *The Confidence Man* revolves around an elaborate charade that has at its heart the proposition that men no longer can believe in anything other men say or do. Confidence—or to consider the term's religious overtones, as Melville clearly intended, *faith*—had become inexpedient, if not impossible, in a society in which language was reduced to rhetorical chicanery, attached neither to thing nor to spirit but only to the selfish whims of those who exploited it for their own purposes. As though offering a proof text of Emerson's dictum that the corruption of language is linked to the corruption of mankind, Melville invites the reader on a topsy-turvy ride aboard the *Fidèle*, displaying at every turn and with every turn of phrase the impracticality and foolishness of having faith in one's fellowman, let alone in God.

Melville's own judgment is heard penetrating his character's when early in the story, as the verbal machinations that form the tale are just commencing, the "man with the wooden leg" exclaims to his gullible fellow passengers: "You fools! You flock of fools, under this captain of fools, in this ship of fools!"[5] The men on board this archetypally American vessel are deceived not only by their inordinate regard for personal interests but also by their thoughtless susceptibility to the confidence man's rhetoric addressing such supposedly worthwhile causes as "charity," "benevolence," and "investment." Further, it is a revealing indication of Melville's sensitivity to one of his culture's most disturbing problems that not the least of the confidence man's ploys involves Scripture itself—in which one is asked to place the ultimate confidence and which comes under its most vicious attack at the conclusion of the story.

Here, having dispensed with the likes of such transcendentalist thinkers as Emerson and Thoreau through his introduction of Mark Winsome and his disciple Egbert—Winsome, for example, is revealed as a man whose language is peppered with comic inconsistencies and whose philosophical propositions are comprehensible only to himself—Melville raises the question of how it is possible that a phrase like "An enemy speaketh sweetly with his lips" can be found in Scripture if admirers of the sacred writings purported that, above all else, the Bible counseled faith and trust among men. The old man with the Bible excuses the phrase by claiming it only part of the Apocrypha and so of "uncertain credit"; but the confidence man—alias the cosmopolitan—pronounces the deeper truth. "Fact is, when all is bound up together [as the two Testaments and the Apocrypha are]," he declares, "it's sometimes confusing."[6] These could serve as the words spoken by a parishioner in Horace Bushnell's Hartford congregation who faced the inconsistencies in scriptural interpretation his pastor tried so hard to explain away. But here the cosmopolitan's reply speaks more to the final worthlessness of Scripture's applicability to the *moral* realm if its messages are, indeed, so self-contradictory. Rather than concluding his story with a cry for more trust and a "Christian comprehensiveness" with regard to religious doctrine, Melville shocks the reader by allowing the old man with the Bible to be led off into darkness by the cosmopolitan, while in his hand he carries a chamber pot full of excrement that

[151]

jokingly has been given him as a "life preserver."[7] *That*, Melville implies, is where serious study of the Bible leads in an age whose most typical representative is not the assiduous biblical scholar but the confidence man himself.

Cecilia Tichi, one of the few critics who has noted how much *The Confidence Man* is a novel about language, has remarked that Melville's tortuous failure of a novel attempts to "teach [Melville's] attentive, select listeners what the immoral Wall Street spirit and its ramifications had done to language in America."[8] But it was more than the "Wall Street spirit"—which, after all, had made Bartleby the Scrivener a creature not of linguistic deception but instead of *silence*—that undercut the possibility of ethical discourse in *The Confidence Man*. Rather, it was the entire culture's inability to have confidence or faith in the kinds of ethical arrangements that prior to 1820 still had been credible to most Americans because of their sound basis in scriptural doctrine. As the "herb doctor" in Melville's novel puts it when counseling the sick man to purchase his vials of medicine, "From evil comes good. . . . Distrust is a stage to confidence."[9] Such specious or (depending on how the reader interprets "confidence") cynical language makes sense only when such terms as "good" and "evil" cease to be rooted in any recognizable, objective reality. Further, as Mark Winsome explains at another point in the story, "Advance into knowledge is like advance upon the ground of the Erie Canal, where from the character of the country, change of level is inevitable." You are locked up and down "with perpetual inconsistencies," he continues, "and yet all the time you get on."[10] When the reader notes that the quasiapocalyptical ending to Melville's story follows closely on the phrase "Jehovah shall be thy confidence," he understands that by 1858 Melville had refused to acknowledge the possibility of any ethical commitment to a society that failed to agree on the meaning of language that hitherto had formed the basis for the social and religious contract.

Admittedly, *The Confidence Man* is an extreme example of Melville's acerbic disillusionment with his contemporaries' failures to provide a moral foundation in a confusingly pluralistic universe; and I have referred to it so prominently only to suggest how questions of language and meaning—particularly as they pertained to religious faith—figured significantly in Melville's artistic imagination. Though not a student of philology as, say, Thoreau was, Melville still had an interest in the meaning and context of rhetoric that was related to the transcendentalists' concerns about language.

Equally important to my purpose here, however, is both Hawthorne's and Melville's imaginative confrontation with the allied proposition that, if the language of religious doctrine failed to create "confidence" among those who still wished to believe in it, religious or ethical truth never again could be unambiguous. Further, their investigation of this topic in their imaginative literature involved the use of literary symbol in a way hitherto untested. This deployment of symbolic reference provided their works with a rhetorical energy at least as powerful as Thoreau's in *Walden*.

Though on one level almost transparently allegorical, stories like Hawthorne's "Young Goodman Brown" and "The Minister's Black Veil," for example, point the reader toward the larger questions of language and meaning that vexed their author. If one's faith were severely shaken, be it from a newly gained knowledge of all humanity's complicity in sin or from a realization that one's most cherished companions were not immune from the darkest of temptations, what would happen to one's religious faith? Could it be readily restored? When Goodman Brown cries wildly for his "Faith" to aid his escape from the devil (who is described similarly to Melville's confidence man), neither Brown's religious principles nor his dearest wife is able to offer any comfort to negate the horrible fact of his appearance for baptism at the devil's fount. With the loss of the ability to believe unequivocally in the direction offered by one's religious tradition also went a concomitant peace of mind never to be recaptured. Young Goodman Brown and the Reverend Hooper, whose relationship to his congregation is jeopardized by his decision openly to typify what he knows of their hypocrisy, both go to their graves as sad and melancholy men, without the consolation they so much needed in the face of their dark vision. The reader leaves such tales with the unsettling realization that Hawthorne did not intend their stories to be at all atypical.

A question of faith, too, animates the structure of Hawthorne's major romance, *The Scarlet Letter*, for in their outward behavior the various inhabitants of the artist's Puritan community typify the options available to the inquiring nineteenth-century mind seeking order amidst increasing moral chaos. Not concerned with theological language per se, *The Scarlet Letter* blatantly displays the disastrous personal results of holding one or another view of morality as it traditionally had been defined from Scripture. The Reverend Wilson, Dimmesdale's older co-worker, represents the conservative doctrinal Christian whose allegiance to the Bible's every word—especially to the Old Testament's law—still is very strong and who has little sympathy for the more "romantic" theology of someone like Hester Prynne, who brings to the community a counterpart of the nineteenth-century liberal's belief in the importance of the emotions in religious life. Setting her punishment so severely, the Puritan community reinforces its belief that what it always has considered to be "truth" indeed still is, even though, as is made apparent at the commencement of the tale, many in the society themselves shared Hester's antinomian longings and, by extension, her theological justifications for them. Even Hawthorne's description of Hester—"an object to remind [a papist] of the image of Divine Maternity"—reinforces the ambiguous nature of her sin. More than just an adulteress, Hester represents the romantic, individualistic challenge to a theology that refused to acknowledge the necessary conjunction of the Me and Not-Me (as Emerson might have put it) in forming the whole personality; that is, the role of self and society in giving sense both to the world and to one's relation to it. In her character Hawthorne very well may have been examining the logical conclusion of the potentially destructive individualism and self-reliance preached by such ministers-manqué as Emerson, who blithely urged such reconstructed souls as Hester on a world not ready for them.[11]

Chillingworth, too, has his place in the doctrinal typology that Hawthorne suggests in *The Scarlet Letter*. His cold-blooded willfulness and tireless devotion to books and study mark one pole of the skepticism that defined the nineteenth century's critical examination of religious thought. Had he lived two centuries later Chillingworth might well have begun his scholarly career in the kinds of scriptural enterprise that defined the heroic exegesis of Andrews Norton or Moses Stuart. But unlike these men, whose faith in the Bible never was shaken, Chillingworth was a man who understood peoples' self-deception as they strove to believe at any cost, and in Hawthorne's mind he represented the theological cynicism that also marked some of the finest nineteenth-century minds. To pursue the Word too single-mindedly led to a realization that the religious edifice of Christianity had become, as Emerson termed it, a "Mythus." At such a point one's only escape was to accept (as Thoreau did) empirical knowledge as the only reality, or to make the Kierkegaardian leap into faith. But in Chillingworth's case, such an "empirical" search led not to a detailed study of the beauties of the natural world or to a transcendent belief but to an obsessive self-interest that manifested itself in hatred for Dimmesdale.

It is Dimmesdale himself, however, who emerges as the most revealing character in *The Scarlet Letter*, for in him the reader views the emotional and intellectual paralysis that results from an awareness of an ambiguity in one's moral values. Torn between the scriptual legalism of the Reverend Wilson and the protoromantic individualism of Hester, Dimmesdale is so immobilized that his personality is defined only by guilt and self-pity, and his unwillingness to adopt a more comprehensive view of the meaning of such words as "love," "sin," and "charity" is as much to blame for his moral confusion as is his psychological confusion over the "head" and the "heart." When after their meeting in the forest Dimmesdale decides to leave with Hester for Europe, he finally attempts to embrace the liberal world view marked by her behavior, but his escape fails because he has given too much of his life—and faith—to the New England Way as expressed in his community's strictly dogmatic understanding of human righteousness. Fittingly, at the end of Hawthorne's tale Dimmesdale's great sermon (as well as the mark of evil upon his breast) is interpreted differently by the different people who witness it. A man whose life had become tortured by the ambiguity of his own moral behavior had himself become nothing less than the occasion for symbolic interpretation of what faith he displayed.[12]

With *The Scarlet Letter* in mind, I think it not farfetched to suggest that Hawthorne's very preoccupation with the "romance" as a prose style originated in the epistemological confusion to which his contemporaries were reduced. His desire to create in his novels "a neutral territory . . . where the Actual and the Imaginary may meet, and each imbue itself with the nature of the other" suggests more than a reaction to America's "commonplace prosperity," which he found so oppressive. Hawthorne knew, for example, that when "romances do really teach anything . . . it is usually through a far more subtle process than the ostensible one"; that is, that the "certain latitude" an author claimed in calling his work a romance allowed an investigation of subtleties and ambiguities that normally were not part of a work of "realistic" fiction. Like it or not, to be successful in depicting the crisis in semantics that characterized nineteenth-century America, novelists had to paint a "Faery Land" in which problems of perception and meaning could be thoroughly explored.[13]

I am suggesting that in his mature romances Hawthorne was concerned, both morally and artistically, with what it meant to live in a world described by someone like Horace Bushnell, but without that minister's confidence in the final justice of God's ways to men. The themes and imagery, if not always the language, of Hawthorne's work declare the necessity of an adoption of some unambiguous truth to restore moral stability. For example, *The Marble Faun*, one of his most explicitly religious novels (set as it is in the Eternal City of Rome), reveals Hawthorne's intense engagement with the problems of religious consolation in an era of increasing skepticism. In this, the last novel he completed, as the shadow of the Civil War began to draw over the nation, Hawthorne again depicted characters who represented moral dilemmas with which he, as well as his culture, had become obsessed. The central complication of the tale—Donatello's impulsive murder of the artist's model—is a romantic deed, without conventional moral sanction; and Miriam and Donatello, like the psychically crippled Dimmesdale, must undergo long penitence to atone for their complicity in the crime. But, while these two are irrevocably marked by their act and genuinely assume their guilt, Hawthorne does not allow them the kind of peace he offers Hilda, his representation of the New England "Puritan" spirit. Donatello and Miriam never totally escape their guilt; in breaking the law of God and so reenacting the Fall from Eden, their souls always will dwell with the pain of their own sinfulness.[14] One result of a profound knowledge of sin, Hawthorne seems to be saying, is a subsequent inability to find respite within the traditional Protestant system, which prohibits any final atonement for sin against an infinite God.

On the other hand, Hilda, who has witnessed the crime and feels as guilty as her two friends, finds peace through, of all institutions, the Roman Catholic church and its sacrament of penance. Although she does not confess to the Catholic clergyman all that she knows—she is too much a loyal child of the Puritans to succumb *that* completely to papal authority—Hawthorne makes it clear that the symbol of the Church's forgiveness, the confessional, goes far toward assuaging her conscience. In a morally troubling world, then, Hawthorne leads his readers back to the bosom of the mother church in Rome and through his sympathetic treatment of Hilda's predicament implicitly counsels, if only briefly, the necessary ecumenicalism that Bushnell sanctioned and that would mark Protestantism's development in the latter part of the century. If men inhabit a world of private symbols, Hawthorne implies, a world in which guilt no longer can be resolved through the conventional forms of Protestant atonement, one of the more viable solutions to the painful introspection brought on by such newly imposed moral responsibility might be spiritual membership in the most complex symbol system of all, the Catholic church. It may be coincidental that Hawthorne's daughter Rose herself became a convert to the Roman Catholic faith, but one cannot help but think that she was led to that commitment by her father's recognition that the moral agony that accompanied the centrifugal social developments of the 1850s demanded a peace only available in the world's most elaborate symbolic construction.

For all Hawthorne's genuinely sympathetic interest in his countrymen's unsettling struggle with the moral complexities engendered by religious skepticism, however, the conclusions to his novels offer resolutions that, while personally acceptable to him, could not always have been so appealing to his readers, particularly those who doubted the ethical accommodations made by characters like Hilda or Hester. Hester's living out her life in resigned expiation while still paying implicit allegiance to the Puritan community that chastised her; young Hilda's returning to America with a conscience soothed by the blessing of the pope's emissary; Holgrave and Phoebe married in a symbolic union that weds liberal transcendentalism to the Pyncheons' outdated Puritanism with its attendant respect for tradition; Miles Coverdale's discovery of the drowned Zenobia, a woman who, like Hester Prynne, represented a religious personality that paid more heed to the promptings of her private spirit than to an omnipotent, divine being: These characters and the ends to which they are brought represent more an escape from the complexity engendered by a pluralistic universe than a wholehearted acceptance of its challenges.

In his symbolic romances, then, Hawthorne began to utilize the concept of rhetorical ambiguity demanded by the moral complexity of his age, but his plots are resolved in ways that at times seem evasive. Like Emerson and Thoreau, he had developed an interest in questions of perception and meaning that led him to investigate the bewildering variety of possible readings of such "natural" emblems as the scarlet *A*, the Pyncheon home, Hilda's dovecote, and Zenobia's flower. But, again like Emerson and Thoreau, Hawthorne always offered some point of secure anchorage (one might even say, of *retreat*) in a morally ambiguous world. This was not the case with his friend Herman Melville, who of all his contemporaries best understood the effects of the revolution in language and meaning that occurred when the centrifugal forces of romanticism were unleashed in theology and philosophy both.

As I already have suggested, Melville was more directly affected than Hawthorne by the crisis in religious and moral
rhetoric that palsied his environment, and he overtly examined the problem of language and meaning in *The Confidence Man*. But we also must recognize that his masterpiece,
Moby Dick, offers readers an intense examination of what
men might do once "meaning" had become, for all intents
and purposes, a privately mediated affair between an individual and his conscience.

The most self-consciously symbolic of Melville's major
works, *Moby Dick* opens with nothing less than an "Etymology" of the word *whale*, "supplied by a late consumptive
usher to a grammar school" who was "ever dusting his old
lexicons and grammars," a task he enjoyed because "it somehow mildly reminded him of his mortality." From the outset,
then, Melville intends to display how the word and the thing,
and (to complete the Emersonian equation) the spiritual
"fact" the whale represents, lend themselves to whole ranges
of phonetic and symbolic interpretation. Indeed, as the first
quotation (from "Hackluyt") in the "Etymology" suggests:
"While you take in hand to school others, and to teach them
by what name a whale-fish is to be called in our tongue,
leaving out, through ignorance, the letter H, which almost
alone maketh up the signification of the word, you deliver
that which is not true."[15] *Moby Dick*, then, is an investigation
of the countless verbal and symbolic representations of the
great white whale, and the different philosophical "grammars" the members of the *Pequod*'s crew use to comprehend
the creature provide many varied readings of the "text" of
the whale.

More importantly, it is hard to overlook Melville's conscious parody of scriptural exegesis, a subject he first introduces in the prefatory "Extracts" supplied by a "Sub-Sub-
Librarian" and continues to explore throughout the novel,
especially in the chapter on cetology. As though he were a
biblical scholar fervently researching the evidences for a Trinitarian God, this "Sub-Sub" appears "to have gone through
the long Vaticans and street stalls on earth, picking up whatever random allusions to whales he could anyways find in

any book whatsoever." But, setting up his audience for an encounter with the complex symbology of the whale that follows (especially in "Moby Dick" and "The Whiteness of the Whale"), through Ishmael Melville warns the reader that he must not "in every case at least, take the higgledy-piggledy whale statements, however authentic . . . for the veritable gospel cetology." The hodgepodge of references that follows bears out the justice of the auctorial warning, but *Moby Dick*'s narrative itself displays how Melville's different characters (Ishmael included) persist in basing their moral response to Ahab's fiery quest on what they consider "gospel" about the white whale and its meaning (*MD*, p. 7).

The "cetology" Melville introduces to give the reader "a thorough appreciative understanding of the more specific leviathanic revelations and allusions" in his novel similarly works to cast doubt on the final authenticity of the text of the whale. Indeed, Melville begins this chapter by admitting that the science of cetology is in such an "uncertain, unsettled condition" that "in some quarters it still remains a moot point whether a whale be a fish" (*MD*, p. 182). Ishmael, a good Protestant who respects traditional exegetical scholarship, cites "holy Jonah" as the strongest authority for his own working definition of the animal, but Melville wishes the reader to compare the business of whaling to the contemporary "profession" of religion by having Ishmael admit that some of the "names" he finds for the whale are "altogether obsolete . . . mere sounds, full of Leviathanism, but signify[ing] nothing" (*MD*, pp. 183, 195). If Melville intends the comparison to the state of biblical scholarship, as I firmly believe he does, he makes Ishmael well aware that even the best "cetology" fails to explicate the most important "facts" about Moby Dick itself, those that originate in the minds of differently constituted individuals as the whale is variously perceived. Soon, Ishmael intimates, we "shall be lost in . . . unshored, harborless immensities" (*MD*, p. 179).

Then, too, what are we to make of the chapter "Jonah Historically Regarded," in which Ishmael discusses an "old Sag-Harbor Whaleman's" reluctance to accept the veracity of the Book of Jonah? Here Melville delights in poking fun at one "German exegetist" who after long study "suppose[d] that Jonah must have taken refuge in the floating body of a *dead* whale" and at other "learned exegetists who have opined that the whale mentioned in the book of Jonah merely meant a life-preserver—an inflated bag of wind—which the endangered prophet swam to" (*MD*, pp. 470–71). Even more telling, however, is Ishmael's pronouncement on the Sag-Harbor whaleman himself, for, good "Presbyterian" that Ishmael is (*MD*, p. 85), he accuses the old skeptic of "evinc[ing] his foolish pride of reason" in so blithely discounting the tale. The quality of his arguments against Jonah's being swallowed by a whale display nothing but an "abominable, devilish rebellion against the reverend clergy" (*MD*, pp. 471–72), a defensive argument used by countless orthodox clergymen themselves in attacking the dangerous corruptions brought on by the Higher Criticism.

If Ishmael bristles at such challenges to his strongly held Presbyterian faith, though, Melville himself knew what the Higher Criticism implied about the final authority of any inspired text—hence his brief but critical excursus into phrenology in "The Prairie," when he has Ishmael admit that no "Physiognomist" has yet deciphered the features of Leviathan (*MD*, p. 445). "Physiognomically regarded," Ishmael declares, "the Sperm Whale is an anomalous creature," for when man stares directly at its brow to decipher its character, "not one distinct feature is revealed; no nose, eyes, ears, or mouth; no face." The whale's visage—like the final meaning of Moby Dick itself, or of God—*cannot* be comprehended through human reason; it must always remain a riddle. Demonstrating his knowledge of contemporary philological research, Melville allows Ishmael directly to set this problem of interpretation to readers of his tale: "If then, Sir William Jones, who read in thirty languages, could not read the simplest peasant's face in its profounder and more subtle meanings, how may unlettered Ishmael hope to read the awful Chaldee on the Sperm Whale's brow? I put that before you. Read it if you can." There was as yet no "Champollion" to "decipher the Egypt of every man's and every being's face" (*MD*, p. 449), and so the whale's mystery, like the mystery of Fate, remained unread.

As the novel unfolds, then, the crew of the *Pequod*, itself

[161]

a symbol of the pluralistic American experiment with its various races "federated along one keel," are forced to construct their own etymologies and so to learn to read the meaning of the whale and the reasons for Ahab's violent hatred of it. Surely *Moby Dick*, being "broiled in hell-fire" as Melville claimed it was, is no sacred Scripture; but its characters behave as though their understanding of the white whale should be grounded in the same certainties that characterized a biblical scholar's interest in his texts. And here, as among the various denominations that tore apart the fabric of American Protestantism, the multiplicity of their individual readings ends not in amicable embrace but in a tragedy of jealousy and revenge.

Given Melville's allusions to biblical exegesis, what needs to be stressed is how much the act of reading itself forms the vital center of *Moby Dick*.[16] Ahab's brash announcement that he must strike through the pasteboard mask of appearances is only the most vivid instance of his challenge to the world's manifold deceptions. For example, Ishmael's experience with the painting in "The Spouter-Inn" typifies his later revelations when, contemplating the whiteness of the whale, he learns that "all deified Nature absolutely paints like the harlot" (*MD*, p. 264). Captivated by the dark, smoke-covered painting in the inn, a work of art that does not easily yield its subject, Ishmael admits to feeling in it "a sort of indefinite, half-attained, unimaginable sublimity," which he yearns to decipher. Whatever was in the painting "fairly froze you to it," he admitted, "till you involuntarily took an oath with yourself to find out what that marvellous painting meant" (*MD*, p. 36). Ishmael finally decides that the canvas depicts a whaleship in a severe storm, but more important has been his decision to fathom its mystery until all its secrets are told, an existential act he repeats in his reveries on the masthead when he stares beneath the surface of the sea to find the "strange, half-seen, gliding, beautiful thing which eludes him" (*MD*, p. 214).

The language of nature—especially as it is made evident at sea, where in their isolation natural facts are so much more striking—must be read by anyone who seeks more than a surface acquaintance with life. And yet, Ishmael notes, as you lean away from the mast, "Over Descartian vortices you hover" (*MD*, p. 215). The danger always remains that a tumble from the masthead heights of one's private thoughts, or lingering too long in those sea chambers where the idiot boy, Pip, had seen "God's foot upon the treadle of the loom" (*MD*, p. 530), will result in one's never again surfacing to the world where men and women ply their mundane trades. Ishmael's later acknowledgment of the disturbing irony that "man's insanity is heaven's sense" brings little comfort to those who will not admit that things are not what they seem, in the moral or the natural world, where it is easier to regard nature with "an opium-like listlessness of vacant, unconscious reverie," believing that nature will reveal its every secret (*MD*, p. 214).

Moreover, the famous chapter dealing with the whiteness of the whale offers the starkest challenge to conventional interpretations of "objective" reality and can be read profitably in light of the controversies over biblical exegesis. As though foreshadowing the question Melville asks about the "Indian Hater" in *The Confidence Man*, in this chapter Ishmael candidly inquires how something can be both good and bad *at the same time*; that is, how whiteness can represent something beautiful and yet terrifying, "not so much a color as the visible absence of color, and at the same time the concrete of all colors" (*MD*, pp. 245–46). The answer lies in the reader's grasp of how Ishmael's ultimate survival depends on his understanding the propositions of such radical thinkers as Bushnell: The whale, like the great truths of the Christian religion, is to be understood not in one way or another but as a *symbol* of the final inapproachability of *any* objective reality. To form a proper conception of what it is the white whale represents one must experience both the terror and the awe its vision brings on. The sum of each man's understanding is what identifies reality for what it is to him, and one man's egotistical vision never can embrace something as enormously complex as a whale-god, or a point of Christian doctrine. Ishmael's and Ahab's visions, then, are not contradictory; rather, each is *part* of the reality of a supernatural realm of which the whale's existence is the outward symbol. The error of men like Ahab, Melville declares, is that they, like Emerson's Swedenborg, or Sherwood Anderson's "grotesques," take one truth to themselves and attempt to call it their own to the exclusion of all others. On the strictly theological level, such men might become Universalists, Swedenborgians, Freewill Baptists, or Unitarians. In the ethical realm they are Starbucks, Ahabs, and Flasks.

Here an understanding of Ahab's inverted Emersonian vision is important, for Ahab refuses to compromise his own understanding of the natural world and the whale's relation to it. In the paragraph that provides the first description the reader has of Ahab, Ishmael suggests that Ahab is a man "of greatly superior natural force, with a globular brain and a ponderous heart." But, more significantly, he had "been led to think untraditionally and independently" and, "receiving all nature's sweet or savage impressions fresh from her own virgin voluntary and confiding breast," he learned "a bold and nervous lofty language." To this point a man we might identify as Emerson's poet, Ahab becomes poisoned by "a half willful overruling morbidness at the bottom of his nature" (*MD*, p. 111). Because of this temperamental disability, he persists in seeing the whale as the incarnation of an "inscrutable malice." "All visible objects," Ahab declares, "are but as pasteboard masks"; but, carrying the theory of correspondence to its farthest limits, Ahab believes he must strike *through* the mask to the reality beyond (*MD*, pp. 220–21). It never occurs to him that his own private reading of the whale might not be absolutely true or that the mask itself may be the ultimate reality. He and his crew, then, must confront the natural world with a latitude that allows for such possibilities, and their failure to do so seals their violent doom.

The mysterious hold the doubloon nailed to the masthead by Ahab exercises over his crew similarly is linked to the problem of pluralistic interpretation. Though a symbol such as the white whale can, in extremis, represent *both* the ultimate beauty of nature *and* its ultimate horror, for most men the epistemological challenge never is as *apparently* contradictory. Men are not always asked to choose between black and white but from among the various shades between—hence, for example, the proliferation of sects all of whom called themselves Protestant and proclaimed their ability to represent the deepest truths of Christianity.

The doubloon, of course, like the doctrine of the Trinity or the meaning of the Eucharist, can be interpreted differently by different individuals. From the meekness and piety of Starbuck to the insanely driven egotism of Ahab there exists a range of possibilities concerning its symbolism, among which are Flask's materialist "reading" of the coin and Queequeg's association of the symbols with his own culture and, in particular, with his sexuality. But the most accurate translation of all is made by Pip, who here represents the contemporary dissociated personality. Symbolically drowned in the immensity of wisdom he possessed after his plunge to the depths of the ocean, Pip responds to the confusion of symbols in what to most observers is a cryptic manner. "I look, you look, he looks; we look, ye look, they look," he declares (*MD*, p. 556). Pip has, indeed, been studying Murray's *Grammar*, as one of the crew suggests; but, in addition, his sinking to the ocean's depths (where "strange shapes of the unwarped primal world glided to and fro") has provided him with the knowledge that any individual object like the coin exists only as the sum of the different "grammars" men bring to their understanding of its objective existence. All objectivity vanishes in acts of personal interpretation. The doubloon's message, like the mystery of the whale's color, is accessible only through a multiplicity of readings. To rest in any one reading is to risk being lost in the labyrinth of one's perceptions.

The *Pequod*'s wreck leaves a survivor, though, for Ishmael surfaces from the disaster on Queequeg's intricately carved coffin, whose message, after all, contained nothing less than "a complete theory of the heavens and the earth, and a mystical treatise on the art of attaining truth" (*MD*, p. 612). Copied from that tattooing on Queequeg's body, the hieroglyphics are a riddle to him as much as to anyone else, "destined in the end to moulder away with the living parchment whereon they were inscribed." But Ishmael's survival, Melville implies, partly entails his belief in, if not his understanding of, the coffin's profound riddle. More importantly, his survival also depends on his ability to assimilate all the views of reality held by the different crewmen aboard the ship, for with this wide sympathy he has become a member of the "ancient Catholic Church" to which "every mother's son and soul of us belong[,] the great and everlasting First Congregation of this whole worshipping world" to which Queequeg himself belonged (*MD*, p. 128). Ishmael has learned to read events through a catholic vision, wrenching a usable meaning from the various natural and moral clues he encounters on the *Pequod*'s mad voyage. Because (unlike the other men) he is not restricted to any single point of view, and because he is so open to the lessons of his education that he finally can accept the whiteness of the whale in all its ambiguity, Ishmael survives the tragic journey of the *Pequod*. All whose private constructions of reality had prevented them from entering into such acts of sympathetic brotherhood and Christian embrace as the "sperm-squeezing" are not allowed a peace that passes understanding. In Melville's tale, then, Ishmael, a brother to all other men, is much more than a supreme democrat. More than any other, he is the man who has learned that to live amidst the multiplicity that characterized the nineteenth century one must listen to Father Mapple as well as to Ahab and so steer a course in which all possibilities, all possible readings of the world, are given their due. Bushnell might have termed Ishmael a perfect example of one who had come to represent "Christian comprehensiveness."

Melville realized, though, that Ishmael, for all his catholicity of judgment, was more an ideal projection than a true representative of the men who populated the Albany or Pittsfield Melville knew. While Ishmael-as-survivor remains an attractive character, the sinister power Ahab holds over the reader is more compelling. It may be that Melville's own dissatisfaction with the moral relativism he embodied in Ishmael is what prompted a further exploration of the topics of language and meaning in *Pierre*, a book begun shortly after the completion of *Moby Dick* and whose very subtitle, *The Ambiguities*, suggests its relevance to this study.[17] In this antiromance, a book as gnarled and misshapen as *The Confidence Man*, Melville explores the downfall of another absolutist, one who takes the world only on his own terms and who forces others to accept that same vision.

What makes the novel particularly disturbing is that Pierre Glendinning is patently *not* an Ahab. Pierre, it is true, has taken a truth to himself and declared it valid over the claims of all "virtuous expediency." But what that truth is— a respect for the ideals of Christianity as they should be practiced if the Bible is studied and heeded carefully—is directly opposed to Ahab's monomaniacal vision. Plotinus Plinlimmon's frightening conclusion that to live by Greenwich meridian time—that is, by a set of unearthly values—in a world where moral relativism is the only guarantor of stability, leads to misunderstanding and inconvenience, if not outright tragedy, directly challenged the Christian tradition by which the majority of Americans professed to live. Pierre, a man who thinks he has understood the Bible, is forced to the grossest of misdeeds because of the world's inability to accept the nature of his scriptural interpretation. Ironically, to them his actions become nothing less than criminal.

Pierre seeks only to do what is right and so to live by the Christian charity and humility counseled in the Bible. But in adopting his half sister, Isabel, and in striving to publish to the world the truths that have seared his heart since that act of charity, he is relegated first to a pauper's and then to an outcast's existence. The "ambiguities" raised by his punishment defy simple enumeration, but one of the more prominent of them suggests that, even when understood as clearly as possible, the Scriptures offer no safe guidance through this morally tangled world. Better to live by "horological" time, in the moral pragmatism of a Mrs. Glendinning or a Glen Stanley, than with the pain and misunderstanding to which Pierre's uncompromisingly Christian acts lead him. It is true that at his death Pierre has around him those whom he loves, but his consolations have been few and the world's chastisement severe. Like Isabel, he "dost not pine for empty nominalness, but for vital realness," and yet the ambiguity of the human race's attitude toward righteousness, while it willingly accepts selfish half-deeds rather than acts of Christian charity, bespeaks a universe in which the "best" (that is, the "safest") form of behavior is merely nominal.[18]

Pierre discovers that Christian truths are not useful to a man seeking earthly peace, for if true adherence to the Bible leads to incest and murder, where then the reasons for bestirring oneself to live like a "good" Christian? "Thou, Pierre, speakest of Virtue and Vice," Isabel says, "What are they, in their real selves, Pierre?" He answers:

"If on that point the gods are dumb, shall a pygmy speak? Ask the air!"
"Then Virtue is nothing."
"Not that!"
"Then Vice?"
"Look: a nothing is a substance, it casts one shadow one way, and another the other way; and these two shadows cast from one nothing; these, seems to me, are Virtue and Vice."
"Then why torment thyself so, dearest Pierre?"
"It is the law."

Into such a labyrinth of semantic madness Pierre has been tossed, and, with his faith shaken, moral choices have lost their meaning. "From nothing proceeds nothing," he proclaims to the dark Isabel. "How can one sin in a dream?"[19]

The absolute reading of Scripture, then, is not useful, Pierre's story concludes. More than being unfashionable, the Bible's counsel is impossible to follow if a man desires temporal happiness. Why then waste years of one's life on a struggle to decipher what supposedly are God's messages to men? *Pierre*, I believe, includes among its many disturbing messages the lowly whispered suggestion that the Bible is meaningless because the world holds "empty nominalness" more dear than "vital realness." Coming at the end of a long period of serious study of the language and meaning of the Bible, a development that caused an erosion in peoples' abilities to believe unequivocally in the word of God, Melville's *Pierre* stands as a coda to that entire enterprise, a signal light declaring the impossibility of anything fruitful's emerging from those lengthy commentaries theologians had devoted to understanding the hitherto infallible words of God. In *Billy Budd* Melville would reexamine the horological and chronometrical values of such theological concepts as "guilt," "innocence," and "depravity," but the outcome of these later ruminations would be the same. If the world still would not allow righteousness to triumph, it was of slight consideration that sailors carried with them sacred pieces of the spar from which Billy Budd was hanged.[20] The dark and sinister world of *The Confidence Man* returns to haunt Melville's readers, for in that cruel vision of linguistic and moral deception one learns that the only certainty to be expected in a world in which the truth of ambiguity is never to be displaced is the mocking irony of the cosmopolitan's "confidence."

The road from Andrews Norton's scriptural studies to the "dark" romanticism of Melville is not direct. I never intended to imply that it was. However, it seems clear that the study of language in its various manifestations—the exegetical scholarship of Norton and Stuart; the Coleridgean speculation on words and their meanings by James Marsh and Horace Bushnell; the preternatural correspondences between words and things, things and the spirit, announced by Sampson Reed, Guillaume Oegger, and Emerson; and the philological explorations into a universal language by Elizabeth Peabody and Henry Thoreau—created the possibility for Hawthorne's and Melville's symbolistic methods. More than a mere extension of the typological methodology of the New England Puritans, their novels are direct responses to a cultural situation that demanded that the serious thinker—be he a theologian or a novelist—seriously explore problems of language and meaning. Because of the centrifugal forces within nineteenth-century society, intellectual and social developments that irrevocably destroyed the possibility of religious "belief" in the way that term once was understood, Hawthorne and Melville had to develop a literary style that could deal constructively with the problems caused by these changes. The topic of language (especially whether or not it had the ability to convey absolute standards of truth and value) was a culturally significant one. The writers I have discussed all responded to it consciously and in such ways that their works were marked distinctively by the various propositions about language and symbol that engaged New England's intellectual community.

In writing this book I did not intend to exhaust the possibilities of further study of the problem of language in the works of these authors. Rather, I have sought to circumscribe or, as Thoreau might have said, to "perambulate" the topic, suggesting how a full understanding of the achievement of those men who revitalized our literature during the New England Renaissance depends on the reader's awareness not only of these authors' concern with the propagation of a literature genuinely responsive to America's conditions but also of how in their various artistic statements they explored questions of epistemology that were closely linked to the crisis within American Protestantism. They responded to problems that at their root were profoundly theological and moral and that had to be resolved if the possibility of an accurate description of spiritual reality was to be resurrected. After the rise of the Higher Criticism, "meaning" never again could be the same. It had to be provided in a new form, that of heuristic symbol. Hawthorne and Melville were pioneers in this American symbolist tradition.

Thus, when in the privacy of his *Journal* Henry Thoreau confided that men never should underestimate the value of any natural fact, for it one day would flower into a truth, he rehearsed one of the most important announcements he and his fellow artists made to their age. Natural facts flowering into various difficult truths had replaced the Old and New Testaments as guideposts to moral direction in the world. And the seriousness with which the chief writers of the New England Renaissance treated the place of language in establishing this new typology should alert readers to the important proposition that, for novelists like Hawthorne and Melville as well as for essayists like Emerson and Thoreau, the wisdom of words, while different from what it once was thought to be, still could not be denied.

Notes

Introduction

1. Henry David Thoreau, *The Writings of Henry David Thoreau*, Walden Edition, 20 vols. (Boston and New York: Houghton Mifflin Co., 1906), 16:233; hereafter cited as *Wr*.

2. M. H. Abrams, *Natural Supernaturalism: Tradition and Revolution in Romantic Literature* (New York: W. W. Norton & Co., 1971), p. 65. Also see Murray Roston, *Prophet and Poet: The Bible and the Growth of Romanticism* (Evanston, Ill.: Northwestern University Press, 1965).

3. Charles Feidelson, *Symbolism and American Literature* (Chicago: University of Chicago Press, 1953). The main shortcoming of this work is Feidelson's neglect of the *immediate* background to the early nineteenth century's interest in philology. Though he does deal in an exploratory manner with the influence of the New England Puritan mind and its propensity toward "symbolic" formulation, he does not investigate how among Emerson's contemporaries the relation of language to theology was still a primary concern. Moreover, his assessment of the seventeenth-century Puritan imagination has been superseded by more recent studies of Puritan typology, for example, Ursula Brumm, *American Thought and Religious Typology* (New Brunswick, N.J.: Rutgers University Press, 1970); Sacvan Bercovitch, ed., *Typology and Early American Literature* (Amherst: University of Massachusetts Press, 1972), and *The Puritan Origins of the American Self* (New Haven and London: Yale University Press, 1975).

4. Hans Aarsleff, *The Study of Language in England, 1780–1860* (Princeton N.J.: Princeton University Press, 1967), p. 4. In this study I seek to combine the assumptions and methodology of critics like Abrams and Aarsleff and to test their insights for the period 1800–60 in America. As I see it, in this country "natural supernaturalism" had a particularly close relationship to conceptions of scriptural language. As religious discourse became more secularized—later in New England than in Old—the possiblity of a symbolic mode of aesthetic discourse developed from some of the premises at first considered only in their *theological* import. However, as Robert D. Richardson, Jr., shows in his *Myth and Literature in the American Renaissance* (Bloomington: University of Indiana Press, 1978), for some of the transcendentalists, particularly Theodore Parker and Bronson Alcott, the issue of the new biblical exegesis centered more on myth than on language. For Emerson, however, that certainly was *not* the case; see Richardson, *Myth and Literature*, pp. 34–64.

5. Aarsleff, *Study of Language*, p. 10.

6. On Emerson's interest in Neoplatonic thought, see, for example, George M. Harper, "Thomas Taylor in America," in Kathleen Raine and George M. Harper,

eds., *Thomas Taylor the Platonist* (Princeton: Princeton University Press, 1969), pp. 49–102; S. G. Brown, "Emerson's Platonism," *New England Quarterly* 18, no. 3 (September 1945): 325–45; and Kenneth Walter Cameron, *Emerson the Essayist*, 2 vols. (Raleigh, N.C.: Thistle Press, 1945), 1:38–46ff.

7. For two recent assessments of the ways in which Hawthorne and Melville rejected the conventional novelistic formulas of their day, see Ann Douglas, *The Feminization of American Culture* (New York: Alfred A. Knopf, 1977), pp. 289–326; and Henry Nash Smith, *Democracy and the Novel: Popular Resistance to Classic American Writers* (New York: Oxford University Press, 1978), passim.

8. See, for example, the introduction to H. Shelton Smith, ed., *Horace Bushnell* (New York: Oxford University press, 1965), for Bushnell's influence on later nineteenth-century theologians.

9. My own view of the transcendentalist revolt against the standing order regards the various reforms—be they individual, as in Thoreau's or Margaret Fuller's case, institutional, as in George Ripley's, or political, as in Theodore Parker's—essentially as part of the need to find a common center against the centrifugal forces unleashed by Jacksonian democracy.

Chapter 1 The Word of God, within Reason

1. A good introduction to Webster is still Henry R. Warfel, *Noah Webster: Schoolmaster to America* (New York: Macmillan, 1936).

2. Noah Webster, *Observations on Language, and on the Errors of the Class-books: Addressed to the New York Lyceum* (New Haven: Babcock, 1839), p. 12.

3. Ibid., p. 31.

4. Ibid.

5. For a general overview of American religious history during this period, see Sydney Ahlstrom, *A Religious History of the American People* (1972; rpt. 2 vols., New York: Doubleday, 1975), especially pt. 4.

6. For the effects of the concept of religious voluntarism on New England's religious establishment, see, for example, William W. Fenn, "The Revolt against the Standing Order," in *The Religious History of New England: King's Chapel Lectures* (Cambridge: Harvard University Press, 1917); George S. Marsden, *The Evangelical Mind and the New School Presbyterian Experience* (New Haven: Yale University Press, 1970); and Sidney Mead, *Nathaniel William Taylor, 1768–1858: A Connecticut Liberal* (Chicago: University of Chicago Press, 1942).

7. Jerry Wayne Brown, *The Rise of Biblical Criticism in America: The New England Scholars* (Middletown, Conn.: Wesleyan University Press, 1969), offers the best introduction to this topic; see also Hans W. Frei, *The Eclipse of Biblical Narrative: A Study in Eighteenth and Nineteenth Century Hermeneutics* (New Haven and London: Yale University Press, 1974), especially pp. 155–244. A fine study of Herder is Robert T. Clark, *Herder: His Life and Thought* (Berkeley: University of California Press, 1955), especially pp. 295–97, for my arguments. For the impact of the German scholarship in literature as well as in theology, see Henry A Pochmann, *German Culture in America: Philosophical and Literary Influences* (Madison: University of Wisconsin Press, 1961), passim.

8. During this period Unitarianism emerged as a separate and powerful denomination in America; see especially Conrad Wright, *The Beginnings of Unitarianism in America* (Boston: Beacon Press, 1955), passim.

9. At present no such all-inclusive study exists; Jerry Wayne Brown's is restricted, as the title suggests, almost exclusively to New England. The other de-

nominations' interests in scriptural interpretation must be pieced together from readings in primary documents.

10. Daniel Walker Howe, *The Unitarian Conscience: Harvard Moral Philosophy, 1805–61* (Cambridge: Harvard University Press, 1970), has become the starting point for any discussions of the Unitarians' intellectual position. On the Scottish Common Sense school, see S. Grave, *The Scottish Philosophy of Common Sense* (Oxford: Oxford University Press, 1960); and Sydney Ahlstrom, "Scottish Philosophy and American Theology," *Church History* 24 (1955): 257–72. Of tangential interest is Terrence Martin, *The Instructed Vision: Scottish Common Sense Philosophy and the Origins of American Fiction* (Bloomington: University of Indiana Press, 1961).

11. Reed quoted in Perry Miller, ed., *The Transcendentalists: An Anthology* (Cambridge: Harvard University Press, 1950), p. 55.

12. Cameron Thompson, "John Locke and New England Transcendentalism," in Brian Barbour, ed., *American Transcendentalism: An Anthology of Criticism* (South Bend, Ind.: University of Notre Dame Press, 1973), p. 94.

13 On Lord Monboddo's *Origin and Progress of Language* (1773), see Arthur O. Lovejoy, *Essays in the History of Ideas* (New York, 1948; rpt. ed., Capricorn Books, 1960), pp. 38–61.

14. See Perry Miller, "The Rhetoric of Sensation," in *Errand into the Wilderness* (Cambridge: Harvard University Press, 1956), pp. 167–83, and *Jonathan Edwards* (New York: William Sloane Associates, 1949), pp. 43–70.

15. John Locke, *An Essay Concerning Human Understanding*, ed. Peter H. Nidditch (Oxford: Clarendon Press, 1975), bk. 3, chap. 2, par. 1. See also Ernest Lee Tuveson, *The Imagination as a Means of Grace* (Chicago: University of Chicago Press, 1960), for a thorough discussion of the implications of Lockean epistemology on the writers who followed Locke.

16. Miller, "Rhetoric of Sensation," p. 169.

17. Ibid.; also see Locke, *Essay Concerning Human Understanding*, bk. 3, chap. 1, par. 5, and chap. 2, pars. 5, 8.

18. See, for example, Norman K. Smith, *The Philosophy of David Hume* (London: Macmillan, & Co., 1941), especially pp. 79–88.

19. Howe, *Unitarian Conscience*, p. 29; A. Woolzey, introduction to Thomas Reid's *Essays on the Intellectual Powers of Man* (London: Macmillan & Co., 1941), offers a good discussion of Reid's importance.

20. Howe, *Unitarian Conscience*, pp. 29–30; and, besides Grave, *Scottish Philosophy*, see James McCosh, *The Scottish Philosophy* (New York: Carter, 1875), and Torgny Segerstedt, *The Problem of Knowledge in Scottish Philosophy* (Lund, Sweden: Gleerup, 1935).

21. Thomas Reid, *Works of Thomas Reid*, 2 vols. (New York: Duyckinck, 1822), 1:101.

22. Howe, *Unitarian Conscience*, pp. 31–36.

23. Reid, *Works*, 1:230, 237.

24. Ibid., p. 219.

25. Howe, *Unitarian Conscience*, p. 29; and Dugald Stewart, *The Works of Dugald Stewart*, 7 vols. (Cambridge, Mass.: Hilliard & Brown, 1829), 1:1–13, 69–77.

26. Stewart, *Works*, vol. 1, especially pp. 119–50.

27. See Brown, *Biblical Criticism*, pp. 10–94, especially 10–44; and Lawrence Buell, "Joseph Stevens Buckminster: The Making of a New England Saint," *Canadian Review of American Studies* 20, no. 1 (Spring 1979): 1–29.

28. On Norton, see Brown, *Biblical Criticism*, pp. 27–34; and Conrad Wright, in George Williams, ed., *Harvard Divinity School* (Boston: Beacon Press, 1949), pp. 43–52. On Henry Ware, see Howe, *Unitarian Conscience*, p. 314; on Buckminster's library, see Brown, *Biblical Criticism*, pp. 23, 27–29.

29. Brown, *Biblical Criticism*, pp. 45–58. For the background to Andover's founding, see Daniel Day Williams, *The Andover Liberals* (New York: King's Crown Press, 1941). On Stuart's near censure, see Pochmann, *German Culture*, pp. 128–31; and Brown, *Biblical Criticism*, p. 44, quoting from Stuart's manuscript concerning the affair.

30. See Brown, *Biblical Criticism*, p. 44; and Moses Stuart, *Letter to the Rev. Wm. E. Channing, Containing Remarks on His Sermon Recently Preached and Published at Baltimore* (Andover, Mass.: Flagg & Gould, 1819), p. 11.

31. Brown, *Biblical Criticism*, p. 65; and Channing, quoted in Clarence Faust, "The Background of the Unitarian Opposition to Transcendentalism," *Modern Philology* 25 (1938): 297–304.

32. Stuart, quoted in Williams, *Andover Liberals*, p. 19.

33. Andrews Norton, *A Statement of Reasons for Not Believing the Doctrines of Trinitarians*, 7th ed. (Boston: American Unitarian Association, 1859) p. 162. Norton first responded to Stuart in two reviews in the *Christian Disciple* for 1819 and later expanded one of these to book length. See Norton, "Defense of Liberal Christianity," *General Repository and Review* 1 (1812): 2ff., for another statement on scriptural language.

34. The book went through many subsequent editions but achieved its final form in the 1833 printing.

35. Norton, *Statement of Reasons*, pp. 16, 20. It is interesting to note how close Norton was to defining the vagaries of "historical Christianity" that so exercised younger ministers like Emerson, Theodore Parker, and George Ripley. See, for example, Parker, "A Discourse of the Transient and Permanent in Christianity," and Ripley, "Jesus Christ, the Same Yesterday, Today, and Forever," in Miller, *The Transcendentalists*, pp. 259–83, 284–99.

36. Norton, *Statement of Reasons*, p. 162.

37. Ibid., pp. 138; 148–49.

38. Ibid., pp. 144, 148.

39. Ibid., p. 148.

40. Brown, *Biblical Criticism*, passim, gives a good sense of this, but we need a more all-inclusive history of biblical scholarship in this country for the years 1800–60 to allow us to see other of its implications, especially among the less popular, yet highly significant denominations like the Universalists, Freewill Baptists, and so on. Richardson, *Myth and Literature*, is helpful in establishing a starting point for the study of Parker's and Bronson Alcott's views of the Bible; see pp. 34–64.

Chapter 2 Transcendental Logic

1. Charles Mayo Ellis, *An Essay on Transcendentalism* (Boston: Crockett & Ruggles, 1842).

2. For "The Transcendentalist," see *The Collected Works of Ralph Waldo Emerson*, eds. Alfred R. Ferguson et al. (Cambridge: Harvard University Press, 1971–), 1:201–16; hereafter cited as *W*. References to other volumes of Emerson's works are from *The Complete Works of Ralph Waldo Emerson*, Centenary Edition, 12 vols. (Boston and New York: Houghton Mifflin Co., 1903–4), hereafter cited as *WC*. Also see Theodore Parker, "Transcendentalism," in *Centenary Edition of The Writings of Theodore Parker*, 15 vols. (Boston: American Unitarian Association, 1907–11) 6:1–38.

3. Ellis, *Essay on Transcendentalism*, p. 22.

4. Ibid., p. 23.

5. Francis Bowen, *Critical Essays, On a Few Subjects Connected with the History*

and Present Condition of Speculative Philosophy (Boston: Williams, 1842), pp. xix, xvi–xvii. On Bowen, a well-known faculty member at Harvard, see Howe, *Unitarian Conscience*, pp. 309–10, and 77–81, for an assessment of his *Critical Essays*.

6. See, for example, Pochmann, *German Culture*, pp. 73–74; and Orie W. Long, *Literary Pioneers: Early American Explorers of European Culture* (Cambridge: Harvard University Press, 1935), pp. 3–76, 108–58.

7. Walter Leighton, *French Philosophers and New England Transcendentalism* (Charlottesville: University of Virginia Press, 1908), p. 5; and Harold C. Goddard, *Studies in New England Transcendentalism* (New York: Columbia University Press, 1908), p. 4.

8. Leighton, *French Philosophers*, p. 1; and Alexander Kern, "The Rise of Transcendentalism," in Henry M. Clark, ed., *Transitions in American Literary History* (Durham, N.C.: Duke University Press, 1953), pp. 252–75, for an elaboration of the Kantian influence. Cf. Réné Wellek, "Emerson and German Philosophy," *New England Quarterly* 16, no. 1 (March 1943): 41–62; also, n. 35, below.

9. Perry Miller (in *The Transcendentalists*, pp. 3–15) is the most prominent among those who regard transcendentalism primarily as a religious movement; and William Hutchison, *The Transcendentalist Ministers: Church Reform in the New England Renaissance* (New Haven: Yale University Press, 1959), lends Miller's arguments strong support.

10. On James Marsh, see Ronald V. Wells, *Three Christian Transcendentalists: James Marsh, Caleb Sprague Henry, Frederic Henry Hedge* (New York: Columbia University Press, 1943); and John J. Duffy, ed., *Coleridge's American Disciples: The Selected Correspondence of James Marsh* (Amherst: University of Massachusetts Press, 1973), introduction. Also valuable are Peter C. Carafiol, "James Marsh: Transcendental Puritan," *ESQ: A Journal of the American Renaissance* 21, no. 3 (3d quarter, 1975): 127–36, and "James Marsh's American *Aids to Reflection*: Influence through Ambiguity," *New England Quarterly* 49, no. 1 (March 1976): 27–45; and Lewis S. Feuer, "James Marsh and the Conservative Transcendentalist Philosophy," *New England Quarterly* 31, no. 1 (March 1958): 3–31. On Bushnell, see especially Smith, *Horace Bushnell*; Barbara Cross, *Horace Bushnell: Minister to a Changing America* (Chicago: University of Chicago Press, 1958); and Mary Bushnell Cheney, *Life and Letters of Horace Bushnell* (New York: Charles Scribner's Sons, 1880).

11. Carafiol, "James Marsh," p. 128; for Bushnell's interest in Coleridge, see Cross, *Horace Bushnell*, p. 20, and Cheney, *Life and Letters*, pp. 208–9.

12. Carafiol, "James Marsh," gives a good summary of the biographical materials found in Joseph Torrey, *The Remains of the Reverend James Marsh, D. D.* (Boston: Crockett & Brewster, 1843).

13. Ibid., p. 128.

14. Ibid. On Marsh's contributions to American education, see Peter C. Carafiol, "James Marsh and John Dewey: The Fate of Transcendentalist Philosophy in American Education," *ESQ: A Journal of the American Renaissance* 24, no. 2 (1st quarter, 1978): 1–13.

15. See Carafiol, "Marsh's *Aids to Reflection*," passim. Odell Shepard, *Pedlar's Progress: The Life of Bronson Alcott* (Boston: Little, Brown & Co., 1937), p. 159, assesses the importance of the *Aids to Reflection* to transcendentalists. Also see introduction to Duffy, *Coleridge's Disciples*; and Ralph Waldo Emerson, *The Letters of Ralph Waldo Emerson*, ed. Ralph L. Rusk, 6 vols. (New York: Columbia University Press, 1939), 1:412–13.

16. [James Marsh], "Ancient and Modern Poetry," *North American Review* 6 (January 1822): 94–131.

17. Carafiol, "James Marsh," p. 127. Ludovico Arborio Gattinara di Breme (1780–1820) was prominent in the Italian romantic movement, holding a place com-

parable to Mme. de Staël's in France. See Duffy, *Coleridge's Disciples*, p. 37n. on Marsh's review of di Breme.

18. Duffy, *Coleridge's Disciples*, p. 16.

19. [Marsh], "Ancient and Modern Poetry," pp. 106, 123–28.

20. Ibid., p. 124.

21. Ibid. pp. 125–28. This idea is premonitory of the fascination Thoreau had for the language not only of the American Indian tribes but of the early American explorers as well—see chap. 4, below. Thoreau was fascinated by the powerfully evocative way these types of peoples were able to use their vocabularies. Elizabeth Palmer Peabody's interest in the work of Herder had its basis in a similar recognition. See her review-essay, "Spirit of the Hebrew Scriptures," *Christian Examiner* 16 (May, July 1834): 174–202, 305–20; and 17 (September 1834): 78–92.

22. [Marsh], "Ancient and Modern Poetry," p. 123.

23. Feuer offers further insight into the particularly conservative postion that Marsh came to represent among his contemporaries. I am indebted to Richard I. Rabinowitz of Boston, Mass., for sharing with me his thoughts on Marsh.

24. James Marsh, "Review of Stuart on the Epistle to the Hebrews," *Quarterly Christian Spectator* 1 (1829): 122ff. Also see Duffy, *Coleridge's Disciples*, pp. 19–21.

25. On Taylor, see Mead, *Taylor*, passim, but especially pp. 171–242. This important volume opens this entire period of religious history to the student.

26. Marsh, "Review of Stuart," p. 147.

27. Ibid., p. 148.

28. Here Marsh, and other of his contemporaries like Emerson and Parker, pointed to a problem that Jonathan Edwards, too, had faced just prior to the Great Awakening: the remarriage of science (or "natural philosophy") and theology. People like Cotton Mather (in *The Christian Philosopher* [1721]) had tried to effect such a reconciliation, but it was not until Edwards rephrased the problem as one between reason and the "affections" that any progress was made toward its solution. See, for example, his *Treatise Concerning Religious Affections* (1746). Marsh, Emerson, Bushnell, and Parker inherited a more romantic vocabulary and defined the problem essentially as one between "head" and "heart."

29. See Duffy, *Coleridge's Disciples*, introduction; and Carafiol, "Marsh's *Aids to Reflection*," passim.

30. Cameron, *Emerson the Essayist*, 1:125, n. 244.

31. Noah Porter, "Coleridge's American Disciples," *Bibliotheca Sacra* 4 (1847): 163. This lengthy review is still one of the best introductions to Marsh's thought, made by a Congregationalist who shared some of his primary concerns.

32. Miller, *The Transcendentalists*, p. 34.

33. See n. 28, above.

34. James Marsh, "Preliminary Essay" to Samuel Taylor Coleridge, *Aids to Reflection in the Formation of a Manly Character*, ed. James Marsh (Burlington, Vt.: Chauncey Goodrich, 1829), p. xxv.

35. For understanding Coleridge's relation to British theology as well as to German thought, see Stephen Prickett, *Romanticism and Religion: The Tradition of Coleridge and Wordsworth in the Victorian Church* (Cambridge: Cambridge University Press, 1976), especially pp. 9–90; James D. Boulger, *Coleridge as Religious Thinker* (New Haven: Yale University Press, 1961); and Robert Barth, *Coleridge and Christian Doctrine* (Cambridge: Harvard University Press, 1969). Not to be neglected at this point is Thomas Carlyle's influence; see, for example, Abrams, *Natural Supernaturalism*, especially pp. 307–14.

36. Coleridge, *Aids to Reflection*, p. 260, Marsh's note.

37. Marsh, "Preliminary Essay," p. viii; and Coleridge, *Aids to Reflection*, p.

261. The important thing is how much Coleridge himself already had changed the meaning of some of Kant's terms; see Pochmann, *German Culture*, pp. 131–38.

38. Marsh, "Preliminary Essay," p. viii.

39. Duffy, *Coleridge's Disciples*, p. 4; and Carafiol, "James Marsh," p. 128.

40. "Coleridge," *North American Review*, n.s. 40 (1835): 316.

41. Quoted in I. A. Richards, *Coleridge on Imagination* (New York: Harcourt, Brace, 1935), p. 12; also in Samuel Taylor Coleridge, *Collected Letters of Samuel Taylor Coleridge*, ed. Earl Leslie Griggs (Oxford: Oxford University Press, 1956–59), 1:625–26.

42. Coleridge, *Aids to Reflection*, p. lviii.

43. Wells, *Three Christian Transcendentalists*, p. 18.

44. Quoted in Duffy, *Coleridge's Disciples*, pp. 22–23.

45. Wells, *Three Christian Transcendentalists*, p. 18. Charles Follen had a significant role in spreading the influence of German thought in America. See, for example, Pochmann, *German Culture*, pp. 114–24; and George W. Spindler, *The Life of Karl Follen: A Study in German-American Cultural Relations* (Chicago: University of Chicago Press, 1917), especially pp. 84–185.

46. Duffy, *Coleridge's Disciples*, p. 3.

47. Ibid.

48. Feuer, "James Marsh," p. 23.

49. Carafiol, "James Marsh," p. 134, quoting a letter from Marsh to Henry Dana, Sr., 14 March 1838.

50. Carafiol, "Marsh's *Aids to Reflection*," p. 20.

51. Cheney, *Life and Letters*, p. 208.

52. Ibid., p. 209.

53. Ibid. There is still need for an entire book on Coleridge's effect on American theology. See Ahlstrom, *Religious History*, 2:16, 27–29, 34, 47–48, 63, 72, 245, for suggestions of the range of that influence.

54. Cheney, *Life and Letters*, p. 209.

55. The phrase is used in Wells, *Three Christian Transcendentalists*, but Carafiol, "James Marsh," works from a similar premise. Wells's other subjects, Frederic Henry Hedge and Caleb Sprague Henry, are interesting in their own right and deserve more study, especially Hedge, who was the convener of the Transcendental Club. See O. W. Long, *Frederic Henry Hedge: A Cosmopolitan Scholar* (Portland, Me.: Anthoensen Press, 1940), and Joel Myerson, "Frederic Henry Hedge and the Failure of Transcendentalism," *Harvard Library Bulletin* 23 (1975): 396–410.

56. The early nineteenth-century theologians' interests in Schleiermacher need to be investigated more fully. For example, Moses Stuart translated an essay of his on the Trinity (*On the Discrepancies between the Sabellian and Athanasian Methods of Representing the Trinity of the Godhead* [Andover, Mass., 1835]), and George Ripley published a long article on the German theologian in the *Christian Examiner* 20 (1836): 1–46. See also Robert R. Williams, *Schleiermacher the Theologian: The Construction of the Doctrine of God* (Philadelphia: Fortress Press, 1978).

57. Feidelson, *Symbolism and American Literature*, pp. 151–57, 311–15, emphasizes Bushnell's importance in theorizing *toward* a symbolic mode in theology, but he does not pay enough attention to the theological complexities of Bushnell's situation. See, for example, Harold Durfee, "Language and Religion: Horace Bushnell and Rowland Gibson Hazard," *American Quarterly* 5, no. 1 (Spring 1953): 57–70; Donald A. Crosby, *Horace Bushnell's Theory of Language* (The Hague: Mouton, 1975); and Frederick Kirschenmann, "Horace Bushnell: Cells or Crustacea?" in Jerald Brauer, ed., *Reinterpretation in American Church History* (Chicago: University of Chicago Press, 1968) pp. 67–90.

58. Mead, *Taylor*, passim, provides a good background to the theological climate at Yale during this period, but also see Joseph Haroutunian, *Piety versus Moralism: The Passing of the New England Theology* (New York: Henry Holt & Co., 1932).

59. Mead, *Taylor*, pp. 38–127. On Dwight, see especially Stephen E. Berk, *Calvinism versus Democracy: Timothy Dwight and the Origins of American Evangelical Orthodoxy* ([Hamden, Conn.]: Archon Press, 1974).

60. Cross, *Horace Bushnell*, p. 18.

61. Quotation from Professor Alan Heimert, in conversation, 28 March 1971. Haroutunian, *Piety versus Moralism*, is best for an introduction to the Edwardsian successors, but see also Alan Heimert's *Religion and the American Mind from the Great Awakening to the Revolution* (Cambridge: Harvard University Press, 1966), an idiosyncratic but brilliant work that only now is receiving the attention it long has deserved.

62. Cross, *Horace Bushnell*, title of chap. 13.

63. Mead, *Taylor*, p. 63; or W. C. Fowler, *Essays: Historical, Literary, Educational* (Hartford: Lockwood & Brainard, 1876), pp. 60–62, letter from Bushnell to Fowler, 4 November 1825.

64. See n. 56, above. Besides Stuart and Ripley, other religious thinkers like Emerson, Parker, and Hedge were influenced by Schleiermacher. See, for example, Emerson, *Letters*, 1:425–26; Parker *Writings*, 13:301, 7:1–38; and Pochmann, *German Culture*, p. 560, n. 430. For Hedge, see Pochmann, p. 560, n. 431, where he quotes Emerson as having heard Hedge read him some things from Schleiermacher's works; or Ralph Waldo Emerson, *The Journals and Miscellaneous Notebooks of Ralph Waldo Emerson*, ed. William H. Gilman et al., 14 vols. to date (Cambridge: Harvard University Press, 1960–), 4:360; hereafter cited as *JMN*.

65. Cross, *Horace Bushnell*, p. 20.

66. Horace Bushnell, *God in Christ: Three Lectures Delivered at New Haven, Cambridge, and Andover, with a Preliminary Dissertation on Language* (Hartford: Brown & Parsons, 1849); throughout I have used a later edition (New York: Charles Scribner's Sons, 1877).

67. Cheney, *Life and Letters*, p. 90.

68. Ibid., p. 213. Bushnell's long relationship with Bartol suggests that he would have been kept abreast of the latest developments in the always-changing Boston theological scene, but there is little information as to how well read Bushnell was in the literature of American transcendentalism. It is to be noted, though, that his *Nature and the Supernatural, as Together Constituting the One System of God* (New York: Charles Scribner's Sons, 1858), consists largely of a virulent if implicit attack on transcendentalism's main premises as applied to religion. Perhaps there he was reacting to critics like Enoch Pond who, in his *Review of "God in Christ"* (Bangor, Me.: Duren, 1849), had proclaimed that Bushnell absorbed his heretical ideas from the "German Transcendental philosophy" (p. 112). In *Nature and the Supernatural*, Bushnell argues for the primacy of the symbolic Christ and says that humanity has need continually to imagine the presence of the God-Man in their lives. Also see Bushnell, "Our Gospel a Gift to the Imagination" in *Building Eras in Religion* (New York: Charles Scribner's Sons, 1881), for his continuing interest in the symbolic elements of the religious life.

69. Cheney, *Life and Letters*, pp. 191–94, for an account of his conversion.

70. Bushnell, *God in Christ*, pp. 10–11; hereafter cited as *GC*.

71. See my section on Swedenborg in chap. 3, below. In Swedenborg's theology there is a one-to-one correspondence between natural objects and spiritual truths, creating an almost allegorical reading of the world of "matter." In his book-length review of Bushnell's *God in Christ*, Enoch Pond had also associated Bushnell with the Swedenborgians; see *Review*, p. 3.

72. In passages like these Bushnell comes close to linking himself with that mystical strain in American theology embraced by such earlier figures as Jonathan Edwards, who studied the "images or shadows of divine things," and Emerson, for whom nature similarly blossomed with meaning. Miller, "From Edwards to Emerson," in *Errand into the Wilderness*, pp. 184–203, is suggestive about this connection.

73. Certainly this idea of confusing the word for the *real* thing had been an issue in Edwards's day as well, but in the 1730s the problem had been more that people heard the words but had no sense of the ideas behind them. In Bushnell's time it was more that the word was *too literally* taken for the thing, especially in theological argument.

74. On Johnson, see Alexander Bryan Johnson, *A Treatise on Language, Edited with a Critical Essay on Johnson's Philosophy of Language*, ed. David Rynin (Berkeley: University of California Press, 1947); and Charles L. Todd and Russell T. Blackwood, eds., *Language and Value* (New York and London: Greenwood Publishing Co., 1969), a collection of essays about Johnson. In 1828 Johnson, a banker in the area around Utica, N.Y., had published *The Philosophy of Human Knowledge; or, A Treatise on Language* and revised it in 1836, when it appeared as *A Treatise on Language; or, The Relation Which Words Bear to Things* (New York: Harper & Bros., 1836). Like Marsh, Sampson Reed, and others, Johnson attacked the Scottish Common Sense philosophers but from an *empirical* viewpoint. He elaborately maintained that words never do justice to the sheer variety of the physical world—he saw human language as a limited construct in the face of nature's overwhelming complexity. He counseled that men had to become more specific in their usage of language and to use words that could be verified by the five senses, not by "abstract" designations. When one removes a word from "all references to sensible existences," he maintained, "the word no longer signifies any sensible existence, but becomes a void." Words—even if they related to abstractions like "God" or "heaven"—somehow had to be presented to our senses if they were to be comprehensible. Implicitly he was suggesting that to have any meaning at all language had to be returned to its roots in experience, a thought with which Emerson and Thoreau would agree.

75. Pond, *Review*, p. 10.

76. Such words as these should bring to mind the later dark fictions of Melville (most notably *Pierre* [1852]), which possess so many "antagonisms" and "crossviews" that the reader is left with a feeling of the futility of all attempts to circumscribe—as Pierre thought he might—such profound theological propositions as, for example, "true virtue." See Epilogue, below.

77. See chap. 1, n. 35, above.

78. Smith, *Horace Bushnell*, pp. 3–39, offers a good introduction to Bushnell's formulations in the more strictly doctrinal vein. Notice, however, how the passages just cited are reminiscent of William James's philosophy of pragmatism. James believed that if an idea "worked" for an individual—that is, if it could be assimilated into one's life without upsetting other deeply felt convictions—then that idea was "true" for that person. Here Bushnell placed a similar emphasis on the value of symbolic ritual, an idea he was to expand in such works as *Christ in Theology* (Hartford: Brown & Parsons, 1851) and *The Vicarious Sacrifice, Grounded in Principles of Universal Obligation* (New York: Charles Scribner's Sons, 1866).

79. Feidelson, *Symbolism and American Literature*, pp. 142–61, especially 157.

80. Cross, *Horace Bushnell*, p. 107. See chap. 3, below, for Emerson on the poet.

81. Quoted in O. B. Frothingham, *Theodore Parker: A Biography* (Boston: Osgood, 1874), p. 160.

82. Bushnell, *Nature and the Supernatural*, p. 118.

83. Ibid., pp. 508–9. This compelling reaffirmation of the mystery of Christ and

his meaning for Bushnell's contemporaries should be read in the context of other "christological" documents of the age—most notably Emerson's "Divinity School Address" (*W*, 1:71–94); and see Joel Porte, *Representative Man: Ralph Waldo Emerson in His Time* (New York: Oxford University Press, 1979), pp. 114–32, for a brilliant reading of that sermon.

Chapter 3 The Example of Emerson

1. Men like Parker and Ripley—and others among their contemporaries, Caleb Sprague Henry and Cyrus Bartol, for example—never moved outward from theology to literature in their philological interests. For them Scripture retained a primacy it no longer possessed in the same degree for Emerson or Thoreau. See, for example, Parker's *Discourse of Matters Pertaining to Religion* (Boston: Little and Brown, 1842), especially bks. 2 and 4; Bartol, "Transcendentalism," in *Radical Problems* (Boston: Roberts, 1872), pp. 61–97; and Ripley's review of Herder in the *Christian Examiner* for 1835, partially reprinted in Miller, *The Transcendentalists*, pp. 89–92.

2. Throughout this chapter I intend to treat Emerson more *representatively* (to use a word he would have been fond of) than definitively. That is, I have no design to give an exhaustive reading to the entire corpus of his essays. Anyone seeking that kind of treatment has a large number of fine studies already available, among them Jonathan Bishop, *Emerson on the Soul* (Cambridge: Harvard University Press, 1964); Vivian C. Hopkins, *Spires of Form: A Study of Emerson's Aesthetic Theory* (New York: Russell & Russell, 1965); Sherman Paul, *Emerson's Angle of Vision: Man and Nature in the American Experience* (Cambridge: Harvard University Press, 1952); and Stephen Whicher, *Freedom and Fate: An Inner Life of Ralph Waldo Emerson* (Philadelphia: University of Pennsylvania Press, 1953). More recent studies include Porte, *Representative Man;* David Porter, *Emerson and Literary Change* (Cambridge: Harvard University Press, 1978); and R. A. Yoder, *Emerson and the Orphic Poet in America* (Berkeley and Los Angeles: University of California Press, 1978). I intend to use the few Emerson essays I have chosen to analyze as benchmarks against which to judge the philological accomplishment or sophistication of figures who came before and after him. And while Emerson the artist is, as Porter calls him, "the central man" (Emerson, p. 1), I do not claim to treat his *overall* aesthetic theory with any degree of completeness. Throughout this chapter my major focus is his concern with what he did with the theological language and symbols he inherited.

3. William Ellery Channing, for example, the patriarch of the Unitarian movement, never concerned himself to any great degree with the problems Emerson (and, later, Bushnell) identified as critical to contemporary Protestant theology. Despite his interest in the speculations on language of Rowland Gibson Hazard, whose *Language: Its Connexion with the Present Condition and Future Prospects of Man* (Providence: Marshall & Brown, 1836) Elizabeth Palmer Peabody read aloud to his approval, not many of Channing's sermons or essays express an explicit concern with the problems of language in religion. See Elizabeth Palmer Peabody, *Reminiscences of Rev. Wm. Ellery Channing, D.D.* (Boston: Roberts Bros., 1880), pp. 185–86; or my "Elizabeth Palmer Peabody and the Philosophy of Language," *ESQ: A Journal of the American Renaissance* 23 (3d quarter, July 1977): 156. Hazard, a Rhode Island industrialist who published a number of philosophical works—including an attack on Jonathan Edwards's *Freedom of the Will*—proposed a theory of language with affinities to the idealistic thought of Kant and Coleridge. The most interesting part of his treatise deals with the "language of ideality," a term by which he meant

poetic discourse that expressed man's "primitive perceptions." Speech had, he thought, degenerated to a "language of narration," which placed no demands on man's imagination. Even the "language of abstraction" failed to be honest to the manner in which speech originally was conceived. Hazard, like Reed and Emerson, urged men to bring poetry back into their discourse; for he believed that, while the languages of narration and abstraction were useful in persuasion, the language of ideality was needed for conviction. See William Gammell, *The Life and Services of the Honorable Rowland Gibson Hazard* (Providence: Reid, 1888); and Rowland Gibson Hazard, *Essay on Language and Other Essays and Addresses*, ed. Caroline Hazard (Boston: Houghton Mifflin Co., 1889).

What should be noted, however, is that during this period there emerged a clearly defined Unitarian aesthetic, a set of organizing principles visible in the more "literary" sermons produced by members of that denomination. It is my belief, though, that while these sermons became more belletristic, practitioners of the form in fact were not advancing the use of figurative language in the ways Emerson, Thoreau, and others after them did. See Lawrence Buell, *Literary Transcendentalism: Style and Vision in the American Renaissance* (Ithaca, N.Y.: Cornell University Press, 1973), especially pp. 21–54; "The Unitarian Movement and the Art of Preaching in Nineteenth Century America," *American Quarterly* 24, no. 2 (May 1972): 166–90; and "Unitarian Aesthetics and Emerson's Poet-Priest," ibid. 20, no. 1 (Spring 1968): 3–20, for good discussions of this aesthetic.

4. See Catherine L. Albanese, *Corresponding Motion: Transcendental Religion and the New America* (Philadelphia: Temple University Press, 1977), passim, for an interesting argument that suggests that "what was new about their [the transcendentalists'] language in the context of Brahmin Boston was its *style* more than its content; it was written in the kinetic mode." All the dominant images used by the transcendentalists, Albanese argues, "proclaimed a new religion of process inaugurating a future of eternal energy." Basing her argument on the comparativist approach of scholars like Mircae Eliade, Albanese concerns herself too much with style rather than substance. Also see Elizabeth A. Meese, "Transcendentalism: The Metaphysics of Theme," *American Literature* 47, no. 1 (March 1975): 1–20.

5. Among the more valuable discussions of *Nature* are Kenneth Burke, "I, Eye, Ay—Emerson's Early Essay *Nature*: Thoughts on the Machinery of Transcendence," in Myron Simon and Thornton Parsons, eds., *Transcendentalism and Its Legacy* (Ann Arbor: University of Michigan Press, 1966), pp. 3–24; Morton Sealts and Alfred Ferguson, eds., *Emerson's "Nature": Origin, Growth, Meaning* (New York: Dodd, Mead & Co., 1969), especially pp. 38–72; Richard L. Francis, "The Architectonics of Emerson's *Nature*," *American Quarterly* 19 no.1 (Spring 1967): 39–52; and Barry Wood, "The Growth of the Soul: Coleridge's Dialectical Method and the Strategy of Emerson's *Nature*," *PMLA* 91 (May 1976): 385–97.

6. Ralph L. Rusk, *The Life of Ralph Waldo Emerson* (New York: Charles Scribner's Sons, 1949), pp. 169–97, for Emerson's European journey and the impressions he brought away from it.

7. Rusk, *Life*, pp. 160–67, gives a good account of Emerson's actions during this critical period. In his journal for that same year (1832), Emerson was formulating the kinds of arguments he would use in "The Lord's Supper." For example, 15 July 1832: "I think Jesus did not mean to institute a perpetual celebration [at the Last Supper], but that a commemoration of him would be useful" (*JMN*, 4:30; also see pp. 45, 92, 95). It should be noted that at this point in his intellectual development Emerson had not yet decided to abandon *altogether* the Christian ministry—during the next few years he continued to supply many pulpits in the Boston area, if only on an occasional basis. See Henry Nash Smith, "Emerson's Problem of Vocation:

A Note on the American Scholar," in Barbour, *American Transcendentalism*, pp. 225–38.

8. Also see *JMN*, 4:45, where Emerson declares that "the whole world holds on to formal Christianity, and nobody teaches the essential truth." To Emerson's mind, too many of his contemporaries partook of the Lord's Supper and then thought they were absolved from being diligent in their religion until the next celebration of that sacrament.

9. See, for example, Stanley M. Vogel, *German Literary Influences on the American Transcendentalists* (New Haven: Yale University Press, 1955), pp. 79, 108; and Frederic Ives Carpenter, *Emerson Handbook* (New York: Hendricks House, 1953), pp. 108–42. Recently, Joel Porte has shown how Emerson, even at the time of his delivery of the famed "Divinity School Address," had been troubled by strictly doctrinal questions that pointed to "antinomian" tendencies; see *Representative Man*, pp. 98–104, and Wesley T. Mott, "Emerson and Antinomianism: The Legacy of the Sermons," *American Literature* 50, no. 3 (November 1978): 369–97.

10. See Clarence P. Hotson, "Sampson Reed, Teacher of Emerson," *New England Quarterly* 2, no. 2 (April 1929): 249–77, and "Emerson and the Swedenborgians," *Studies in Philology* 27 (1930): 517–45; Cameron, *Emerson the Essayist*, 1:253–94; and Carl F. Strauch, "Emerson Rejects Reed and Hails Thoreau," *Harvard Library Bulletin* 26 (1968): 257–73.

11. Miller, *The Transcendentalists*, p. 49.

12. Cameron, *Emerson the Essayist*, 1:230. Also see Marguerite Block, *The New Church in the New World* (New York: Henry Holt & Co., 1932), a dated, but still the best, account of Swedenborgianism in America.

13. Miller, *The Transcendentalists*, p. 53.

14. Block, *New Church*, p. 21, quoting from Swedenborg's *Adversaria*.

15. Austin Warren, *The Elder Henry James* (New York: Macmillan Co., 1934), p. 70. In the 1838 edition of his *Observations on the Growth of the Mind*, Reed denied any connection to the transcendentalists; Miller, *The Transcendentalists*, p. 205.

16. See Miller, *The Transcendentalists*, pp. 49–50, 53; Block's earlier chapters; and n. 10, above.

17. Peabody, *Reminiscences of Channing*, pp. 185–86. See *JMN*, 5:51 n., for discussion of Reed's oration in manuscript form. There the editor states that Emerson's brother Charles was given a copy as early as 1830.

18. The entire oration has been reprinted in Cameron's *Emerson the Essayist*; for this section, see 2:9–11.

19. Ibid., p. 11.

20. Quoted in Miller, *The Transcendentalists*, p. 53.

21. Sampson Reed, *Observations on the Growth of the Mind* (Boston: Hilliard & Metcalf, 1826), p. 13.

22. Ibid., pp. 20–21, 23.

23. Ibid., pp. 22–24.

24. Ibid., p. 24.

25. On Clarke's exposure to Reed, see Oliver Wendell Holmes, *Ralph Waldo Emerson*, American Men of Letters Series (Boston: Houghton Mifflin Co., 1885), p. 80. For Alcott, see Shepard, *Pedlar's Progress*, p. 258.

26. On Oegger, see Cameron, *Emerson the Essayist*, 1:295–302.

27. Rusk, *Life*, p. 236. The publication of this selection from Oegger's book was important enough to receive a notice in the *Dial* (3 [1842]: 131), with the reviewer claiming it a "very remarkable tract" and intimating that the remainder of Oegger's work could be printed "in a like manner, if it appeared wanted." Apparently the demand was not sufficient to warrant this.

28. G[uillaume] Oegger, *The True Messiah; or, the Old and New Testaments Examined According to the Principles of the Language of Nature* (Boston: Peabody, 1842), p. 5; reprinted in Cameron, *Emerson the Essayist*, 2:83–98.

29. Oegger, *True Messiah*, pp. 3, 6, 7.

30. Ibid., p. 9.

31. Ibid., pp. 13–14.

32. Emerson, *Letters*, 2:26.

33. Burke, "I, Eye, Ay," pp. 5, 11–13.

34. An important point here is that, while Oegger and others were concerned mainly with the correspondence between the natural world and scriptural revelation, Emerson was catholic enough to extend the equation to revelation *apart from* its intrinsically Christian overtones.

35. Francis Bowen, "Transcendentalism," *Christian Examiner* 21 (1837): 371.

36. Ibid., pp. 372, 378.

37. Ibid., p. 379.

38. The connection between Edwards and Emerson has been suggested by Perry Miller in "From Edwards to Emerson," but Miller does not stress to any great degree their common problem concerning the ineffectiveness of religious discourse upon their contemporaries.

39. On Coleridge, see, for example, Prickett, *Romanticism and Religion*, pp. 9–33.

40. Here Emerson certainly eschews, if unconsciously, James Marsh, who in many of his writings lamented the lack of vigor in contemporary theological discourse compared to, for example, the inspired texts of the Hebrews. See above, pp. 41–43.

41. Bushnell, *Nature and the Supernatural*, pp. 261–71, claims that one of the main errors made by some of the transcendentalists (particularly Parker) was in lauding the advance of science *indiscriminately*. What they neglected to realize was that, though natural law had its place, scientific discoveries were always *more* significant in allowing man to create new metaphors for the never-ending task of trying to comprehend God.

42. See *W*, 1:45, for the conclusion of *Nature*, where Emerson's sense of an impending revelation from God is highly apparent in his "prospects" for those who have learned how properly to regard nature.

43. Here one can see how concerned Emerson still was with the connection between human and divine Logos; he always maintained that there indeed was such a connection. As we shall see in my next chapter, however, Thoreau came to perceive them as one and the same.

44. See Porte, *Representative Man*, pp. 114–33; and Bishop, *Emerson on the Soul*, pp. 87–91.

45. *W*, 1:214, for the similar passage in "The Transcendentalist."

46. For Cranch's amusing caricatures of Emerson and his acquaintances, see F. de Wolfe Miller, *Christopher Pearse Cranch and His Caricatures of New England Transcendentalism* (Cambridge: Harvard University Press, 1951).

47. See, for example, Parker's *Discourse of Religion*, bk. 3; and "The True Idea of a Christian Church" and "Transcendentalism," in Henry Steele Commager, ed., *Theodore Parker: An Anthology* (Boston: Beacon Press, 1960), pp. 83–98.

48. See *W*, 1:117–40; 201–16; *WC*, 3:167–96; and Stephen Whicher et al., eds., *The Early Lectures of Ralph Waldo Emerson*, 3 vols. (Cambridge: Harvard University Press, 1959–72), 3:271–85.

49. Feidelson, *Symbolism and American Literature*, p. 131.

50. Recently, William J. Scheick, in *The Slender Human Word: Emerson's Artistry in Prose* (Knoxville: University of Tennessee Press, 1978), argues for Emerson's pro-

longed interest in "hieroglyphs," but Scheick does not address the whole problem of language. Also see John Irwin, "The Symbol of the Hieroglyphics in the American Renaissance," *American Quarterly* 26, no. 2 (May 1974): 103–26.

Chapter 4 Farther Afield

1. William Ellery Channing, *Thoreau: The Poet-Naturalist* (Boston, 1873; rpt., Boston: Goodspeed, 1902).
2. Ibid., p. 77.
3. See David Skwire, "A Checklist of Wordplays in *Walden*," *American Literature* 31, no. 3 (November 1959): 282–89, where the compiler lists 122 of the more apparent puns in that book; Richard Poirier, *A World Elsewhere: The Place of Style in American Literature* (New York: Oxford University Press, 1966), especially pp. 85–88; and Stanley Cavell, *The Senses of "Walden"* (New York: Viking Press, 1972), pp. 1–34. To date, Michael West is the most profound student of Thoreau's philological interests; see his "Charles Kraitsir's Influence on Thoreau's Theory of Language," *ESQ: A Journal of the American Renaissance* 20, no. 4 (4th quarter, 1973): 262–74; "Scatology and Eschatology: The Heroic Dimensions of Thoreau's Wordplay," *PMLA* 89, no. 5 (October 1974): 1043–64; and *"Walden's* Dirty Language: Thoreau and Walter Whiter's Geocentric Etymological Theories," *Harvard Library Bulletin* 22 (1975): 117–28. My "Henry Thoreau and the Wisdom of Words," *New England Quarterly* 52, no. 1 (March 1979): 38–54, extends West's analysis and links Thoreau's language study to larger philosophical concerns.
4. See, for example, Arthur E. Christy, *The Orient in American Transcendentalism* (New York: Columbia University Press, 1932), pp. 185–234; and Jonathan Bishop, "The Experience of the Sacred in Thoreau's *Week*," *ELH* 33, no. 1 (March 1966): 66–91.
5. Edward Tyrell Channing, *Lectures Read to the Seniors at Harvard College*, ed. Richard Henry Dana, Jr. (Boston: Ticknor & Fields, 1856); and Richard H. Dillmann, "The Psychological Rhetoric of *Walden*," *ESQ: A Journal of the American Renaissance* 25, no. 2 (2d quarter, 1979): 79–91. Thoreau's early college themes are included in Henry D. Thoreau, *Early Essays and Miscellanies*, ed. Moldenhauer, Moser, Kern, in *The Works of Henry D. Thoreau* (Princeton: Princeton University Press, 1975).
6. Channing, *Lectures*, p. 220.
7. Ibid., p. 223. On Horne Tooke, see Aarsleff, *Study of Language*, pp. 44–114.
8. Channing, *Lectures*, pp. 224–27.
9. Ibid., p. 234.
10. Ethel Seybold, *Thoreau: The Quest and the Classics* (New Haven: Yale University Press, 1951), p. 12.
11. The relationship—both intellectual and personal—between Emerson and Thoreau has been explored most provocatively by Joel Porte, *Emerson and Thoreau: Transcendentalists in Conflict* (Middletown, Conn.: Wesleyan University Press, 1966). Although Porte stresses the two men's differences, there is ample proof of strong early connections between Thoreau's thoughts on language and Emerson's.
12. See ibid., especially chaps. 5 and 6, and Poirier, *A World Elsewhere*, p. 89.
13. For a good introduction to Trench's influence, see Aarsleff, *Study of Language*, pp. 230–47. Also see Gordon V. Boudreau, "Thoreau and Richard C. Trench: Conjectures on the Pickerel Passage in *Walden*," *ESQ: A Journal of the American Renaissance* 20, no. 2 (2d quarter, 1974): 117–24, where concise biographical material on Trench is provided. Boudreau, passim, notes several instances of Trench's refer-

ences to Emerson; see Richard C. Trench, *On the Study of Words* (New York: Macmillan Co., 1892), p. 4, for the passage cited here.

14. Trench, *Study of Words*, pp. viii, ix, 6; Thoreau, *Walden*, ed. J. Lyndon Shanley, in *The Works of Henry D. Thoreau* (Princeton: Princeton University Press, 1971), p. 101; hereafter cited as WP.

15. Trench, *Study of Words*, pp. 11–15.

16. Thoreau, *Early Essays and Miscellanies*, pp. 226, 228. J. J. G. Wilkinson's essay "Correspondence" appeared in Elizabeth Peabody's *Aesthetic Papers* (Boston: Peabody, 1849), the periodical in which Thoreau's "Civil Disobedience" first appeared. Wilkinson was a prominent British Swedenborgian, so well known that Henry James, Sr., named one of his sons after him. On Carlyle, see John Holloway, *The Victorian Sage: Studies in Argument* (1953; rpt., New York: W. W. Norton & Co., 1965), pp. 41–45.

17. F. O. Matthiessen, *American Renaissance: Art and Expression in the Age of Emerson and Whitman* (New York: Oxford University Press, 1941), p. 116. Also see my "Thoreau and John Josselyn," *New England Quarterly* 48, no. 4 (December 1975): 505–18, for a detailed study of Thoreau's interest in one of these explorers.

18. Thoreau, *Early Essays and Miscellanies*, p. 226.

19. Thoreau, *A Week on the Concord and Merrimack Rivers*, ed. Carl Hovde et al., in *The Works of Henry D. Thoreau* (Princeton: Princeton University Press, 1980), p. 106–7; cited hereafter as *Week*.

20. Thoreau, *The Maine Woods*, ed. Joseph J. Moldenhauer, in *The Works of Henry D. Thoreau* (Princeton: Princeton University Press, 1972), pp. 136–37, 142, 169.

21. The most accessible information on Kraitsir is in West, "Kraitsir's Influence." My "Elizabeth Peabody" discusses the intellectual relationship of Peabody and Kraitsir and comments upon the latter's philological activity. *Karoly Kraitsir* (n.p., n.d.), a scarce pamphlet, is the main source of biographical material. The copy I examined was donated to the Harvard College Library in 1863 by Charles Sumner.

22. See my "Elizabeth Peabody," passim; Bruce Ronda, "Elizabeth Palmer Peabody's Views of the Child," *ESQ: A Journal of the American Renaissance* 23, no. 2 (2d quarter, 1977): 106–13, is of some service, as is John B. Wilson, "Grimm's Law and the Brahmins," *New England Quarterly* 38, no. 2 (June 1965): 234–39. Professor Margaret Neussendorfer is presently preparing a new biography of Peabody.

23. [Peabody], "Spirit of the Hebrew Scriptures," pp. 174–75.

24. Ibid., pp. 175–76. On Hazard, whose papers Peabody republished in 1857, see Durfee, "Language and Religion"; and chap. 3, n. 3, above.

25. Alcott's interest in language still has not been sufficiently explored; Elizabeth Peabody's *Record of a School: Exemplifying the General Principles of Spiritual Culture* (Boston: Munroe, 1835), in which she details Alcott's educational methods at the Temple School, is a good source with which to commence such an examination; see also Peabody's preface to the second (1836) edition.

26. Charles Kraitsir, *The Significance of the Alphabet* (Boston: Peabody, 1846), and *Glossology: Being a Treatise on the Nature of Language and on the Language of Nature* (New York, 1852; 2nd ed., New York: C. B. Norton, 1854). For documentation of Thoreau's reading in Kraitsir, see West, "Kraitsir's Influence."

27. Kraitsir, *Glossology*, p. 10.

28. Ibid., pp. 19–20.

29. Ibid., p. 23.

30. Ibid., pp. 25–26. It should be noted that other scholars were proposing similar theories. For example, in an article called "The Relation of Language to Thought" (*Bibliotheca Sacra* 5 [1848]), W. G. T. Shedd—a disciple of James Marsh—claimed that the "motions of the mouth, the position of the organs, and the tension

of the muscles of speech in utterance of such words as shock, smite, writhe, slake, quench, are produced by the force and energy and character of the conceptions which these words communicate, just as the prolonged relaxation of the organs and muscles in the pronunciation of soothe, breathe, dream, calm, and the like, results naturally from the nature of the thoughts of which they are the vocal embodiment" (p. 654). Hans Aarsleff has informed me that such arguments about the organic production of speech were particularly common in the seventeenth century. See, for example, Franciscus Mercurius von Helmont, whose *Alphabeta naturae* (c.1688) bears interesting similarities to Kraitsir's theory; and Murray Cohen, *Sensible Words: Linguistic Practice in England, 1640–1785* (Baltimore: Johns Hopkins University Press, 1977), pp. 1–42.

31. Kraitsir, *Glossology*, p. 170.

32. Ibid., p. 213. This proposition is similar to that advanced by Hazard in his *Language*; see my "Elizabeth Peabody," p. 156. In 1839 Josiah Gibbs, one of Bushnell's teachers at Yale, had noted that the "natural significance of sounds is now beginning to be regarded as one of the deepest and most important doctrines in philology. . . . For in order to explain the existence of language it is not enough that man has the organ of speech, that he has sensations of ideas, and that he has a desire to communicate them to others; but it is also necessary that sounds should have a natural adaptedness to express the particular sensations and ideas" ("On the Natural Significancy of Articulate Sounds," *Biblical Repository*, 2d ser. 2 [1839]: 167).

33. Kraitsir, *Glossology*, p. 213.

34. Ibid., pp. 71–72.

35. Here, of course, is where Thoreau's philology differs from Emerson's, which always implied a correspondential relation between this world and a world of spirit (even if it were only mentally conceived). See Brian Harding, "Swedenborgian Spirit and Thoreauvian Sense: Another Look at Correspondence," *American Studies* 8, no. 1 (April 1974): 65–79, where Harding claims that Thoreau worked within a Swedenborgian vision; and Sherman Paul, "The Wise Silence: Sound as the Agency of Correspondence in Thoreau," *New England Quarterly* 22, no. 4 (December 1949): 511–27.

36. Kraitsir, *Glossology*, pp. 22, 159.

37. Ibid., p. 197.

38. W, 3:24. Charles R. Anderson, *The Magic Circle of Walden*, (New York: Holt, Rinehart and Winston, 1968), pp. 243–44, speculates that the leaf imagery of this passage may have come from Goethe's *Metamorphosis of Plants* (1790) but that "the metaphoric embodiment of it in sand foliage is entirely original. So are the punning etymologies by which Thoreau extends the universal leaf form." Obviously, in light of Kraitsir's glossology, I disagree with Anderson's statement. Also see Perry Miller, ed., *Consciousness in Concord: The Text of Thoreau's Hitherto "Lost Journal"* Boston: Houghton Mifflin Co., 1958), pp. 126–27.

39. For example, West notes that Emerson's library contained a copy of Walter Whiter's *Etymologicon Magnum; or, Universal Etymological Dictionary, on a New Plan* (London, 1800) and hypothesizes that Thoreau, who frequently borrowed books from his neighbor, would have noticed any such work. Whiter's wildly speculative theory was based on the idea that the secret to all languages resided in the *earth* itself; that is, in the very consonants *RTH*, of which the word was formed. He noted the resemblances between the English *earth*, the Hebrew *aretz*, and the Arabic *erd*, and concluded that "the name of an object so important as the Earth, would supply the origins of a great race of words expressing the various operations which are attached to it." As West succinctly puts it, Whiter's implied solution to the riddle of the origin of language was that "the earth apparently generated it." The analogies

of Whiter's geocentric theory to Thoreau's vision in the railroad cut seem plausible. See West, *"Walden's* Dirty Language," passim, and Aarsleff, *Study of Language,* pp. 78–79.

40. Harding, "Swedenborgian Spirit," tries to make a strong argument for Thoreau's use of a modified correspondential theory. It now seems more profitable to stress Thoreau's philosophical differences from his onetime mentor, as Porte does in *Emerson and Thoreau.* See Christopher Collins, *The Uses of Observation: A Study of Correspondential Vision in the Writings of Emerson, Thoreau, and Whitman* (The Hague: Mouton, 1971), for a more conservative view.

41. Harding, "Swedenborgian Spirit," pp. 69–70. Thoreau (*Wr*, 9:310) offers a direct statement about personal mortality, drawn from a natural lesson. "When I realize," he noted, "that the mortality of suckers in the spring is as old a phenomenon, perchance, as the race of suckers itself, I contemplate it with serenity and joy even, as one of the signs of spring. . . . [This] proves its necessity and that it is part of the *order*, not the disorder, of this universe."

42. It is interesting to note that the most recent revaluations of Emerson's poetics have stressed—albeit with a different emphasis from that of this study—Emerson's gradual acceptance of this world as the true home of the poet, if not of the philosopher. See Porter, *Emerson,* and Yoder, *Emerson and the Orphic Poet.*

43. Walter Benn Michaels, in *"Walden's* False Bottoms," *Glyph I,* Johns Hopkins Textual Studies (Baltimore: Johns Hopkins University Press, 1977), pp. 132–149, argues for the paradoxical nature of Thoreau's writing in *Walden.* Also see Anderson, *Magic Circle,* pp. 13–56.

Chapter Five Ambiguity and Its Fruits

1. See, for example, Merton M. Sealts, Jr., *Melville's Reading: A Checklist of Books Owned and Borrowed* (Madison: University of Wisconsin Press, 1966), and M. L. Kesserling, "Hawthorne's Reading, 1828–1850," *Bulletin of the New York Public Library* 53 (1949): 55–71, 121–38, 173–94.

2. Studies of Hawthorne's religious interests include Leonard J. Fick, *The Light Beyond: A Study of Hawthorne's Theology* (Westminster, Md.: Newman Press, 1955); and John T. Frederick, *The Darkened Sky: Nineteenth Century Novelists and Religion* (South Bend, Ind.: University of Notre Dame Press, 1969), especially pp. 27–122. James K. Folsom, *Man's Accidents and God's Purposes: Multiplicity in Hawthorne's Fiction* (New Haven: College and University Press, 1963), while provocative, has not been unequivocally accepted. On Melville and religion, see Lawrance Thompson, *Melville's Quarrel with God* (Princeton: Princeton University Press, 1952); T. Walter Herbert, *"Moby Dick" and Calvinism: A World Dismantled* (New Brunswick, N.J.: Rutgers University Press, 1977); Nathalia Wright, *Melville's Use of the Bible* (1949; rpt., New York: Octagon, 1974); and William Braswell, *Melville's Religious Thought: An Essay in Interpretation* (1943; rpt., New York: Octagon, 1973), especially pp. 3–18, 107–26. Herbert, pp. 23–56, is especially good on demonstrating how questions of religion affected Melville in his younger years; within his own family, for example, there were relatives expressing both Dutch Reformed and Unitarian traditions. Thomas Vargish, "Gnostic Mythos in *Moby Dick*," *PMLA* 81, no. 3 (June 1966): 272–77, speculates that in *Moby Dick* Melville may have been reacting to none other than Andrews Norton.

3. Folsom, *Man's Accidents,* offers a solid introduction to the topic of ambiguity in Hawthorne's works, though I differ with some of the author's readings. Henry Nash Smith, *Democracy and the Novel,* in his chapter on Hawthorne, comes to some

of the same conclusions I do concerning that author's use of ambiguity and suggests that his use of that rhetorical mode confused many of his contemporary readers. Paul Brodtkorb, Jr., *Ishmael's White World: A Phenomenological Reading of "Moby Dick"* (New Haven: Yale University Press, 1965), while overemphasizing Melville's modernity, still contributes greatly to our knowledge of Melville's philosophical intentions, in this case, primarily in *Moby Dick*. Feidelson's remains the classic exposition of the symbolic mode as Melville developed it, but his treatment of Hawthorne is not as extensive.

4. Cecilia Tichi, in "Melville's Craft and the Theme of Language Debased in *The Confidence Man*," *ELH* 39, no. 4 (December 1972): 639–58, is among the few critics who note Melville's concern with rhetoric in *The Confidence Man*. Also useful are Ernest Tuveson, "The Creed of the Confidence Man," *ELH* 33, no. 2 (June 1966): 247–70; Malcolm O. Magaw, "*The Confidence Man* and Christian Deity: Melville's Imagery of Ambiguity," in Rima Reck, ed., *Explorations of Literature* (Baton Rouge: Louisiana State University Press, 1966); and Henry Sussman, "The Deconstructor as Politician: Melville's *Confidence-Man*," *Glyph IV*, Johns Hopkins Textual Studies (Baltimore: Johns Hopkins University Press, 1978), pp. 32–56. Throughout this chapter I will refer to *The Confidence Man* in the edition prepared by Hershel Parker (New York: W. W. Norton & Co. 1971).

5. Melville, *Confidence Man*, p. 12.

6. Ibid., pp. 161–71, 209. For Melville's attitude toward Emerson, see, for example, Perry Miller, "Melville and Transcendentalism," in Elizabeth Miller, ed., *Nature's Nation* (Cambridge: Harvard University Press, 1967), pp. 184–96; and Matthiessen, *American Renaissance*, especially pp. 184–86.

7. Melville, *Confidence Man*, pp. 216–17.

8. Tichi, "Melville's Craft," p. 644.

9. Melville, *Confidence Man*, p. 71. Herbert, *"Moby Dick" and Calvinism*, p. 135, notes that "Melville exploited a situation in which the distinction between 'fact' and 'allegory' had become problematic. Orthodox Biblicists took Biblical 'fact' to have doctrinal meaning and resisted new 'fact' which seemed to undermine its sacred and moral meaning. . . . Melville's symbols gain peculiar equivocal bearings from this situation."

10. Melville, *Confidence Man*, p. 165.

11. The parallels between Hester and a powerful, nineteenth-century woman like Margaret Fuller are striking and often have been noted. However, it seems plausible that, in addition to disliking Margaret Fuller for what he considered her obnoxious personality, Hawthorne may have seen in her the result of the Emersonian emphasis on *self*. When one juxtaposes this to Hawthorne's obsessive concern with monomania—as evidenced in his characters Ethan Brand and Aylmer, for example—his particularly bitter animus toward women characters like Zenobia or Hester becomes more understandable. They were not only women but Emersonians to boot.

12. See, for example, Edward H. Davidson, "Dimmesdale's Fall," *New England Quarterly* 36, no. 3 (September 1963): 358–70; and William H. Nolte, "Hawthorne's Dimmesdale: A Small Man Gone Wrong," *New England Quarterly* 38, no. 2 (June 1965): 168–86, for an essay that sees Hester's role in the novel as more significant than Dimmesdale's.

13. See the prefaces to Hawthorne's four novels in Norman Holmes Pearson, ed., *The Complete Novels and Selected Tales of Nathaniel Hawthorne* (New York: Modern Library, 1937). Joel Porte, *The Romance in America: Studies in Cooper, Poe, Hawthorne, Melville, and James* (Middletown, Conn.: Wesleyan University Press, 1969), offers a good introduction to this genre in American prose; see especially pp. 95–151.

14. Good studies with which to start consideration of this underrated work

include Merle E. Brown, "The Structure of *The Marble Faun*," *American Literature* 28, no. 3 (November 1956): 302–13; Frederick Crews, *The Sins of the Fathers: Hawthorne's Psychological Themes* (New York: Oxford University Press, 1966), pp. 213–39; and Porte, *Romance in America*, pp. 137–51.

15. Herman Melville, *Moby Dick; or, The Whale*, ed. Charles Feidelson (Indianapolis: Bobbs-Merrill Co., 1964), pp 3–5; hereafter cited as *MD*.

16. Brodtkorb, *Ishmael's White World*, offers the most detailed exposition of this theory of *Moby Dick*'s organization. Many studies (most notably Feidelson's *Symbolism and American Literature*) stress the symbolic acts of reading that occur in the book; but few critics have noted how that act of interpretation itself is related to the cultural crisis over the interpretation of scriptural doctrine. Herbert, *"Moby Dick" and Calvinism*, is among the few who make such an assessment; see particularly pp. 127–30, 135–36. Also germane is Rodolphe Gasché, "The Scene of Writing: A Deferred Outset," *Glyph 1*, Johns Hopkins Textual Studies (Baltimore: Johns Hopkins University Press, 1977), pp. 150–71.

17. On *Pierre*, see especially Tyrus Hillway, "Pierre, the Fool of Virtue," *American Literature* 21, no. 2 (May 1949): 201–11; Mary Dichmann, "Absolutism in Melville's *Pierre*," *PMLA* 67, no. 5 (September 1952): 702–15; Thompson, *Melville's Quarrel*, pp. 247–94; Henry A. Murray, introduction to Melville's *Pierre; or, The Ambiguities* (New York: Hendricks House, 1949); and Milton R. Stern, *The Fine Hammered Steel of Herman Melville* (Urbana: University of Illinois Press, 1957), pp. 150–205.

18. Melville, *Pierre*, p. 225.

19. Ibid., pp. 321–22.

20. See, for example, Wendell Glick, "Expediency and Absolute Morality In *Billy Budd*," *PMLA* 68, no. 1 (March 1953): 102–10; Roland A. Duerkson, "The Deep Quandary of *Billy Budd*," *New England Quarterly* 41, no. 1 (March 1968): 51–66; John B. Noone, "*Billy Budd*: Two Concepts of Nature," *American Literature* 29, no. 3 (November 1957): 249–62; and Porte, *Romance in America*, pp. 184–92.

Selected Bibliography
of Primary Sources

Alcott, Amos Bronson. *Conversations with Children on the Gospels*. 2 vols. Boston: Munroe, 1836–37.

Balch, William. *Lectures on Language*. Providence: Cranston, 1838.

Bartol, Cyrus. *Radical Problems*. Boston: Roberts, 1872.

Bowen, Francis. *Critical Essays, On a Few Subjects Connected with the History and Present State of Speculative Philosophy*. Boston: Williams, 1842.

Brownson, Orestes. *Brownson's Works*. Edited by Henry F. Brownson. 20 vols. Detroit: H. F. Brownson, 1882–87.

Bushnell, Horace. *Building Eras in Religion*. New York: Charles Scribner's Sons, 1881.

———. *Christ in Theology*. Hartford: Brown & Parsons, 1851.

———. *God in Christ: Three Lectures Delivered at New Haven, Cambridge, and Andover, with a Preliminary Dissertation on Language*. Hartford: Brown & Parsons, 1849. Reprint. New York: Charles Scribner's Sons, 1877.

———. *Nature and the Supernatural, As Together Constituting the One System of God*. New York: Charles Scribner's Sons, 1858.

———. *The Vicarious Sacrifice, Grounded in Principles of Universal Obligation*. New York: Charles Scribner's Sons, 1866.

Cameron, Kenneth Walter. *Emerson the Essayist*. 2 vols. Raleigh, N.C.: Thistle Press, 1945.

Cardell, William S. *Essay on Language, as Connected with the Faculties of the Mind, and as Applied to Things in Nature and Art*. New York: C. Wiley, 1825.

Channing, Edward Tyrell. *Lectures Read to the Seniors at Harvard College*. Edited by Richard Henry Dana, Jr. Boston: Ticknor & Fields, 1856.

Channing, William Ellery. *The Works of William E. Channing*. Boston: American Unitarian Association, 1875.

Coleridge, Samuel Taylor. *Aids to Reflection in the Formation of a Manly Character*. Edited by James Marsh. Burlington, Vt.: Chauncey Goodrich, 1829.

Selected Bibliography of Primary Sources

[Ellis, Charles Mayo.] *An Essay on Transcendentalism*. Boston: Crockett & Ruggles, 1842.

Emerson, Ralph Waldo. *The Collected Works of Ralph Waldo Emerson*. Edited by Alfred R. Ferguson et al. 2 vols. to date. Cambridge: Harvard University Press, 1971–.

———. *The Complete Works of Ralph Waldo Emerson*. Centenary Edition. 12 vols. Boston and New York: Houghton Mifflin Co., 1903–4.

———. *The Early Lectures of Ralph Waldo Emerson*. Edited by Stephen E. Whicher, Robert E. Spiller, and Wallace E. Williams. 3 vols. Cambridge: Harvard University Press, 1959, 1964, 1972.

———. *The Journals and Miscellaneous Notebooks of Ralph Waldo Emerson*. Edited by William H. Gilman et al. 14 vols. to date. Cambridge: Harvard University Press, 1960–.

———. *The Letters of Ralph Waldo Emerson*. Edited by Ralph L. Rusk. 6 vols. New York: Columbia University Press, 1939.

Gammell, William. *The Life and Services of the Honorable Rowland Gibson Hazard*. Providence: Reid, 1888.

Gibbs, Josiah Willard. "On the Natural Significancy of Articulate Sounds." *Biblical Repository*, 2d ser. 2 (July 1839): 166–73.

———. *Philological Studies with English Illustrations*. New Haven: Durrie & Peck, 1857.

Goodwin, Henry M. "Thoughts, Words, and Things." *Bibliotheca Sacra* 6 (1849): 271–300.

[Hazard, Rowland Gibson.] *Language: Its Connexion with the Present Condition and Future Prospects of Man*[,] *by a Heteroscian*. Providence: Marshall & Brown, 1836.

Hazard, Rowland Gibson. *Essay on Language and Other Papers*. Edited by Elizabeth Peabody. Boston: Phillips, Sampson & Co., 1857.

———. *Essay on Language and Other Essays and Addresses*. Edited by Caroline Hazard. Boston and New York: Houghton Mifflin Co., 1889.

Herder, J. G. *The Spirit of Hebrew Poetry*. Edited by James Marsh. 2 vols. Burlington, Vt.: Smith, 1833.

Hodge, Charles. *Essays and Reviews*. New York: Carter & Bros., 1857.

Hubbard, F. M. "Study of the Works of Nature." *Biblical Repository*, 1st ser. 6 (1835): 173–87.

Johnson, Alexander Bryan. *A Treatise on Language, edited with a Critical Introduction on Johnson's Philosophy of Language*. New York: Harper & Bros., 1836. Reprint. Edited by David Rynin. Berkeley: University of California Press, 1947.

Kraitsir, Charles. *Glossology: Being a Treatise on the Nature of Language and on the Language of Nature*. New York: G. P. Putnam, 1852. 2d ed. New York: C. B. Norton, 1854.

———. *The Significance of the Alphabet*. Boston: Peabody, 1846.

Selected Bibliography of Primary Sources

Locke, John. *An Essay Concerning Human Understanding.* Edited by Peter H. Nidditch. Oxford: Clarendon Press, 1975.

Lowth, Robert. *Lectures on the Sacred Poetry of the Hebrews.* Edited by Calvin Stowe. Andover, Mass.: Flagg & Gould, 1829.

Marsh, James. "Ancient and Modern Poetry." *North American Review* 6 (January 1822): 94–131.

———. *Coleridge's American Disciples: The Selected Correspondence of James Marsh.* Edited by John J. Duffy. Amherst: University of Massachusetts Press, 1973.

———. "Preliminary Essay," in Samuel Taylor Coleridge, *Aids to Reflection in the Formation of a Manly Character*, edited by James Marsh. Burlington, Vt.: Chauncey Goodrich, 1829.

———. "Review of Stuart on the Epistle to the Hebrews." *Quarterly Christian Spectator* 1 (1829): 121–50.

Miller, Perry. *The Transcendentalists: An Anthology.* Cambridge: Harvard University Press, 1950.

Norton, Andrews. "Defense of Liberal Christianity." *General Repository and Review* 1 (1812): 2–13.

———. *A Statement of Reasons for Not Believing the Doctrines of Trinitarians, Concerning the Nature of God and the Person of Christ.* 7th ed. Boston: American Unitarian Association, 1859.

Oegger, G[uillaume]. *The True Messiah; or, The Old and New Testaments Examined According to the Principles of the Language of Nature.* Boston: Peabody, 1842.

Parker, Theodore. *Centenary Edition of the Writings of Theodore Parker.* 15 vols. Boston: American Unitarian Association, 1907–11.

———. *A Discourse of Matters Pertaining to Religion.* Boston: Little & Brown, 1842. Reprint. New York: G. P. Putnam's Sons, 1876.

Peabody, Elizabeth. "Language," in *Aesthetic Papers.* Boston: Peabody, 1849.

———. *Record of a School: Exemplifying the General Principles of Spiritual Culture.* Boston: Munroe, 1835. Reprint. Boston: Russell, Shattuck & Co., 1836.

———. *Reminiscences of Rev. Wm. Ellery Channing, D.D.* Boston: Roberts Bros., 1880.

———. "Spirit of the Hebrew Scriptures." *Christian Examiner* 16 (May, July 1834): 174–202, 305–20; and 17 (September 1834): 78–92.

Pond, Enoch. *Review of "God in Christ."* Bangor, Me.: Duren, 1849.

Porter, Noah. "Coleridge's American Disciples." *Bibliotheca Sacra* 4 (1847): 117–71.

Reed, Sampson. *Observations on the Growth of the Mind.* Boston: Hilliard & Metcalf, 1826.

Reid, Thomas. *Works of Thomas Reid.* 2 vols. New York: Duyckinck, 1822.

Selected Bibliography of Primary Sources

Schlegel, Frederick von. *The Philosophy of Language in a Course of Lectures.* Translated by A. J. W. Morrison. London: Bohn, 1847.

Shedd, W. G. T. "The Relation of Language to Thought." *Bibliotheca Sacra* 5 (1848): 650–63.

Smith, George. *The Origin and Progress of Language.* New York: Lane & Scott, 1849.

Stewart, Dugald. *The Works of Dugald Stewart.* 7 vols. Cambridge, Mass.: Hilliard & Brown, 1829.

Stuart, Moses. "Letter to Dr. Channing on the Trinity," in *Miscellanies.* Andover, Mass.: Allen, Morrill, & Wardwell, 1846.

Taylor, Benjamin. *The Attractions of Language.* Hamilton, N.Y.: Atwood & Griggs, 1843.

Thoreau, Henry David. *Early Essays and Miscellanies.* Edited by Joseph J. Moldenhauer and Edwin Moser, with Alexander Kern. In *The Works of Henry D. Thoreau.* Princeton: Princeton University Press, 1975.

———. *The Maine Woods.* Edited by Joseph J. Moldenhauer. In *The Works of Henry D. Thoreau.* Princeton: Princeton University Press, 1972.

———. *Walden.* Edited by J. Lyndon Shanley. In *The Works of Henry D. Thoreau.* Princeton: Princeton University Press, 1971.

———. *A Week on the Concord and Merrimack Rivers.* Edited by Carl Hovde et al. In *The Works of Henry D. Thoreau.* Princeton: Princeton University Press, 1980.

———. *The Writings of Henry David Thoreau.* Walden Edition. 20 vols. Boston and New York: Houghton Mifflin Co., 1906.

Torrey, Joseph. *The Remains of the Reverend James Marsh, D.D.* Boston: Crockett & Brewster, 1843.

Trench, Richard C. *On the Study of Words.* New York: Redfield, 1852. Reprint. New York: Macmillan Co., 1892.

Whiter, Walter. *Etymologicon Magnum; or, Universal Etymological Dictionary, on a New Plan.* Cambridge, 1800.

Index

Index

Bushnell, Horace (*cont*)
transcendentalism, 69–70, 178 (n. 68); education of, 52–53, 186 (n. 32); and Emerson, 68–70; *God in Christ*, 8, 57–68, 79, 134; on language, 52–53, 58–71; *Nature and the Supernatural*, 97, 178 (n. 68), 183 (n. 41); poetry and theology, 8, 57, 67, 70–71, 103, 149; "Preliminary Dissertation on Language," 8, 57, 59–67; and Swedenborgianism, 178 (n. 71); and Nathaniel W. Taylor, 54–56

Cameron, Kenneth Walter: on Marsh's "Preliminary Essay," 44; on Swedenborg, 80
Campbell, George, 21
Carlyle, Thomas, 120; Thoreau and, 118–19, 121, 123
Channing, Edward Tyrell, 111–13, 122–23
Channing, William Ellery, 25, 49, 83, 84, 113, 124, 180 (n. 3); on language, 25–27; on the Trinity, 25
Channing, William Ellery, the younger, 109, 113; *Thoreau: The Poet-Naturalist*, 109
Christian Examiner, 8, 30, 76, 91
Clarke, James Freeman, 86
Coleridge, Samuel Taylor, 36, 38, 44–49, 58, 76, 87, 89, 116, 176 (n. 35), 180 (n. 3); *Aids to Reflection*, 39, 46, 48, 56; Bushnell and, 52; Emerson and, 93–94, 99; *The Friend*, 47; on language, 46, 48; Marsh's edition of *Aids to Reflection*, 40, 44, 49, 77; "Reason" in religion, 46–49
Commentary on St. Paul's Epistle to the Hebrews (Marsh), 42–43
Common Sense philosophy, 9, 18, 19, 21–23, 27, 46, 48, 173 (n. 10), 179 (n. 74); influence on Unitarians, 18–24; influence on Nathaniel W. Taylor, 55
Compendious Dictionary of the English Language (Webster), 15
Confidence Man (Melville), 150–53
Contextuality in language, 20–21, 23,

24; Emerson on, 78–79; Norton on, 26, 28–29
Correspondence, 148, 169; Bushnell's theory of, 59–60; in Emerson, 94–97, 104; between natural and spiritual worlds, 9, 80–81; Oegger on, 86–88, 183 (n. 34); Reed on, 84–86; Swedenborg on, 80–81; in Thoreau, 114, 130, 137–38, 142
Cranch, Christopher, 102
Cross, Barbara, on Bushnell, 68

Denominationalism: influence on biblical criticism, 7, 8, 16–17, 62
Descartes, 21
Dial, The, 49, 182 (n. 27)
di Breme, Ludovico Gatinara, 40–42, 175 (n. 17)
"Discourse of the Transient and Permanent in Christianity" (Parker), 26, 65, 89
Diversions of Purley (Tooke), 117
"Divinity School Address" (Emerson), 79, 89, 99
Dwight, Timothy, 55; *Theology Explained and Defended*, 56

Education: language study in, 9, 126; Reed on, 84
Edwards, Jonathan, 36, 39, 47, 53, 93, 97, 98, 176 (n. 28); interest in Locke, 19, 26
Edwards, Jonathan Jr., 55
Eichhorn, J. G., 17, 24
Elements of Logick (Hedge), 22
Elements of the Philosophy of the Human Mind (Stewart), 23
Ellis, Charles Mayo, 35–36; *An Essay on Transcendentalism*, 35
Emerson, Ralph Waldo, 4, 7, 9, 18, 25, 35, 37, 40, 45, 49, 60, 63, 71, 75–105, 110, 113, 118, 125, 130, 132, 142, 143, 144, 148, 149, 150, 151, 154, 169, 170; background to language theory of, 77–88; and Bushnell, 68–70; on Christ as poet, 98–102; correspondential theory in his works, 94–96; interest in language,

[196]

Index

10, 64, 93–98; and Marsh, 77; and
Oegger, 86–88, 96; and the poet, 68,
77, 164; and Reed, 79–86; and
Thoreau on language, 114, 127, 186
(n. 35); on Swedenborg, 77, 81–82,
164; and Unitarianism, 76, 78. *Works*:
"Divinity School Address," 79, 89,
99; *Essays: Second Series*, 99; funeral
oration on Thoreau, 109; "The
Lord's Supper," 77–79, 99, 181 (n.
7); "The Method of Nature," 104;
Nature, 77, 79, 86, 89–97, 99;
"Nature," 104, 123; "The Poet," 79,
88, 90, 92, 99–103; 116–17, 136; "The
Present Age," 104; *Representative
Men*, 81–82; "The Transcendentalist,
35, 100, 104
Empiricism, 20–22, 24, 35, 37, 45–46,
50, 65; basis for philosophy at
Harvard, 22; in Bushnell's theory of
language, 59, 61; Ellis on, 35–36;
Reed's attack on, 19–20, 83–84
Essay Concerning Human Understanding
(Locke), 11, 20–22
Essay on the Intellectual Powers of Man
(Reid), 22
Essay on Transcendentalism (Ellis), 35
Essays: Second Series (Emerson), 99
Etymology, 112–13, 118; Thoreau's
interest in, 115, 130; *see also*
Philology
Everett, Edward, 40
Exegesis, scriptural. *See* Biblical
criticism

Feidelson, Charles, 4, 77, 171 (n. 3),
177 (n. 57); on Bushnell, 68, 71; on
Emerson, 68, 104; *Symbolism and
American Literature*, 4
Follen, Charles, letter to Marsh, 54
Friend, The (Coleridge), 47
Frost, Barzillai, 99
Frost, Robert, 102

Gibbs, Josiah Willard, 186 (n. 32)
*Glossology: Being a Treatise on the Nature
of Language and on the Language of
Nature* (Kraitsir), 126–29

God in Christ (Bushnell), 8, 57–68, 79,
134
Godwin, William, Coleridge's letter to,
48
Goethe, J. W. von, 64, 186 (n. 38)
*Grammatical Institute of the English
Language* (Webster), 15
Griesbach, Johann J., 24
Griffin, Edward Dorr, 54

Harvard College: Common Sense
philosophy and, 22
Harvard Divinity School, 25, 39, 54;
Emerson's address to, 79, 98
Hawthorne, Nathaniel, 6, 7, 8, 10, 11,
18, 64, 71, 79, 105, 119, 132, 143,
169, 170; *The Marble Faun*, 156–58;
"The Minister's Black Veil," 153–54;
and romance, 156–57; *The Scarlet
Letter*, 10, 154–56; "Young
Goodman Brown," 153–54
Hazard, Rowland Gibson, 125, 180 (n.
3)
Hedge, Frederic Henry, 49, 177 (n. 55)
Hedge, Levi, 22; *Elements of Logick*, 22
Henry, Caleb Sprague, 177 (n. 55), 180
(n. 1)
Herder, Johann G. von, 17, 24, 75,
111, 124–26, 130; Peabody on *The
Spirit of Hebrew Poetry*, 124–26
Higher Criticism, 17, 24, 28, 30, 75,
170; Emerson and, 103; Melville on,
160–61; relation to language study,
17, 28, 75
Hopkins, Samuel, 55
Howe, Daniel Walker, on
Unitarianism, 18
Human Body and Its Connexion to Man
(Wilkinson), 118
Hume, David, 21
Hutchinson, Anne, 16

Idealism: influence on language, 9, 19,
20, 24, 37, 45, 49, 75, 78, 80, 89, 91,
93
Imagination: place of in religion, 41,
43, 44

Index

"Jesus Christ, the Same Yesterday, Today, and Forever" (Ripley), 65
Johnson, Alexander Bryan, 61, 179 (n. 74); Bushnell's interest in, 61–62; *Treatise on Language*, 61, 179 (n. 74)
Josselyn, John, Thoreau on, 119–21

Kant, Immanuel, 24, 36, 46, 56, 180 (n. 3)
Kraitsir, Charles, 9, 110, 124, 126–29, 133–34, 136, 142, 148; *Glossology*, 126–29; influence on Thoreau, 129–37; on scriptural language, 127; *The Significance of the Alphabet*, 126; theory of glossology, 126–29, 131, 133

L'Allemagne, De (Staël), 37
Language. *See* Ambiguity in Language; Arbitrariness in language; Contextuality in language
Language, American Indian: Thoreau's interest in, 113, 119, 121–22, 124, 176 (n. 21)
Language, organic. *See* Language of nature
Language, scriptural, 4, 7, 8, 15, 16, 28; Bushnell on, 52–53, 58–71; Emerson on, 76–78; Marsh on, 42–43, 50; Norton on, 27–30; Stuart on, 25–26
Language, universal, 9, 85, 96, 117, 125–26, 169
Language of nature, 10, 31, 33, 76, 77, 88–89, 110, 114–15, 118, 120; and American Indian language, 122–23; Emerson on, 95–103; Kraitsir on, 126–29, 133–34; Melville on, 162–64; Oegger on, 87–88; Reed on, 83–85; Thoreau on, 118–23, 138, 142
Language study: importance of, 5, 15, 40, 45–46, 48, 143; influence of Neoplatonic thought on, 6, 9; relation to biblical criticism, 15
Leaves of Grass (Whitman), 103
Locke, John, 9, 18, 19, 30, 36, 48; *Essay Concerning Human Understanding*, 11, 20–22; Reed's criticism of,

19–20, 83–84; theory of language, 20–22
"Lord's Supper, The" (Emerson), 77–79, 99

Mann, Horace, 9
Marble Faun (Hawthorne), 156–58
Marsh, James, 9, 20, 24, 31, 38, 39–51, 54, 56, 58–59, 65, 71, 76, 79, 85, 87, 91, 93, 110, 123, 124, 130, 149, 169, 179 (n. 74); American edition of *Aids to Reflection*, 40, 49; and Coleridge, 44–51; on di Breme, 40–42; education of, 39–40; and Emerson, 77; on Locke, 46; on poetry of the ancients, 41–42, 87–88, 124; "Preliminary Essay," 44–47, 59; relation to transcendentalism, 42, 49–50, 69; on scriptural language, 42–43, 50; on Stuart, 42
Matthiessen, F. O., on Thoreau, 119
Melville, Herman, 4, 7, 8, 10, 11, 18, 64, 71, 79, 105, 131, 132, 143, 150–52, 159–69, 170; on ambiguity, 151–52, 162–66; *Billy Budd*, 168–69; *The Confidence Man*, 150–53, 159, 167, 169; and Emerson, 164; *Moby Dick*, 10, 159–66; *Pierre; or, The Ambiguities*, 150, 166–69, 179 (n. 76); on scriptural language, 151, 159–62, 188 (n. 9).
"Method of Nature" (Emerson), 104
Miller, Perry, on Swedenborg, 80
Milton, John, 112
"Minister's Black Veil" (Hawthorne), 153–54
Moby Dick (Melville), 10, 159–66
Monboddo, Lord (James Burnett), 19

Natural Supernaturalism (Abrams), 4
Nature: influence on language in Emerson, 94–96; in Oegger, 86–88; in Reed, 82–86
Nature (Emerson), 77, 79, 86, 89–97, 99
"Nature" (Emerson), 104, 123
Nature and the Supernatural (Bushnell), 97, 178 (n. 68), 183 (n. 41)

Index

[199]

Index

Index

About the Author

Philip F. Gura was born and raised in Ware, Massachusetts, a hill town on the edge of the Connecticut Valley, a region that has been the focus of many of his scholarly interests. He has published many articles on colonial and nineteenth-century New England, especially on American transcendentalism and Thoreau. In 1977, the MLA awarded the Foerster Prize to Gura for his essay, "Thoreau's Maine Woods Indians: More Representative Men." Associate professor of English at the University of Colorado at Boulder, Gura was named a fellow at the Charles Warren Center for Studies in American History at Harvard University for 1980–81. He is a graduate of Harvard College and received his Ph.D. from Harvard University in the history of American civilization.